Great Americana

Journal of a Voyage to North-America
VOLUME I

Pierre de Charlevoix

Journal of a Voyage
to North-America

VOLUME I

by Pierre de Charlevoix

READEX MICROPRINT

Foreword

The *Journal of a Voyage to North America* by Pierre de Charlevoix was first published in French in 1744 as an appendix to the author's *History of New France*. The journal proved so popular that it was subsequently printed separately. An English translation appeared in 1761. In the journal Charlevoix described his voyage to Canada in 1720, his journey up the St. Lawrence River, across the Great Lakes, and down the Mississippi River to New Orleans. He concluded with an account of his shipwreck off the Florida Keys and his return to France at the close of 1722. Though Charlevoix made no new discoveries, the accuracy of his observations and the dispassionate character of his judgments gave to his journal an inestimable value. A century later American explorers continued to cite him and to compare their own observations with his.

A Jesuit, Father Charlevoix first visited Canada in 1705 and taught at the Jesuit seminary in Quebec until his return to France in 1709. When in 1719 the Regent of France wished to send an agent to New France for various secret reconnaissance purposes involving boundaries and routes to the West, he selected Father

Charlevoix. Charlevoix concealed the real purpose of his trip by pretending to visit Jesuit missions in North America.

Father Charlevoix differed considerably in temperament from Jesuits like Father Marquette who had preceded him. He was essentially a scholar and a teacher, a man accustomed to move in the best circles of French society. Unlike Marquette, no all-consuming zeal drove him to spend his life in the wilderness converting the Indians to Christianity. His interests were, in fact, extremely varied. Whether he wrote about the development of New France, about the Indians, about the wild life in North America, or about the nature of the country, he gave to each subject a searching and thoughtful examination.

He foresaw a great future for New France. He expected that one day the capital, Quebec, "shall have become as flourishing as that of Old France (and we should not despair of any thing, Paris having been for a long time much inferior to what Quebec is at this day)." Although Quebec then boasted a population of only 7,000, "yet you find in it a small number of the best company, where nothing is wanting that can possibly contribute to form an agreeable society." Furthermore, he wrote, "no where in the world is our language spoken in greater purity. There is not even the smallest foreign accent remarked in their pronunciation."

If New France had not yet fully lived up to its promise, the fault lay with those who had neglected its development because the country lacked deposits of precious metals. If only an adequate population had existed to support the fur trade and the fisheries of New France, Charlevoix felt certain the colony could have sent "greater returns to France, than Spain has drawn from the richest provinces of the New World."

Charlevoix cast his journal in the form of successive letters addressed to the Duchess of Lesdiguières. In doing so he resorted to a literary device often employed in the 18th century. Actually the "letters" were never sent. Charlevoix apparently composed them by supplementing notes taken on the trip with information he derived from other sources, written and oral.

The map included in the English edition of 1761 is based on that of Bellin, hydrographer to the King of France, who prepared it for the first French edition. Louise P. Kellogg has provided additional information about Charlevoix and his *Journal* in her edition of Pierre F. X. de Charlevoix, *Journal of a Voyage to North America* (Chicago, 1923), I, xi-xxviii.

JOURNAL

OF A

VOYAGE

TO

NORTH-AMERICA.

A MAP OF THE WESTERN OCE...

Intended to Illustrate the VOYAGE made by F. CHAR...

N.B. The Roads by land...

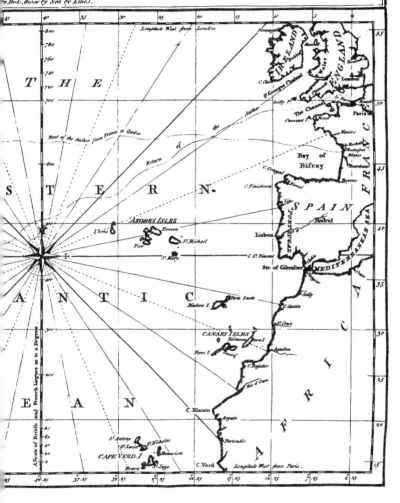

JOURNAL

OF A

VOYAGE

TO

NORTH-AMERICA.

Williamson

Undertaken by ORDER of the

FRENCH KING.

CONTAINING

The GEOGRAPHICAL Defcription and Natural
Hiftory of that Country, particularly

CANADA.

TOGETHER WITH

An Account of the CUSTOMS, CHARACTERS,
RELIGION, MANNERS and TRADITIONS
of the original Inhabitants.

In a Series of Letters to the Duchefs of LESDIGUIERES.

Tranflated from the French of P. DE CHARLEVÓIX.

IN TWO VOLUMES.

VOL. I.

LONDON:
Printed for R. and J. DODSLEY, in Pall-Mall.
MDCCLXI.

THE

CONTENTS

OF THE

FIRST VOLUME.

LETTER

LETTER IV.

LETTER V.

LETTER VI.

LETTER VII.

LETTER VIII.

L E T T E R

L E T T E R XIV.

L E T T E R XV.

L E T T E R XVI.

Preliminary

Preliminary Difcourfe

ON THE

O R I G I N

OF THE

A M E R I C A N S.

AFTER reading almoft every thing that has been writ on the manner in which America might have been peopled, we feem to be juft where we were before this great and interefting queftion began to be agitated; notwithftanding, it would require a moderate volume to relate only the various opinions of the learned on this fubject. For moft part of them have given fo much into the marvellous, almoft all of them have built their conjectures on foundations fo ruinous, or have had recourfe to certain refemblances of names, manners, cuftoms, religion and languages, fo very frivolous, which it would, in my opinion, be as ufelefs to refute, as it is impoffible to reconcile with each other.

It is not, perhaps, to be wondered at, that thofe who have firft treated this matter, fhould wander in a way which had not as yet been marked out, and in which they muſt travel without a guide. But what I am ſurprized at is, that thoſe who have gone deepeſt into this affair, and who have had the advantage of helps beyond all thoſe who have gone before them, ſhould have been guilty of ſtill greater miſtakes, which at the ſame time they might eaſily have avoided, had they kept to a ſmall number of certain principles, which ſome have eſtabliſhed with ſufficient judgment. The ſimple and natural conſequences they ought to have drawn from them, would have been, in my opinion, ſufficient to ſatisfy and determine the curioſity of the publick, which this unſeaſonable and erroneous diſplay of erudition throws back into its original uncertainty. This is what I flatter myſelf I ſhall be able to make appear, by that ſmall portion of theſe conjectures which I am now going to relate.

Thoſe of our hemiſphere were, no doubt, much ſurprized, when they were told of the diſcovery of a new world in the other, where they imagined nothing was to be ſeen, but an immenſe and dangerous ocean. Notwithſtanding, ſcarce had Chriſtopher Columbus found out ſome iſlands, and amongſt others that of Hiſpaniola, in which he diſcovered gold mines, but he was preſently of opinion, ſometimes that this was the Ophir of Solomon, and at others the Zipangri, or the Cipango of Mark Pol the Venetian. Vatablus and Robert Stephens were likewiſe perſuaded, that it was to America that Solomon ſent fleets in queſt of gold, and Columbus thought he ſaw the remains of his furnaces in the mines of Cibas, by much the fineſt and richeſt of the iſland of Hiſpaniola, and perhaps of all the new world.

Arius Montanus not only places Ophir and Parvaim in the new world, but likewise makes Joctan, the son of Heber, the founder of Juctan, a chimetical city in Peru; and also pretends, that the empire of Peru, and that of Mexico, which he will have to be the same with Ophir, were founded by a son of Joctan of that name. He adds, that another son of the same patriarch, called in the scripture Jobab, was the father of the nations on the coast of Paria, and that the eastern mountain Sephar, to which Moses says the children of Joctan penetrated after departing from Messa, is the famous chain of the Ardes, extending from North to South quite thorough Peru and Chili. The authority of this learned interpreter of the scriptures has drawn Postel, Becan, Possevin, Genebrard, and many others, into the same opinion. Lastly, the Spaniards have asserted, that in the time when the Moors invaded their country, part of the inhabitants took refuge in America. They even pretended in the fifteenth century, that they discovered certain provinces of their empire, which the misfortunes of those times had robbed them of, and to which, if you believe them, they had an incontestable right. Oviedo, one of their most celebrated authors, was not afraid to affirm, that the Antilles are the famous Hesperides, so much vaunted of by the poets; and that God, by causing them to fall under the dominion of the kings of Spain, has only restored what belonged to them three thousand one hundred and fifty years ago in the time of king Hesperus, from whom they had this name; and that St. James and St. Paul preached the gospel there, which he supports by the authority of St. Gregory in his morals. If we add to this what Plato has advanced, that beyond his own island of Atalantis, there were a great number of

islands,

iſlands, and behind them a vaſt continent, and behind this continent the true ocean, we ſhall find, that the new world was very far from being new to the ancients. What then muſt become of the opinion of Paracelſus, who maintains, that each hemiſphere had its own Adam?

Poſtel, whom I have already cited, and who has made himſelf famous by his adventurous conjectures, believed that all North America was peopled by the Atlantides, inhabitants of Mauritania; and he is the firſt who has made ſuch a difference between the two America's, by means of the Iſthmus of Panama; that according to him, and thoſe who have adopted his opinions, the inhabitants of thoſe two continents have nothing common in their original. But in this caſe, I ſhould rather be for placing with Budbecks the Atalantis in the North, as well as the pillars of Hercules, and maintaining, that North America has been peopled from Scandinavia, than by ſending thither the Moors from the coaſt of Africa. On the other hand, Gomara and John de Lery make the Americans come from the Canaanites, driven out of the promiſed land by Joſhua: Some, on the contrary, make thoſe Iſraelites, whom Salmanazus led captive into Media, paſs into America by the North of Aſia. But Thevet, who believed, like them, that the Iſraelites peopled the new world, concludes, that they muſt have ſpread themſelves over the whole world, from the circumſtance of the finding a tomb with Hebrew characters on it in one of the Azores or weſtern iſlands. This author was miſinformed as to the fact. It was not a tomb that was diſcovered in Corvo, the moſt northernly of thoſe iſlands, but an equeſtrian ſtatue, erected upon a pedeſtal, on which were certain characters, which could not be deciphered.

Au-

Auguftine Torniel is of opinion, that the defcendants of Shem and Japhet have paffed to America, and from thence to the countries lying to the fouthward of the ftreights of Magellan, by the way of Japan, and the Continent, to the Northward of the Archipel, or clufter of iflands. A Sicilian, whofe name is Marinocus, makes no doubt of the Romans having fent a Colony into this country, for which he has no other reafon, than a report current in his time, that a medal of Auguftus was found in one of the mines of Peru; as if it had not been more natural to fuppofe, that fome Spaniard had accidentally dropt this medal, when vifiting thefe mines. Paulus Jovius has dreamt that the Mexicans have been among the Gauls, which ridiculous opinion he founds upon the human facrifices which thofe two nations offered to their falfe divinities. But if this pretended refemblance proves any thing, it would much rather prove that the Gauls had been in Mexico, a people whom we know to have been always of a wandering difpofition, and to have peopled many provinces by the colonies they fent out.

The Frifelanders have likewife had their partifans with refpect to the origin of the Americans. Juffridus Petri and Hamconius affert, that the inhabitants of Peru and Chili came from Frifeland. James Charron and William Poftel do the fame honour to the Gauls, Abraham Milius to the antient Celtæ, Father Kirker to the Egyptians, and Robert Le Compte to the Phenicians; every one of them at the fame time excluding all the reft. I pafs by a great many other opinions, ftill lefs tenable than the foregoing, equally founded on fimple conjecture, and void of all probability, to come to thofe who have made the deepeft refearches into this affair.

The

The firſt is Father Gregorio Garcia, a Spaniſh Dominican, who having been a long time employed in the miſſions of Peru and Mexico, publiſhed at Valencia in the year 1607, a treatiſe in Spaniſh, on *the Origin of the Indians of the New World*, where he both collects and examines a great number of different opinions on this ſubject. He propoſes every opinion, as if it were ſome theſis or queſtior. in philoſophy: names its authors and advocates, ſets down the arguments, and laſtly, anſwers the objections, but gives no deciſion. To theſe he has added the traditions of the Peruvians, Mexicans, and iſlanders of *Haiti*, or Hiſpaniola, all which he was informed of, when on the ſpot. In the ſequel, he gives his own opinion, which is, that ſeveral different nations have contributed to the peopling of America : and here I think he might have ſtopt. This opinion is ſomewhat more than probable, and it appears to me, that he ought to have been contented with ſupporting it, as he does, with ſome arguments drawn from that variety of characters, cuſtoms, languages and religions, obſervable in the different countries of the new world. But he admits ſuch a number of theſe, which the authors of other opinions had before made uſe of, that inſtead of ſtrengthening, he really weakens his own. In the year 1729, Don André Gonzales de Garcia reprinted the work of this Father at Madrid, with conſiderable augmentations ; but though he has made many learned additions to it, he has contributed nothing to the farther ſatisfaction of his readers.

The ſecond is Father Joſeph de Acoſta, a Spaniſh Jeſuit, who had likewiſe ſpent a great part of his life-time in America, and has left behind him two very valuable works ; one in the Caſtilian language, intituled, *The natural and moral Hiſtory of the Indies* ;

dies ; the other in Latin, the title of which is, *De promulgando Evangelio apud Barbaros, five de procuranda Indorum falute.* This author, in the firſt book of his hiſtory, after taking notice of the opinion of Parmenides, Ariſtotle, and Pliny, who believed there were no inhabitants between the Tropicks, and that there never had been any navigation farther to the weſtward of Africa than the Canary Iſlands, gives it as his opinion, that the pretended prophecy of Medea in Seneca, could be no more than a bare conjecture of that poet, who, feeing that the art of navigation was beginning to receive confiderable improvements, and not being able to perſuade himſelf that there was no land beyond the Weſtern Ocean, imagined that in a ſhort time fome difcoveries would be made on that fide of the globe. At the fame time, this Spaniſh hiſtorian looks upon the paſſage I have already cited from the Timæus of Plato, as a mere fiction, in which, in order to fave his reputation, the difciples of that philoſopher, zealous for his glory, ſtrained their imagination to find out fome ingenious allegory.

In his ſixteenth chapter, Father Acoſta begins to examine by what means the firſt inhabitants of America might have found a paſſage to that immenſe Continent, and at the firſt view he rejects the direct and premeditated way of the fea, becauſe no ancient author has made mention of the compaſs. However, he fees no improbability in faying, that fome veſſels might have been thrown upon the coaſt of America by ſtreſs of weather, and on this occaſion he mentions *, as a certain fact, the ſtory of a pilot, driven by a tempeſt on the Brazils, who,

* Chap. xix.

at his death, left his memoirs to Chriftopher Columbus. Afterwards, he takes notice of what Pliny relates concerning fome Indians, who being driven by bad weather on the coaft of Germany, were given in a prefent to Quintus Metellus Celes, by the king of the Suevi. In the fame manner, he finds nothing improbable in the report which goes under Ariftotle's name, *viz.* that a Carthaginian veffel having been driven very far to the weftward by a ftrong eafterly wind, the people on board difcovered lands, which had, till that time, been unknown; and from thofe facts he concludes, that, according to all appearance, America has, by fuch like means, received one part of its inhabitants; but adds, that we muft of neceffity have recourfe to fome other way to people that quarter of the world, were it only to account for the tranfportation of certain animals found in thofe parts, which we cannot reafonably fuppofe to have been embarked on board of fhips, or to have made fo long a paffage by fwimming.

The way by which this has been done, continues father Acofta, could only be by the north of Afia or Europe, or by the regions lying to the fouthward of the ftraits of Magellan; and, were only one of thefe three paffages practicable, we may fufficiently comprehend how America has been peopled by degrees, without having recourfe to navigation, of which there are no traces in the traditions of the Americans. In order to ftrengthen this argument, he obferves, that thofe iflands, fuch as Bermudas, which were too remote from the Continent to fuppofe that fuch fmall veffels as were ufed in that part of the world could find their way thither, were upon their firft difcovery uninhabited; that the Peruvians teftified an extreme furprize at the firft fight of fhips on their coafts;

coasts; and that those animals, such as tygers and lions, which might probably have got thither by land, or at most by traversing small arms of the sea, were altogether unknown even in the best peopled islands of that hemisphere.

In chapter twenty-second, he returns to the Atalantis of Plato, and refutes, with a great deal of gravity, the notion of some who believed the reality of this chimera, and who fancied, that there was but a very short passage from this imaginary island to America. In the following chapter, he rejects the opinion of those who have advanced on the authority of the fourth book of Esdras, that this vast country was peopled by the Hebrews. To these he objects, First, that the Hebrews were acquainted with the use of characters, which no nation of America ever was. Secondly, that these latter held silver in no manner of estimation, whereas the former have always sought after it with extreme avidity. Thirdly, that the descendants of Abraham have constantly observed the law of circumcision, which is practised in no part of America. Fourthly, that they have always preserved with the greatest care their language, tradition, laws and ceremonies; that they have always, without ceasing, looked for the coming of the Messiah; that ever since their dispersion over all the earth, they have never in the least relaxed from all those particulars; and that there is no reason to believe they should have renounced them in America, where not the smallest vestige of them remains.

In the twenty-fourth chapter, he observes, that in a discussion of this nature, it is much easier to refute the system of others than to establish any new one, and that the want of writing and certain

tain traditions, have rendered the difcovery of the origin of the Americans extremely difficult, fo that nothing could be determined in it without being guilty of great temerity ; and that all that can be allowed to the uncertainty of conjecture is, that this great continent has been peopled by degrees in the way we have juft now mentioned ; that he cannot believe thefe tranfmigrations to be very antient, and that according to all human appearance the firft who attempted this paffage were hunters, or wandering nations, rather than a civilized people ; but even granting the firft inhabitants of the new world to have been fuch, there would be but little caufe to wonder, that their defcendants fhould degenerate and vary from the religion and manners of their anceftors : that the want of feveral things was enough to make them forget the ufe of them, and that for want of certain helps for tranfmitting their traditions from age to age, they fhould come by degrees altogether to forget them, or at leaft to disfigure them in fuch manner as to render it impoffible to diftinguifh them : That the example of feveral nations of Spain and Italy, who feem to have had nothing belonging to the human fpecies befides the figure, gives all thefe reafons a great air of probability : That the deluge, of which the Americans have preferved the remembrance, does not appear to him to be that fpoken of in fcripture, but fome particular inundation, whereof fome perfons of great ability pretend there ftill remain certain marks in America : Laftly, that it cannot be proved, that the moft ancient monuments in America are older than the thirteenth or fourteenth century, and that all beyond this is nothing but a confufed heap of fables and tales, and thofe fo very childifh as to render it impoffible to form one reafonable conjecture from them.

The

The third author John de Laët, whose opinion I ought to relate, acknowledges that there is a great deal of good sense and solid reasoning in that of father de Acosta. What he does not approve of is what follows. First, he pretends that the Jesuit is in the wrong to suppose that long passages by sea cannot be made, without the help of the needle, since we may navigate by the help of the stars only; and, that he even seems to contradict himself, by asserting that the compass is a late invention, after telling us, that the use of it was very antient on the coast of Mozambique in the fifteenth Century; that he advances without proof that the Orientals were unacquainted with it, till it had been found out by the people of the west; lastly, that it was very evident either that we could do without it, or that it must have been known in the earliest times, since several islands, even of our hemisphere, and those at a considerable distance from the continent, were peopled very soon after the deluge.

Secondly, that he relates as a thing certain, the story of the Pilot, from whose memoirs it is pretended Christopher Columbus learned the route of the New World, as also that of the Indians sent to Metellus Celer by the king of the Suevi; that we know that the Spaniards spread abroad the first report merely out of jealousy of that great man to whom they owed the obligation of having put them in possession of so many rich countries, and whose only misfortune it was not to have been born in Spain; and that the occasion of their publishing the second was only to rob the Portuguese of the glory of having first opened a way to the Indies by sailing round Africa; that he is deceived if he thinks it possible to make the passage from Terra Australis to the Streights of Magellan, without crossing the

sea,

sea, the discovery of the Streights of Le Maire having shewn its utter impracticability. The error of Father de Acosta, if it is one, was, however, excusable, as at the time when he wrote Le Maire had not as yet discovered the Streights which bear his name.

Thirdly, That he makes the peopling of America too late; and that it is contrary to all probability, that this vast Continent, and some of the islands which surround it, should have so great a number of inhabitants at the end of the fifteenth century, had they only begun to be inhabited two hundred years since. John de Laët pretends, that there is no reason to think, that the Deluge, the tradition of which is still preserved amongst the Americans, is not the universal deluge which Moses mentions in the book of Genesis.

Besides the Spanish Jesuit, three other writers, a Frenchman, an Englishman, and a Dutchman, who have handled the same topick, have passed under the examination of this learned Fleming. These are Lescarbot, Brerewood, and the famous Grotius. He probably knew nothing of the work of Father Garcia, whereof I have already spoken, no more than of that of John de Solorzano Pereyra, a Spanish lawyer, entituled, *De Jure Indiarum* ; whereof the first volume, in which the author relates all the opinions of the learned on the origin of the Americans, was printed in 1629.

Be this as it will, Mark Lescarbot, advocate in the parliament of Paris, was a man of sense and learning, but a little addicted to the marvellous. I have spoken of him in several places of my history. In relating the different opinions on the present question,

tion, which were in vogue in his time, he rejects, as frivolous, the applications made of certain prophecies on this subject, and especially that of Abdias, which had been applied to the conversion of the West-Indies by the ministry of the French and Spaniards, the only nations who have truly undertaken this great work; for the Portuguese, to whom the Brazils owe their conversion, may be comprehended under the name of Spaniards, and the missionaries of the other nations of Europe who have had a share in the publication of the gospel in the new World, went thither under the banner of the crowns of France, Spain, and Portugal. In fact, Abdias could possibly have had the Idumeans only in view, and there is not a single word in his prophecy that can be applied to America with any degree of probability.

Lescarbot leans somewhat more towards the sentiment of those who have transported into the new world the Canaanites, who were driven out of the promised land by Joshua. He thinks there is at least some probability in this notion, because these nations, as well as the Americans, were accustomed to make their children pass through the fire, and to feed upon human flesh, whilst they invoked their idols. He approves what Father Acosta says of the accidents which might have caused certain ships to land in America, and also with respect to the passage by the north of Asia and Europe. He believes that all the parts of the Continent are contiguous, or at least, that if there be any Streight to pass, like that of Magellan, which he supposes separates two Continents from each other, the animals which are to be found in the New World might have made their passage good notwithstanding, since Jacques Cartier saw a bear, as large as a cow, swim over an

arm

arm of the fea fourteen leagues in breadth. Laftly,
he propofes his own opinion, which he feems to give
only by way of fimple conjecture.

Is it, fays he, to be believed, that Noah, who
lived three hundred and fifty years after the Deluge,
fhould be ignorant that a great part of the world
lay beyond the weftern ocean ; and if he did know
it, could be deftitute of means to people it ? Was
it more difficult to pafs from the Canaries to the
Azores, and from thence to Canada, or from the
Cape Verd iflands to Brazil, than from the Continent of Afia to Japan, or to other iflands ftill more
remote ? On this occafion he relates, all that the
antients, and efpecially Ælian and Plato, have faid
of thofe veftiges, which according to him ftill remained in their time, with refpect to the knowledge
of America. He fees nothing to hinder us from
faying, that the Hefperides of the ancients were the
fame with the iflands of the Antilles ; and he explains the fable of the Dragon, which according to
the poets guarded the golden apples, to be the different ftreights winding in a ferpent-like manner
round thofe iflands, and which the frequency of the
fhipwrecks might have caufed to be looked upon as
unnavigable. To this he adds many geographical
obfervations, which are far from being altogether
exact, and which John de Laët very well refutes.

The fame critick juftly remarks, that if the Canaanites facrificed their children to their idols, we,
however, read in no place of the fcripture of their
being Anthropophagi. He acknowledges the pof-
fibility and probability of the paffage of men and
animals into America by the North ; and confeffes,
that it is eafy to conceive that men thus tranfplanted into a defart and remote country fhould there
become

become favage and barbarous ; but he looks upon it as a real and moſt ridiculous paradox to ſuppoſe that Noah ever entertained any thoughts of peopling that immenſe Continent. The ill-humour he is in, and which is no doubt excited by ſome of Leſcarbot's arguments, which to tell truth, are far from being without alloy, hinders him from ſeeing what is ſolid and ſenſible in this conjecture. But this proceeding is common enough to the learned ; as if truth and probability ceaſed to be ſuch from the mixture of real proofs amongſt thoſe others by which they may happen to be ſupported.

Edward Brerewood, a learned Engliſhman, after having refuted the ill-grounded opinion, which makes all the Tartars deſcend from the Iſraelites, and after ſhowing that the ignorance of the true etymology of the name of Tartar, which comes neither from the Hebrew nor the Syriack, but from the river Tartar, will have the New World to have been entirely peopled from this numerous nation ; his proofs are theſe following. Firſt, America has always been better peopled on the ſide towards Aſia, than on that towards Europe. Secondly, the genius of the Americans has a very great conformity with that of the Tartars, who never applied themſelves to any art ; which is, however, not univerſally true. Third-ly, the colour of both is pretty much alike ; it is certain, the difference is not conſiderable, and is, perhaps, the effect of the climate, and of thoſe mixtures with which the Americans rub themſelves. Fourthly, the wild beaſts that are ſeen in America, and which cannot reaſonably be ſuppoſed to have been tranſported thither by ſea, could only have come by the way of Tartary. Laſtly, he anſwers an objection made to him with reſpect to the cir-cumciſion of the Tartars, and maintains, that this

rite

rite was never in ufe with that nation, till after they had embraced the Mahometan religion.

De Laët is contented with barely narrating the opinion of this learned Englishman, which confifts in rejecting the notion of thofe who make the Tartars defcendants of the Ifraelites, who were tranfported by Salmanafar; and in making the Tartars anceftors to all the Americans. We fhall fee what he himfelf thinks, when we come to relate his own opinions on this article. But it is neceffary in the firft place, to examine what paffed between him and the famous Grotius upon this fubject. The difpute was very hot on both fides, and as is ufual in fuch cafes, only embroiled the queftion.

In the year 1642, Grotius publifhed a fmall treatife in *Quarto*, intituled, *De Origine Gentium Americanarum*, which he begins, with fuppofing that the Ifthmus of Panama had been looked upon, before the difcovery of the new world by the Spaniards, as an impenetrable barrier between the two continents of America: whence he concludes, that the inhabitants of both could have nothing common in their original. Milius, whom he does not cite, had advanced this paradox before him. Now, if we may credit the learned Dutchman, excepting Yucatan, and fome other neighbouring provinces, whereof he makes a clafs apart, the whole of North America has been peopled by the Norwegians, who paffed thither by way of Iceland, Greenland, Eftotiland and Narembega. He, notwithftanding, confeffes, that they were followed fome ages after by the Danes, Swedes, and other German nations.

He draws the greateft part of his proofs from the conformity of their manners, and the refemblance

of

of names. But we muſt acknowledge, that nothing can be farther fetched than theſe pretended reſemblances, of which he ſeems, notwithſtanding, fully perſuaded, though very few will be convinced beſides himſelf. What obliges him to place Yucatan apart by itſelf, is the cuſtom of circumciſion, of which he has taken it into his head to believe, he has found ſome traces in this province, and a pretended ancient tradition amongſt the inhabitants, which ſaid, that their anceſtors had eſcaped being ſwallowed up by the waves of the ſea ; and this according to him is what gave riſe to the opinion of ſome that they were deſcended from the Hebrews. Notwithſtanding he refutes this opinion, with much the ſame arguments which Brerewood made uſe of, and believes with Don Peter Martyr d'Anglerie, that the firſt who peopled Yucatan were ſome Ethiopians caſt away on this coaſt by a tempeſt, or by ſome other accident. He is even of opinion, that theſe Ethiopians were Chriſtians, a conjecture which he infers from a kind of baptiſm in uſe in the country. He could not help allowing that the language of the northern Americans is quite different from either the Ethiopian or Norwegian, but this difficulty does not ſtop his career ; he ſearches in the beſt manner he can for a ſolution to it, in the mixture of different nations, who, in proceſs of time, eſtabliſhed themſelves in this part of the New World, and in their wandering way of life, and which according to him reduced them to the neceſſity of inventing new jargons.

Hence he paſſes to the nations in the neighbourhood of the Streights of Magellan, and imagining he has found a ſtrong reſemblance between thoſe ſettled on this ſide of it in the Continent of South-America, and thoſe who have their abode beyond

it,

it, he gives it as his decision that the former derive their original from the latter, and that these as well as the inhabitants of New Guinea have come from the Moluccoes and the island of Java. Yet for all that the peculiar genius of the Peruvians, their laws, their customs, their police, the superb edifices they had built, and the wrecks of Chinese vessels, which, he says, the Spaniards found at the entry of the Pacifick Ocean, after coming through the Straits of Magellan, permit him not to doubt that this nation is, originally, a Chinese colony, which is confirmed, adds he, by the worship of the Sun, which prevails equally in both empires, by the resemblance of their characters and manner of writing, and by the reputation of the ancient Chinese of excelling in the art of navigation. Lastly, he rejects the Tartar or Scythian original of the Americans from the little conformity that is found according to him between the manners and customs of both nations: He insists chiefly on the circumstance of the Americans having no horses, which we know, says he, the Scythians cannot be without. To destroy this system, it will be sufficient to prove, that it leads constantly to false conclusions, a point, which the Flemish critick has rendered extremely evident. He proves with equal clearness, that Grotius is every whit as unhappy in attacking the opinions of others, as he is in establishing his own. In effect, he proves that all the Scythians have not the use of horses, several of them inhabiting countries utterly incapable of maintaining them ; to which he adds, that according to the opinion of those, who pretend that Scythia is not the country whence America has been peopled, it is not necessary to say, that all those who have penetrated that way into the New World were Scythians or Tartars ; that the countries they must of necessity traverse, were no way proper for horses ;

that

that the cuftom of the Scythians, when they find themfelves under the neceffity of croffing an arm of the fea, is to kill their horfes, to flea them, and to cover the boats in which they embark with their hides. Laftly, he maintains, that according to all appearance, thefe tranfmigrations happened very foon after the difperfion of Noah's grandfons, and that at that time, the Scythians and Tartars might as yet be unacquainted with the ufe of horfes.

He proves the antiquity of thefe colonies by the multitude of people inhabiting North-America when it was firft difcovered; and as to the pretended impoffibility of getting paft the Ifthmus of Panama, he fhows the abfurdity of it by the few obftacles the Europeans met with in that paffage. He afterwards undertakes to fhew, that the moft northern Americans have much greater refemblance, not only in the features of their countenances, but alfo in their complexion, and in their manner of living, with the Scythians, Tartars, and Samoeides, than with the Norwegians and German nations: And with refpect to what Grotius fays, in making thefe pafs from Iceland, he very well remarks, that this ifland began to be peopled only towards the end of the ninth century; that even then there paffed only a few families thither, and that thus this ifland could not prefently be in a condition to fend over to America fuch numerous colonies as to have produced fo many thoufands of inhabitants as replenifhed thofe vaft regions in the fifteenth century.

The route which Grotius makes his Norwegians take, likewife furnifhes his adverfary with dangerous weapons againft him. He makes him obferve, that Greenland is cut thorough with vaft and deep arms of the fea, almoft always frozen up, that the

whole

whole country is covered with snows of a prodigious depth, and which are never entirely melted; that Friezeland, if such a country is in being, can be no more than a part of Greenland, or of Iceland, and that there is no reliance to be had on all that the two Zani's have published about it: that Estotiland, according to the account of these two noble Venetians, is at a great distance from Friezeland, since in their time there was very little correspondence between these two countries, and that it was a matter of pure chance that some fishermen happened on this latter: that this enchanted kingdom, the monarch of which had such a magnificent library, has entirely disappeared since the discovery of the northern parts of America; that Norembega, whither Grotius conducted his Norwegians, is no less fabulous; that this name in which this learned man finds with a secret complacency so strong a conformity with that of Norvegia, or Norway, is not the name of any country, but a fictitious one whereof nobody knows the original; that the natives of the country call it Agguncia; that this country lies very far to the south of the place where Estotiland was supposed to be, since it makes part of the south-coast of New France, between Accadia and New-England.

Grotius had relied very much on the termination in *are*, so common in old and new Mexico. Laët draws him from this intrenchment, by shewing that almost all of these names are modern, and of Spanish extraction. He overthrows, with the same ease, the argument which Grotius drew from the traditions of the Mexicans, by observing, that when these nations placed themselves in the neighbourhood of the lake of Mexico, they found great numbers of barbarians, who spoke all sorts of languages, between

tween which there was no manner of affinity or
analogy; so that after having conquered them, they
were obliged to make use of interpreters to be able
to govern them. This frivolous resemblance of
names likewise made Grotius imagine in California
a nation called Alavard, which he makes descend
from the Lombards; Laët, in answer, says, that
the name of Alavard, might possibly have no other
original than that of *Alvarado*, a Spanish Captain,
that had followed Ferdinand Cortez into Mexico,
and perhaps too into California, of which we know
this conqueror made the first discovery.

Laët, as he goes on, makes it appear, that Grotius is equally unsuccesful in his attempts to shew a
conformity of manners, customs, traditions, and
form of government, between the northern Americans and the Norwegians; every thing he advances
on that head being founded on false memoirs. He
then proceeds to consider the argument which his
antagonist draws from the pretended circumcision
and baptism of the people of Yucatan. He maintains, that it is contrary to all probability to look out
for a country surrounded by Norwegian colonies
for a settlement to his Africans, who must have
been much more naturally supposed to have landed
in Brasil, or at least to have stopped at the Antilles,
which islands they must have met with in their
passage, supposing them to have crossed the line.
He confesses that Don Peter Martyr d' Anglerie,
when speaking of the people of Yucatan, affirms,
that many of them were circumcised; but he al-
ledges, that this Italian author has been misinform-
ed, since neither Antonio de Herrera, father de
Acosta, nor Oviedo, writers of much better credit
than him, have ever mentioned the circumcision,
baptism, or crosses upon the tombs of this people

C 3   but

but as meer fables. Laftly, before the Abyffinians could have paffed to America, they muft have taken their departure from the weftern coaft of Africk; and Laët is confident, that the dominions of the king of Ethiopia do not extend fo far that way. In the mean time, it is certain, from the accounts of the Portuguefe, that the king of Benin had his crown of the emperor of Abyffinia.

Laët fays but little of the manner in which Grotius imagines South-America has been peopled by the inhabitants of thofe countries, which lie to the fouthward of the Streights of Magellan; he is fatisfied with obferving that they are only iflands, beyond which, as far as Terra Auftralis, there is nothing but an immenfe extent of ocean : that we are not as yet well acquainted with what lies between that country and New Guinea, and that all the fouthern American nations, not excepting thofe under the dominion of the incas of Peru, fpoke an infinite variety of different languages. The reafons on which Grotius eftablifhes the Chinefe original of the Peruvians, appear no lefs frivolous to this critick.

In the firft place, fays he, the character of the two nations and their tafte for the arts are extremely different. In the fecond place no one has ever faid that the Chinefe pay any religious adoration to the fun; and were this even granted, that worfhip is common to fo many nations, that no arguments could be drawn from hence of any weight in the prefent queftion. It is true, that the incas of Peru, as well as the Chinefe emperors, called themfelves the defcendants of the Sun; but how many other princes have either ufurped themfelves, or received that title from their fubjects : Did not the Mexicans give

give the fame name to Cortez, either to do him honour, or becaufe he came from the eaft. In the
third place, Grotius is ftill more grofsly miftaken in
affirming that the Peruvians made ufe of characters
like the Chinefe, and which were written like theirs
in perpendicular lines, feeing that Father Acofta,
who refided a long time in Peru, and Garcilaffo de
la Vega, defcended by the mother's fide from the
blood of the incas, inform us that they were neither acquainted with characters, nor had the ufe of
any fort of writing. What is added by the learned
Dutchman, that Mango Capa, the firft of the incas,
was himfelf a Chinefe, is no more than a bare conjecture, or a fable invented by fome traveller, there
not being the leaft notice taken of it in the traditions of Peru.

In the laft place, Laët declares that he has never,
in any author, read of any wrecks of Chinefe veffels in the Pacifick Ocean. The fact itfelf appears
to him very improbable, becaufe in the paffage from
China to Peru, the winds are contrary during the
whole year fo that by making the great round
of the ocean by the weft, would be a fhorter paffage, in point of time, than the direct courfe. He
adds, that fuppofing the Peruvians had defcended
from the Chinefe, they muft have preferved at leaft
fome veftiges of the art of navigation, or of the
ufe of iron, whereas they were acquainted with neither; fo that it is much more natural to fuppofe the
Peruvians and their neighbours, the inhabitants of
Chili, came from fome of the Indian nations, fome
of which have always been fufficiently civilized to
be capable of giving birth to an empire fuch as was
that of Peru.

To

To this Grotius makes anfwer, but with the air of the embaffador, and of a perfon of profound learning, and feems perfectly aftonifhed, that any one fhould dare to contradict him. Laët, fomewhat piqued at this behaviour, treats him in his reply with lefs ceremony than before ; and maintains, that in a difpute purely literary, the character of an ambaffador neither gives one writer any manner of advantage over another, nor any additional weight to his reafoning.

Grotius triumphed upon his adverfary's agreeing that Greenland had been peopled by the Norwegians : See here, faid he, one part of America, the inhabitants of which derive their origin from Norway. Now what could have hindered thefe Norwegian Greenlanders from advancing farther ? The queftion is not, anfwered Laët, to determine, Whether or not any of the Northern people paffed to America by the way of Greenland ; but if all the Americans came from Norway, which I maintain to be impoffible. Angrimus Jonas, an Icelander, affirms, that Greenland was not difcovered till the year 964. Gomara and Herrera inform us, that the Chichimeques were fettled on the lake of Mexico, in 721. Thefe favages came from New Mexico, and the neighbourhood of California, fuch is the uniform tradition of the Mexicans : confequently North-America was inhabited many ages before it could receive any from Norway by the way of Greenland.

It is no lefs certain, that the real Mexicans founded their empire in 902, after having fubdued the Chichimeques, Otomias, and other barbarous nations, who had taken poffeffion of the country round the lake of Mexico ; and Father Acofta tells us,

each

each of them fpoke a language peculiar to themfelves. From other authorities we learn, that the
Mexicans themfelves came from California, or from
New Mexico, and that they performed their journey
at leaft for the moft part by land ; confequently, they
could not have come from Norway.

Grotius having thus fet out with an evident ana-
chronifm, every thing he has built on that foundation is a confequence of that original error ; and
his antagonift, who, with all the liberty of a Fleming, imagined he had a right to confider him
only as a man of letters, whofe fyftem appeared
to him erroneous ; and offended at the fame time,
becaufe having attacked him with fufficient moderation, he had not met with the polite return he
expected, fails not to purfue him through all his
blunders, and to place them continually before his
eyes.

The learned embaffador imagined he had read in
Herrera, that the iflanders of *Baccalaos* bore a perfect refemblance to the Laplanders. Laët, after
declaring he could meet with no fuch fact in the
Spanifh hiftorian, repeats what he had already faid,
that he does not deny but fome of the Americans
might have had their original from Europe ; then
bringing his adverfary back to Mexico, he afks
him what connection there was between the Mexicans and the inhabitants of the ifland Baccalaos ?
He acknowledges afterwards, that Herrera mentions
a fort of baptifm and confeffion, that were practifed
in Yucatan and the neighbouring iflands ; but he
maintains, that the worfhip of thofe barbarians was
mixed with fo many impieties, and thofe fo plainly
idolatrous, that it could not reafonably be fuppofed
to be derived from the Abyffinian Chriftians. He
adds,

adds, that it is much more natural to attribute all those equivocal marks of Christianity and Judaism, which have been believed to subsist in divers provinces of the New World, to the Devil, who has always affected to counterfeit the worship of the true God. This remark is made by all good authors, who have spoken of the religion of nations newly discovered, and is besides founded on the authority of the fathers of the church.

Grotius having advanced, without any hesitation, that the Ethiopians might in time have changed their colour in a climate not so sultry as that which they had quitted, Laët makes answer, that though Whites might possibly lose some of their colour, by removing to a warmer climate than that where they were born, yet that there is no example of the descendants of the Blacks becoming white in a cold country ; and that the colour of the Negroes proceeds not solely from the heat of the sun, since the Brazilians, and many others inhabiting the same latitudes, have it not. Lastly, he takes notice of another error of Grotius, who suffered his prejudices to carry him so far, as to be persuaded that the Chinese were not acquainted with the art of printing before the arrival of the Portugese in their country, that he might thereby obviate an objection which might have been started against his system of making the Peruvians descend from the Chinese.

There can nothing, in my opinion, be added to the criticism, which John de Laët has published on the hypothesis of the celebrated Grotius. We are now going to see whether he has been equally happy in establishing his own. He sets out with relating, on the authority of some authors quoted by Pliny, but who do not appear to have been very able geographers,

graphers,

graphers, that in fome iflands near the coaft of Africa, amongft which are the Canaries, fome ancient edifices have been feen, and which are a certain proof that thefe iflands were inhabited before they were difcovered by the Europeans : now it is certain, fays he, that fince they were afterwards entirely deferted, the inhabitants muft have retired elfewhere ; and there is great reafon to believe that they paffed over to America, the paffage being neither long nor difficult.

This migration, according to the calculation of thefe authors, muft have happened about two thoufand years ago : at that time, the Spaniards were much infefted by the Carthaginians, and a fhort while afterwards, no lefs fo by the Romans. Now is it not natural to think, that feveral amongft thofe fhould bethink themfelves of taking refuge in a country, where they might have nothing to fear from the ambition of their enemies ; and what could have hindered them from retiring to the Antilles by way of the weftern iflands, which are fituated exactly half way in that voyage ? the veffels of the Carthaginians were very proper for this navigation, and might very well ferve the Spaniards for models, by which to build others of the fame conftruction. They had the ftill recent example of Hanno, the famous Carthaginian, before their eyes, who had failed very far to the weftward. It is no lefs probable, that people might have croffed from the Cape Verd Iflands to Brazil. The Autololes, whom Pliny has placed in their neighbourhood, were Getulians, and not Ethiopians ; their colour and manners fufficiently correfpond with thofe of the Brafilians.

Great Britain, Ireland, and the Orcades, appear also to the learned Fleming, extremely proper for founding a like conjecture in favour of North America; he relates on this head, what is recorded in the history of Wales, written by Dr. David Powel, under the year 1170. Madoc, says this historian, one of the sons of prince Owen Gwynnith, being tired and disgusted with the civil wars which broke out between his brothers after the death of their father, fitted out several vessels, and after providing them with every thing necessary for a long voyage, went in quest of new lands to the westward of Ireland; there he discovered very fertile countries, and destitute of inhabitants; wherefore, landing a part of his people, he returned to Britain, where he made new levies, and afterwards transported them to his colony. Laët seems to rely much on this story, and concludes from it, that the like enterprizes might possibly have been carried into execution from all the Britannic islands. It were to be wished, adds he, that some persons had applied themselves to compare the languages of some parts of America with those of Ireland and Wales.

From thence he comes to the Scythians, and draws a parallel of their manners with those of the Scythians; first, he proves, by the testimony of Pliny, that this name was formerly common to all the nations living in the north of Asia and Europe; that it was even sometimes given to the Sarmatians and Germans, although it was afterwards restrained to the nations inhabiting the northern extremities of the two continents, where several of them have been for a long time unknown to the rest of the world. He pretends, that amongst those, many were Anthropophagi, that all of them might have sent colonies into America; and that if it be objected,

ed,

ed, that there never were any Anthropophagi, except in South America, it is becaufe all thofe nations, amongſt whom this deteſtable cuſtom prevailed, paſſed thither. He might, no doubt, have ſaved himſelf the labour of making ſo weak an anſwer to an objection, which no perſon would probably ever have made, ſince ſeveral of the North Americans have ever been, and ſtill are, Anthropophagi: but let us proceed to follow him in the explication of his hypotheſis. I call it hypotheſis, becauſe where memoirs are wanting for eſtabliſhing the truth, he is reduced, like all thoſe who have handled this queſtion, to the neceſſity of having recourſe to probability, and it muſt be eſteemed ſufficient to keep within ſight of it.

Pliny indeed, ſays, that the Scythians valued themſelves for having many horſes; but he does not ſay, that all the Scythians did ſo. Strabo mentions ſeveral nations of them living north of the Caſpian Sea, and part of whom led a wandering life: what he ſays of their manners and way of living, agrees, in a great many circumſtances, with what has been remarked in the Indians of America: now it is no great miracle, adds Laët, that theſe reſemblances are not abſolutely perfect; and thoſe people, even before they left their own country, already differed from each other, and went not by the ſame name: their change of abode effected what remained. We find the ſame likeneſs between ſeveral American nations and the Samoeides, ſettled on the great river Oby, ſuch as the Ruſſians have repreſented them to us; and it is much more natural to ſuppoſe, that colonies of theſe nations paſſed over to America, by croſſing the icy ſea on their ſledges, than to cauſe the Norwegians to travel all the way that Grotius has marked out for
them.

them. Befides that the Americans have much lefs refemblance to thefe, than to the Samoeides and the Scythian Nomades.

From North, Laët paffes to South America, and examines whether that continent could have received part of its inhabitants, by way of the Pacifick Ocean, The Iflands of Solomon are fituated eight hundred leagues from the coafts of Peru, and we now know them to be feparated from Terra Auftralis by a fea, the extent of which is not as yet fully afcertained. Father de Acofta believes it to be not very diftant from New Guinea, which he imagines is a continent. But Sir Richard Hawkins, an Englifhman, pretends to have certainly difcovered it to be an ifland. We muft therefore, continues the learned Fleming, fay that South America has been peopled by way of this great continent of Terra Auftralis, and the coaft of which, Don Pedro Hernando Giros, a Portuguefe, and Don Hernando de Quiros, a Spaniard, ranged along for the fpace of eight hundred leagues in the years 1609 and 1610. The latter, who has given his name to part of this continent, obferves in his letter to his Catholick Majefty, that this country, in feveral places where he landed, was extremely well peopled, and that too with men of all complexions. But is it not ftrange, that Laët fhould rather chufe to people South America from a country, feparated from it by a much greater extent of ocean than the reft of the world, than from North America, which, on the fuppofition that it was firft peopled, ought naturally to have fupplied all the New World with inhabitants ?

In order to fupport his affertion, that America could not have been peopled by means of the Pacifick Ocean, he obferves, that eafterly winds, which
conftantly

conftantly prevail there, prevent all navigation from the Weft to the Eaft ; then he examines feveral American languages, in order to compare them with one another, which is not the beft part of his work, at leaft, if we may form a judgment from the extract he has given us of a vocabulary of the Haron language, in order to compare it with that of Mexico ; for he has taken it from brother Gabriel Saghart, a Recollet, who underftood very little of that tongue.

He does not appear to be better acquainted with the religion of the Indians of Canada, in which he endeavours to difcover traces which might have led him to their firft original ; and indeed, all this difplay of learning does not much conduce to the end he has in view : befides, although no one of his age has made a better connected work, or treated of the Weft Indies with fo much accuracy, yet we now meet with feveral things in his performance, which ftand in need of correction.

He concludes, with a fhort explication of the opinion of Emanuel de Moraez, a Portuguefe, extracted from the twentieth book of his Hiftory of Brazil ; a work, which has not as yet been publifhed. According to this author, America has been wholly peopled by the Carthaginians and Ifraelites. With regard to the firft, his proof is, that they had made difcoveries at a great diftance from Africa, the progrefs of which being put a ftop to by the fenate of Carthage, hence it came to pafs, that thofe who happened to be then in the newly difcovered countries, being cut off from all commerce with their countrymen, and deftitute of many neceffaries of life, fell foon into a ftate of barbarity. As to the Ifraelites, Moraez pretends, that nothing but circumcifion is wanting, in order to conftitute a

perfect

perfect refemblance between them and the Brazilians. Even this would be of great importance, were
we to confider the invincible attachment of the
former to that ceremony. But there are many
other points equally effential, wherein the two nations differ. I can fafely affirm, that this pretended refemblance, which appears fo ftriking to the
Portuguefe hiftorian, is at beft a falfe fhow, which
feizes one at the firft glance, but difappears, when
looked into more narrowly and without prejudice.

John de Laët having, in a fatisfactory manner,
refuted what opinions had been advanced before his
time, but not having been equally fuccefsful in
eftablifhing his own, George de Hornn, a learned
Dutchman, entered the lifts, which he did with the
greater confidence, as he believed he fhould draw
great advantages from the new difcoveries his countrymen and the Englifh had lately made in the
northern parts of Afia, Europe, and America.

After relating every thing that has been imagined
on the fubject he undertakes to handle, that is to
fay, all that is found in father Garcia and Solorzano, he fets in the ftrongeft light the difficulty of
determining this queftion; a difficulty occafioned
by the imperfect knowledge we have of the extremities of the globe towards the North and South,
and the havock which the Spaniards, the firft difcoverers of the New World, made amongft its
moft ancient monuments; as witnefs the great
double road between Quito and Cuzeo; fuch an
undertaking, as the Romans have executed nothing
that can be compared to it. However, he is not
afraid to promife himfelf a happy conclufion to his
enquiries, and condemns father Acofta for too haf-
tily determining, that no one can engage to fucceed

in

in such an enterprize, without great rashness. Let us now see whether he himself is not an example of what he finds fault with in the Spanish historian.

He sets out with declaring, that he does not believe it possible America could have been peopled before the flood, considering the short space of time which elapsed between the creation of the world and that memorable event. Very able men have, notwithstanding, believed that there were more men on the face of the earth at that early period, than there are at this present; the thing is at least possible, and this is sufficient to prevent the destroying the absolute certainty of the opinion. Nevertheless, it must be owned, that de Hornn is not single in this opinion; but what he adds, gives us no great notion either of his accuracy or of his probity. According to him, Lescarbot places Noah's birth in the New World; whereas, this French historian has said nothing that bears the smallest resemblance to such a paradox.

In the next place, he lays it down for a principle, that after the deluge, men and other terrestrial animals have penetrated into America both by land and by water, and both too out of a formed design, and by accident; and that birds have got thither by flight, which does not appear to be improbable, seeing that they have been observed to follow vessels without stopping, for the space of three hundred leagues together, and since there are rocks and islands, where they might rest themselves, scattered about every where in the ocean. Thus, according to him, John de Laët had reason to say, that the article of birds occasioned no manner of difficulty. All the world, however, will not be of their opinion; for do not we know many of the fea-

thered

thered species, which are neither able to fly nor to swim so far ? Father Acosta has likewise very well observed, in the opinion of this learned Dutchman, that wild beasts might have found a free passage by land, and that if we do not meet in the New World with horses or cattle, to which he might have added, elephants, camels, rhinoceros's, and many others; it is, because those nations who passed thither, either were not acquainted with their use, or had no convenience to transport them : yet there are cattle in America, but of a species very different from any of those known in our hemisphere.

As to what relates to the human species, de Hornn excludes from America, 1. The Ethiopians, and all the Blacks, both of Africa and Asia; the few Negroes found in the province of Careta, having, without doubt, been brought there by accident, a short time before. 2. The Norwegians, Danes, Swedes, Celtes, and in a word, all the northern and middle countries of Europe and Asia. Mean while it may be observed, the Celtes and ancient Britons were much addicted to navigation, and as likely as any other people to transport themselves to America. 3. The Samoeides and Laplanders. His reason for excluding all these nations is this, that there are no Americans who have white curled hair and beards, excepting the *Miges*, in the province of *Zapoteca*, the *Scheries*, on the river of *Plate*, and the *Malopoques* in Brazil. The Esquimaux have likewise white hair ; which exceptions embarrass the question not a little.

All the Indians of Asia, continues de Hornn, believe the Metempsychosis : therefore that people could not have passed into America, where this doctrine is not so much as known. Yet good authors,

thors, and particularly the learned Koempfer, alledge that the doctrine of the Metempfychofis was first carried into India by Xaca, who was probably an Egyptian priest, driven from his native country by Cambyfes, when he conquered it. Before him, the religion of fire, and the worship of the fun, were spread all over Perfia and the East Indies, both of which are of great antiquity in a good part of North America. Here follows another argument, which, though fupported by the authority of Diodorus Siculus, does not appear to me a whit more convincing. The Indians, fay they, have never fent colonies abroad; confequently they could not have contributed to the peopling of the New World. But fuch general propofitions are not fufceptible of demonftration, efpecially with refpect to fuch a country as the Indies, poffeffed by fo many nations, differing from one another in manners, cuftoms, and genius.

The Greeks and the Latins are likewife excluded from the New World. They could not, according to our author, fail beyond Cadiz, becaufe the Carthaginians, who had the command of the Atlantick Ocean, would not have fuffered them. This argument appears to me very weak, efpecially with regard to the Greeks, who having founded Cadiz, might very well be able to keep thofe feas in fpite of the Carthaginians. I fhould rather imagine, that Hercules being perfuaded that there was nothing beyond that ocean, his countrymen had never thought of embarking upon it, which, however, is a conjecture, that might eafily be deftroyed.

In the laft place, neither Chriftians, Hebrews, nor Mahometans, if we believe de Hornn, have ever fettled in the New World; and if this learned man does not abfolutely reject thofe accounts of

croffes,

croffes, baptifm, circumcifion, confeffion, fafts, and other religious ceremonies, fome veftiges of which have been pretended to have been found in Yucatan and elfewhere, we fhall foon fee what regard he pays to them in the arrangement of his own fyftem, of which here follows the plan.

In the firft place, he fuppofes that America began to be peopled by the North; and regarding the barrier of the Ifthmus of Panama, which Grotius imagines was not open before the time of the Spaniards, as a fuppofition void of all foundation, he maintains, that the primitive colonies fpread themfelves far beyond it, fince through the whole extent of that continent, and both in the northern and fouthern parts of it, we meet with undoubted marks of a mixture of the northern nations with thofe who have come from other places. He believes that the firft founders of thofe colonies were the Scythians; that the Phenicians and Carthaginians afterwards got footing in America by way of the Atlantick Ocean, and the Chinefe by way of the Pacifick; and that other nations might, from time to time, have landed there by one or other of thefe ways, or might poffibly have been thrown on the coaft by tempefts; and laftly, that fome Jews and Chriftians might have been carried there by fome fuch like event, but at a time when all the New World was already peopled.

He, in my opinion, very well obferves, that thofe giants, who may have been feen in fome parts of America, prove nothing; that though in the firft ages, they might poffibly have been more frequently met with, yet it cannot be faid, they ever compofed the body of a nation; that as their pofterity did not all inherit their gigantic ftature, fo men of

a

a common fize might have probably at firft produced thofe Coloffus's, as may be feen in the modern accounts of Virginia and Senegal. Hitherto he has advanced nothing new, moft of thefe obfervations having been made before: afterwards he has fomething, which is not only new, but which is alfo peculiar to himfelf; he paffes from probability to certainty, and from conjectures to pofitive affertions; and this method once tried, he carries it to a great length; fo that if we follow him, we fhall find him fufficiently entertaining, and at times faying very good things.

Omitting the confideration of the Scythians, whom he fuppofes to have entered America by the North, and there to have made the firft fettlements, he eftablifhes a firft migration of the Phenicians, by laying it down for a principle, that from the earlieft times they have been great navigators, and have replenifhed all our hemifphere with their colonies: but it is to be obferved, that under the name of the Phenicians, he likewife comprehends the Canaanites. From Strabo he learns, that the Phenicians failed into the Atlantick Ocean, and built cities beyond the pillars of Hercules. Appian, continues he, and Paufanias inform us, that the Carthaginians, who were originally Phenicians, covered all the ocean with their fleets; that Hanno made the tour of Africk; and that the Canaries were known to the ancients. We know, from other authorities, that the Phenicians, fettled in Africa, waged long and bloody wars with the natives of the country, who deftroyed above three hundred of their cities in Mauritania. Eratofthenes is his warrant for this, and he prefers the authority of that ancient writer to that of Strabo and Artemidorus, who contradict him. Whither could the Phenicians, adds he, have

retired,

retired, after so many and great losses, but to America?

This migration being possible, he looks upon it of course as certain, and to have been very ancient; but he laughs at Opmeer, who had advanced, that the Africans living in the neighbourhood of Mount Atlas, sailed to America before the deluge. He imagines Plato may possibly be mistaken in some things he has said of Atalantis, but that his description is notwithstanding founded on truth. He observes, that all those islands to the westward of Africa, have been called Atlantides, and he reckons it probable, that the Atalantis of Plato lay in America, and that it was drowned in a deluge, of which there still remain some slender traditions among the Americans. Further, he says, that according to Peter Martyr d'Anglerie, the inhabitants of the Antilles report, that all their islands were formerly joined to the continent, and had been separated from it by earthquakes and great inundations : that the vestiges of a deluge are found in Peru to this day, and that all South America is full of water. He might have added, that the north part of America, or New France, alone contains a greater quantity of water than all the rest of that vast continent besides.

Diodorus Siculus relates, that the Phenicians sailed far into the Atlantick Ocean, and that being constrained by tempestuous weather, they landed upon a large island, where they found a fruitful soil, navigable rivers, and magnificent edifices. De Hornn takes this to be the second migration of that people to America. Diodorus adds, that in the sequel the Phenicians being harrassed by the Carthaginians and the inhabitants of Mauritania, who
would

would neither grant them peace nor a truce, sent colonies to that ifland, but kept the affair fecret, in order that they might always have a fecure retreat in cafe of neceffity. Other authors, whom de Hornn does not mention, have alledged, that thefe voyages were carried on without the knowledge of the government, who, perceiving that the country began to diminifh in the number of its inhabitants, and having found out the caufe of this diforder, prohibited that navigation under very fevere penalties.

The third and laft migration of the Phenicians to the New World was occafioned, according to this author, by a three year's voyage, made by a Tyrian fleet in the fervice of Solomon. He afferts, on the authority of Jofephus, that Efion Geber, where the embarkation was made, is a port in the Mediterranean. This fleet, he adds, went in queft of elephants teeth and peacocks to the weftern coaft of Africa, which is *Tarfifh*: this is likewife the opinion of Huet: then to *Ophir* for gold, which is *Haïti*, or the ifland Hifpaniola : Chriftopher Columbus was of the fame opinion, according to fome, as Vetablus certainly was. De Hornn returning afterwards to the Atlantick iflands, would fain perfuade us, that the Phenicians have, at divers times, fent colonies thither, and that the *Cerné* of the ancients is Grand Canaria, for which name it is indebted to the Canaanites, who took refuge there.

One of the Canary Iflands is called *Gomera* : de Hornn makes no doubt that it derives its name from the Amorites, who went to fettle there after they had been driven out of Paleftine by the Hebrews. Ought we to be furprized, if after this he finds the *Cham* of the Phenicians in the *Chemez* of

the

the island Haïti, in the *Camis* of Japan, and in the *Chile Cambal* of Yucatan? The detail which he afterwards enters into, in order to discover traces of of the Phenician religion and manners in the New World, is pretty nearly in the same taste, and carries the same conviction along with it. But what ought not to be (he observes in this place) passed over in silence, is that the first Phenicians, who settled in Africa and the Balearick Islands, had neither any letters or characters, nor knew the use of them; and that Cadmus, a Phenician, carried into Greece, not the characters which his countrymen afterwards made use of, but those which in his time were known among the Egyptians.

All those migrations preceded the Christian æra many ages: here follow such as are of a later date. Our author distinguishes three sorts of Scythians, who passed into the New World, namely, Huns, Tartars of Cathay, and the Chinese. Undoubtedly the partizans for the antiquity of the Chinese nation, will not excuse his making Scythians the founders of this great empire, neither will those, who reject what is doubtful in the pretensions of certain Chinese, be of his opinion; for it is now past doubt, that the Chinese empire cannot be much later than Noah's grand-children. But we should never have done, were we to repeat all the false and arbitrary conjectures of this Dutch writer.

Under the name of Huns, he comprehends numberless nations, who possessed an immense country; the occasion of the passage of many of them to America, was, according to him, their overgrown numbers, and the intestine wars raging amongst them. He pretends, that the route they made choice of, was by the extremity of the North, where they met with frozen seas. Then forgetting

what

what he had juft been faying of the infinite numbers of thofe barbarians, whofe vaft countries could no longer contain them ; as he had already forgotten what he faid at firft, that the firft fettlements in America were compofed of Scythians, he informs us, that the reafon why the northern regions of America are fo thinly inhabited, is, becaufe it was very late before the country of the Huns was peopled at all, and that even at this day, they are far from being populous.

But did they all take the fame road ? No ; for while the greateft number turned off to the right towards the Eaft, thofe whom he calls *Finnes*, and the Samoeides and Carolians, whom Tacitus places in Finland, went off to the Eaft by the weftward, traverfed Nova Zembla, Lapland and Greenland ; whence he reckons that the Norwegians, who had before this time landed in Greenland, and whereof not one was to be found in the year 1348, penetrated into the northern parts of America in queft of more habitable countries. Nothing can reafonably hinder us from believing, that the Efhimaux, and fome other nations in the neighbourhood of Hudfon's Bay, draw their original from the Norwegians of Greenland, fuppofing fuch ever to' have exifted. What is certain, is, that the Efhimaux have nothing in common either in their language, manners, or way of living, complexion, or in the colour of their hair with the people of Canada proper, who are their neareft neighbours.

As to certain animals, fuch as lions and tigers, which, according to all appearance, have paffed from Tartary and Hircania into the New World, their paffage might very well ferve for a proof, that the two hemifpheres join to the northward of Afia ; and

this

this argument is not the only one we have of this circumstance, if what I have often heard related by father *Grollon*, a French jesuit, as undoubted matter of fact may be depended on. This father, say they, after having laboured some time in the missions of New France, passed over to those of China. One day as he was travelling in Tartary, he met a Huron woman, whom he had formerly known in Canada: he asked her, by what adventure she had been carried into a country so distant from her own? She made answer, that having been taken in war, she had been conducted from nation to nation, till she arrived at the place where she then was. I have been assured, that another jesuit passing by way of Nantz, in his return from China, had there related much such another affair of a Spanish woman of Florida: she had been taken by certain Indians, and given to those of a most distant country, and by these again to another nation, till she had thus been successively passed from country to country, had travelled regions extremely cold, and at last found herself in Tartary, and had there married a Tartar, who had passed with the conquerors into China, and there settled. It is indeed true, that those who have sailed farthest to the eastward of Asia, by pursuing the coasts of Jesso or Kamtschatka, have pretended to have perceived the extremity of this continent, thence concluding, that between Asia and America, there could possibly be no communication by land; but besides that, Francis Guella, a Spaniard, if we may believe John Hugh de Linschooten, hath confirmed, that this separation is no more than a streight, a hundred miles over; the last voyages of the Japonese give grounds to think that this streight is only a bay, above which there is a passage over land.

Let us return to George de Hornn. This writer does not exprefs himfelf with accuracy, when he tells us, that North America is full of lions and tigers. It is true, we find in the country of the Iroquoife, a kind of tigers, the hair of which is of a light grey, which are not fpotted, but which have very long tails, and whofe flefh is good eating: but except this, it is not till towards the Tropick that you begin to fee true tigers and lions, which is, however, no proof that they could not have come from Tartary and Hircania; but as by advancing always fouthwards, they met with climates more agreeable to their natures, we may believe they have therefore entirely abandoned the northern countries.

What Solinus and Pliny relate, that the Scythian Anthropophagi depopulated a great extent of country as far as the promontory *Tabin*; and what Mark Pol, the Venetian, tells us, that to the north-eaft of China and Tartary, there are vaft uninhabited countries, might be fufficient to confirm our author's conjecture concerning the retreat of a great number of Scythians into America. We find in the ancients the names of fome of thefe nations: Pliny fpeaks of the Tabians: Solinus mentions the Apuleans; who, he fays, had for neighbours the Maffagetes, and whom Pliny affures us to have entirely difappeared. Ammianus Marcellinus exprefly fays, that the fear of the Anthropophagi obliged feveral of the inhabitants of thofe countries to take refuge elfewhere. All thefe authorities form, in my opinion, at leaft a ftrong conjecture, that more than one nation of America have a Scythian or Tartar original.

Hitherto

Hitherto de Hornn keeps pretty close to his point, and is sure to return to it from time to time, and we discover the man of learning even in his greatest flights, but on the whole, one would say, that by dint of forming conjectures upon the agreement of names, he fails prodigiously in point of judgment. Who, for example, would not laugh to hear him seriously advance, that the Apalaches, a nation of Florida, are the Apaleans of Solinus, and that the Tabians of Ptolomy are the ancestors of the Tombas of Peru ? What follows is still more ridiculous. There is, says he, a people, who are neighbours to the Moguls called Huyrons; these are the Hurons of Canada. Herodotus calls the Turks Yrcas; these are the Iroquoise and Souriquois of Arcadia. Unhappily for such rare discoveries, this conjecture leads to a false conclusion; all, or most of the names of the Indians of New France being of French extraction.

Nay more, the Hurons and Iroquoise, to whom our author gives so very different originals, speak almost the same language, the one being a dialect of the other; whereas the Souriquois, to whom Hornn gives the same ancestors as to the Iroquoise, have absolutely nothing in common with them either in their language or genius. The language they speak is a dialect of the Algonquin; and the Huron is as different from the Algonquin as the Latin is from the Hebrew. Must not one then have his imagination very strongly impressed to be able to persuade himself that the *Meyro Humona* of the Brasilians, and the *Paicuma* of the inhabitants of Santa Cruz come from St. Thomas, and are derived from the language of the Turks, who before they passed over to America, had some knowledge of this Apostle ?

Our

Our author's usual confidence deserts him, when he seems to have most occasion for it, and he dares not decide whether South-America has peopled the Terra Austral, or whether that country may have thence received its own inhabitants; but he very soon recovers it, and by means of it undertakes to unravel the origin of the empires of Peru and Mexico. He agrees with several historians, that these monarchies were not very ancient when the Spaniards destroyed them, and that their founders had to fight against barbarous nations, that had been long settled in the country they had made choice of, and chiefly Mexico, where the manners were much more rugged in the time of Cortez, than they were amongst the Peruvians. This difference probably was owing to this, that the conquerors of Mexico were not so much civilized as those of Peru.

Both the one and the other, if we may believe Hornn, are, notwithstanding, originally from the same parts; these are, says he, the nations of Cathey ; the Japonese, who are originally descended from thence, the Chinese, whom he always supposes to be descended from the Scythians ; some Egyptians, and some Phenicians, from the time that these two empires attained to perfection, in policy, religion, and arts. Here is certainly a very miscellaneous and capricious original. But in fine, the learned Dutchman will have it, that all these nations have sent colonies into America, and to prove this, it is scarce conceivable, where he goes in quest of Cathayan, Corean, Chinese, and especially Japonese names, in all parts of the New World. Between these, there is often much the same relation as the *Alfana*, and *Equus* of Menage ; but he likewise causes them to take so very long a journey,
that

that we ought not to be surprized if they undergo very confiderable changes by the way.

He even goes fo far as to derive the name of the Chiquites of Paraguay, which is purely of Spanifh extraction from that of Cathay. The name of Inca, which was that of the imperial family of Peru, has, according to him too great a refemblance with the fame name of Cathay, to fuffer any doubt that thefe fovereigns derive their original from this great country. In a word, to feek for the Cathayans in America, is, according to him, the fame with fearching for the Greeks in Italy, and the Phenicians in Africk. The Coreans called their country *Caoli*; therefore, California has been peopled by a Corean Colony. *Chiapa*, a province of Mexico, whence can it come but from *Giapon*, a name which fome give to the ifland of Japan? Montezuma, emperor of Mexico, had a beard after the Chinefe fafhion; he wants no more to make him come originally from China. It is not, however, without fome fcruple, that our author quits his etymologies for the figure of the beard; but this beard is very fingular in a Mexican. He, moreover, finds that the name of monarch has a great affinity with that of Motuzaïuma, which he pretends on I know not what authority, to be a title of honour in Japan: thus this prince might very well derive his original from thefe iflands.

However, it is neither the Cathayans, nor the Japonefe who have founded the Mexican monarchy: De Hornn afcribes that honour to Facfur, king of China, who being dethron'd by Cublay, great cham of Tartary, fled with a hundred thoufand Chinefe, in a thoufand veffels into America, and there became the founder of a new empire. Manco, another

ther Chinese prince, originally of Cathay, had two ages before founded that of Peru. Here are many names, of which the Fathers Couplet, Le Compte, and Du Halde were entirely ignorant. Manco had carried the arts to very great perfection, and it was he who reared those magnificent edifices which so much astonished the Spaniards. He brought no horses into America, because, in his time, says Mark Pol the Venetian, there were none in China. But it may be asked, why the Chinese of Peru have not preserved their characters? It is, answers Hornn, because they were too difficult to write; they found that it was a shorter and easier way to supply the use of them by symbolical figures.

This is a part of what has been written on the present question; and I am much mistaken if the bare setting down of so many different opinions is not sufficient to furnish the attentive reader with all the lights necessary to lead him to the choice of the proper side in this great controversy, which, by endeavouring to explain they have hitherto rendered only more obscure. It may be reduced as appears to me to the two following articles. 1. How the New World might have been peopled? 2. By whom and by what means it has been peopled.

Nothing it would seem may be more easily answered than the first. America might have been peopled, as the three other quarters of the world have been. Many difficulties have been formed upon this subject which have been deemed insolvable, but are far from being so. The inhabitants of both hemispheres are certainly the descendants of the same father. This common father of mankind received an express order from heaven to people the whole world, and accordingly it has been peopled.

To

To bring this about, it was neceſſary to overcome all difficulties in the way, and they have alſo been got over. Were thoſe difficulties greater with reſpect to peopling the extremities of Aſia, Africa, and Europe, and the tranſporting men into the iſlands, which lie at a conſiderable diſtance from thoſe Continents, than to paſs over into America? Certainly not. Navigation which has arrived at ſo great perfection within theſe three or four centuries, might poſſibly have been ſtill more perfect in thoſe firſt times than at this day. At leaſt, we cannot doubt, but it was then arrived at ſuch a degree of perfection as was neceſſary for the deſign which God had formed of peopling the whole earth.

Whilſt thoſe authors whom I have cited, have kept to this poſſibility which cannot be denied, they have reaſoned very juſtly; for if it has not been demonſtrated, that there is a paſſage into America over land, either by the north of Aſia and Europe, or by the ſouth, the contrary has not been made appear; beſides, from the coaſt of Africa to Brazil; from the Canaries to the weſtern Iſlands, from the weſtern Iſlands to the Antilles; from the Britannic iſles, and the coaſt of France to Newfoundland, the paſſage is neither long nor difficult: I might ſay as much of that from China to Japan, and from Japan and the Philippines to the *Iſles Mariannes*, and from thence to Mexico. There are iſlands at a conſiderable diſtance from the Continent of Aſia, where we have not been ſurprized to find inhabitants. Why then ſhould we wonder to find people in America? And it cannot be imagined, that the grandſons of Noah, when they were obliged to ſeparate and to ſpread themſelves in conformity to the deſigns of God over the whole earth, ſhould be in

an

an abfolute impoffibility of peopling almoft one half
of the globe ?

They ought therefore to have kept to this; but
the queftion was too fimple and too eafy to be anfwered. The learned muft make difquifitions, and
they imagined they were able to decide how and by
whom America has been peopled; and as hiftory
furnifhed no materials for this purpofe, rather than
ftop fhort they have realized the moft frivolous conjectures. The fimple refemblance of names, and
fome flight appearances, feemed, in their eyes, fo
many proofs, and on fuch ruinous foundations they
have erected fyftems of which they have become
enamoured, the weaknefs of which the moft ignorant are able to perceive, and which are often overturned by one fingle fact which is inconteftable.
Hence it happens, that the manner in which the
New World has received its firft inhabitants remaining in very great uncertainty, they have imagined
difficulties where none really were, and they have
carried this extravagance to fuch a height, as to believe, that the Americans were not the defcendants
of our firft parents; as if the ignorance of the manner in which a thing hath happened, ought to make
us look upon it as impoffible, or at leaft as extremely difficult.

But what is moft fingular in this, is, that they
fhould have neglected the only means that remained to come at the truth of what they were in fearch
of; 1 mean, the comparing the languages. In effect, in the refearch in queftion, it appears to me,
that the knowledge of the principal languages of
America, and the comparing them with thofe of
our Hemifphere, that are looked upon as primitive,
might poffibly fet us upon fome happy difcovery;

an

and that way of afcending to the original of nations, which is the leaft equivocal, is far from being
fo difficult as might be imagined. We have had, and
ftill have travellers and miffionaries, who have worked on the languages that are fpoken in all the provinces of the New World. It would only be neceffary to make a collection of their grammars and
vocabularies, and to collate them with the dead and
living languages of the Old World that pafs for originals. Even the different dialects, in fpite of the
alterations they have undergone, ftill retain enough
of the mother-tongue to furnifh confiderable lights.

Inftead of this method, which has been neglected, they have made enquiries into the manners,
cuftoms, religion, and traditions of the Americans,
in order to difcover their original. Notwithftanding, I am perfuaded, that this difquifition is only
capable of producing a falfe light, more likely to
dazzle, and to make us wander from the right path,
than to lead us with certainty to the point propofed.
Ancient traditions are effaced from the minds of
fuch as have not, or, who, during feveral ages,
have been, without any helps to preferve them;
and half the world is exactly in this fituation. New
events, and a new arrangement of things give rife
to new traditions, which efface the former, and are
themfelves effaced in their turn. After one or two
centuries have paffed, there no longer remain any
marks capable of leading us to find the traces of
the firft traditions.

The manners very foon degenerate by means of
commerce with foreigners, and by the mixture of
feveral nations uniting in one body, and by a change
of empire always accompanied with a new form of
government. How much more reafon is there to
be-

believe fuch a fenfible alteration of genius and manners amongft wandering nations become favage,
living, without principles, laws, education, or civil
government, which might ferve to bring them back
to the antient manners. Cuftoms are ftill more eafily deftroyed. A new way of living introduces
new cuftoms, and thofe which have been 'forfaken
are very foon forgotten. What fhall I fay of the
abfolute want of fuch things as are moft neceffary
to life? And of which, the neceffity of doing without, caufes their names and ufe to perifh together.

Laftly, nothing has undergone more fudden, frequent, or more furprizing revolutions than religion.
When once men have abandoned the only true one,
they foon lofe it out of their fight, and find themfelves entangled and bewildered in fuch a labyrinth
of incoherent errors, inconfiftency and contradic-
tion being the natural inheritance of falfhood, that
there remains not the fmalleft thread to lead us back
to the truth. We have feen a very fenfible example of this in the laft age. The Buccaneers of St.
Domingo, who were chriftians, but who had no
commerce except amongft themfelves, in lefs than
thirty years, and through the fole want of religious
worfhip, inftruction, and an authority capable of
retaining them in their duty, had come to fuch a
pafs, as to have loft all marks of chriftianity, except baptifm alone. Had thefe fubfifted only to
the third generation, their grandchildren would have
been as void of chriftianity as the inhabitants of
Terra Auftralis, or New-Guinea. They might
poffibly have preferved fome ceremonies, the reafon
of which they could not have accounted for, and
is it not precifely in the fame manner, that fo many
infidel nations are found to have in their idolatrous

wor-

worſhip ceremonies which appear to have been copied after ours.

The caſe is not the ſame with reſpect to languages.
I allow that a living language is ſubject to continual
changes, and as all languages have been ſo, we may
ſay with truth, that none of them have preſerved
their original purity.. But it is no leſs true, that in
ſpite of the changes, introduced by cuſtom, they
have not loſt every thing by which they are diſtinguiſhed from others, which is ſufficient for our preſent purpoſe; and that from the rivulets, ariſing
from the principal ſprings, I mean the dialects, we
may aſcend to the mother-tongues themſelves; and
that by attending to the obſervation of a learned
academician *, that mother-tongues are diſtinguiſhed
by being more nervous than thoſe derived from
them, becauſe they are formed from nature; that
they contain a greater number of words imitating
the things whereof they are the ſigns; that they are
leſs indebted to chance or hazard, and that that
mixture which forms the dialects, always deprives
them of ſome of that energy, which the natural
connection of their ſound with the things they re-
preſent always give them.

Hence, I conclude, that if thoſe characteriſtical
marks are found in the Americans languages, we
cannot reaſonably doubt of their being truly original; and, conſequently, that the people who ſpeak
them have paſſed over into that hemiſphere, a ſhort
time after the firſt diſperſion of mankind; eſpecially, if they are entirely unknown in our Continent.
I have already obſerved, that it is an arbitrary ſuppoſition that the great grandchildren of Noah were

* M. l'Abbé du Bos, *Hiſtory of Painting and Poetry.*

not able to penetrate into the New World, or that they never thought of it. In effect, I fee no reafon that can juftify fuch a notion. Who can ferioufly believe that Noah and his immediate defcendants knew lefs than we do; that the builder and pilot of the greateft fhip that ever was, a fhip which was formed to traverfe an unbounded ocean, and had fo many fhoals and quickfands to guard againft, fhould be ignorant of, or fhould not have communicated to thofe of his defcendants who furvived him, and by whofe means he was to execute the order of the great Creator, to people the univerfe, I fay, who can believe he fhould not have communicated to them the art of failing upon an ocean, which was not only more calm and pacifick, but at the fame time confined within its ancient limits?

Is it even determined on fufficient grounds, that America had not inhabitants before the deluge? Is it probable, that Noah and his fons fhould have been acquainted with only one half of the world, and does not Mofes inform us, that all, even the remoteft Continents and iflands were once peopled? How fhall we reconcile this with the fuppofition of thofe who maintain, that the firft men were ignorant of the art of navigation; and can it ferioufly be faid, contrary to the authority of fo refpectable a teftimony, as John de Laët has done, that navigation is an effect of the temerity of mankind; that it does not enter into the immediate views of the Creator, and that God has left the land to the human fpecies, and the ocean to fifhes? Befides, are not the iflands a part of the earth, and are there not many places on the Continent, to which it is much more natural to go by fea, than by long circuits frequently impracticable, or at leaft fo very

diffi-

difficult, as to induce men to undertake almost any thing in order to avoid them.

It is certain, that the art of navigation has shared the same fate with many others, of which we have no proof that our early ancestors were entirely ignorant, some of which are now lost, and others again preserved only among a few nations; but what does this prove? We must always return to this principle, that the arts necessary to the designs of God have never been unknown to those whose business it was to put them in execution. Industry, has, perhaps, invented some which were useful only, and luxury discovered others which served only to gratify the passions. We may also believe, that what has caused many to fall into oblivion, is their having become no longer necessary, and that such has been the making long voyages as soon as all the parts of the world were supplied with inhabitants. It was sufficient for the purposes of commerce to range along the coasts, and to pass over to the nearest islands. Need we then be surprized, if men, for want of practice, lost the secret of making long voyages on an element so inconstant, and so frequently tempestuous.

Who can ever affirm that it was lost so soon? Strabo says in several places, that the inhabitants of Cadiz, and all the Spaniards, had large vessels, and excelled in the art of navigation. Pliny complains, that in his time, navigation was not so perfect as it had been for several ages before; the Carthaginians and Phenicians were long possessed of the reputation of being hardy and expert mariners. Father Acosta allows, that Vasco de Gama found, that the use of the compass was known among the inhabitants of Mozambique. The islanders of Madagascar have

a

a tradition, importing, that the Chinese had sent a colony into their country. And is it not a meer begging of the question, to reject that tradition on account of the impossibility to sail so far without the help of the compass. For if the compass is necessary for sailing from China to Madagascar, I have as much right to say, on the faith of a tradition, universal in that great island, that the Chinese have sailed to Madagascar, therefore they had the use of the compass; as any other person has to reason in this manner, the Chinese were unacquainted with the compass, therefore they never were at Madagascar. However, I do not undertake to support this as matter of fact, which I might safely do with very good authors; I only say I am as well grounded in advancing, as they are in rejecting it.

The Chinese, whose original reaches up as high as the grandsons of Noah, have anciently had fleets; this is a fact sufficiently established in history: What could have hindered them from passing to Mexico by way of the Philippines? The Spaniards perform this voyage every year; from thence by coasting along shore, they might have peopled all America on the side of the South-sea. The *Isles Mariannes*, and many others, of which discoveries are every day made in that extent of ocean, which separates China and Japan from America, might have received their inhabitants in the same manner, some sooner and some later. The inhabitants of the islands of Solomon, those of New-Guinea, new Holland, and Terra Australis, bear too little resemblance to the Americans, to leave room to imagine they could have sprung from the same original, unless we trace it up to the remotest ages. Such is their ignorance that we can never know from whence they really draw their descent; but in fine, all these countries

E 4 are

are peopled ; and it is probable, fome have been fo
by accident. Now if it could have happened in
that manner, why might it not have been done at
the fame time, and by the fame means with the
other parts of the globe ?

It cannot be denied, that the original of the ancient Celtes and Gauls, fo renowned for their ex-
pertnefs in navigation, and who have fent fo many
colonies to the extremities of Afia and Europe, af-
cends as high as the children of Japhet ; and might
not they have penetrated into America by way of
the Azores ? Should it be objected that thefe iflands
were uninhabited in the fifteenth century, I anfwer,
that their firft difcoverers, had, undoubtedly, neglected them, in order to fettle themfelves in larger
and more fertile countries, in an immenfe Continent,
from which they were at no great diftance. The
Efkimaux, and fome other nations of North-America, bear fo ftrong a refemblance to thofe of the
north of Europe and Afia, and fo little to the reft
of the inhabitants of the New World, that it is
eafy to perceive they muft have defcended from the
former, and that their modern original has nothing
in common with the latter ; I fay, modern original,
for there is not the leaft appearance of its being ancient ; and it is reafonable to fuppofe, that countries fo very far from being tempting, have been
inhabited much later than others.

The fame does not hold good with refpect to the
reft of America, and I can never think that fo confiderable a portion of the globe was unknown to,
or neglected by the firft founders of nations ; and
the argument drawn from the characters of the A-
mericans, and the frightful picture which was at
firft given of them, proves nothing againft their an-
quity.

quity. It is three thousand years at most since
Europe was full of people as savage and as little civilized, as the greatest part of the Americans; and
of these there are still some remains. Does not Asia,
the first seat of religion, policy, arts, and sciences,
and the centre of the purest and most ancient traditions, still behold her most flourishing empires en-
vironed by the grossest barbarity? Egypt which has
boasted of having been the source of the finest improvements, and which has relapsed into the pro-
foundest ignorance; the empire of the Abyssinians so
ancient, and heretofore so flourishing; Lybia, which
has produced so many great men; Mauritania which
has sent forth so many men learned in all sciences:
have not these always had in their neighbourhood
people who seemed to possess nothing human but
the figure? Why then should we be surprized that
the Americans, so long unknown to the rest of the
world, should have become barbarians and savages,
and that their most flourishing empires should be
found destitute of so many articles which we reckon
indispensably necessary in our hemisphere.

Let us enquire what has rendered the moun-
taineers of the Pyrenees so fierce as many of them
are at this day; what is the original of the Laplanders and Samoeides, the Cafres, and Hottentots;
why under the same parallels of latitude there are
blacks in Africa, and not elsewhere; and we shall
then find an answer to the same questions, respecting
the Eskimaux and Algonquins, the Hurons and
Sioux, the Guayranis and Patagonians. If it be
asked, why the Americans have no beards, nor hair
on their bodies, and why the greatest part of them
are of a reddish colour, I shall ask in my turn,
why the Africans are mostly black? This question

is

is of no confequence in the difpute on the original
of the Americans.

Primitive nations have been mixed and divided
by various caufes, foreign and domeftick wars as
ancient as the luft of dominion, or the paffion for
domineering, the neceffity of feparating and removing to greater diftances, either becaufe the country
was no longer able to contain its inhabitants multiplied to an infinite degree, or becaufe the weaker
were obliged to fly before the ftronger ; that reft-
lefsnefs and curiofity, fo natural to mankind, a thoufand other reafons eafily to be imagined, and which
all enter into the defigns of Providence ; the manner in which thofe migrations have been made ; the
difficulty of preferving arts and traditions amongft
fugitives tranfplanted into uncultivated countries,
and out of the way of carrying on any correfpond-
ence with civilized nations : All this I fay is eafy
to conceive. Unforefeen accidents, tempefts, and
fhipwrecks, have certainly contributed to people all
the habitable part of the world ; and ought we to
wonder after this, at perceiving certain refemblances
between the remoteft nations, and at finding fuch a
difference between nations bordering upon one another.

We may likewife further underftand, that fome
part of thefe wanderers, either forced by neceffity to
unite for mutual defence, or to withdraw from the
domination of fome powerful people, or induced by
the eloquence and abilities of a legiflator, muft have
formed monarchical governments, fubmitted to
laws, and joined together in regular and national
focieties. Such have been the beginnings of the
moft ancient empires in the Old World ; and fuch
might have been the rife of thofe of Peru and
Mex-

Mexico in the New; but we are deftitute of hifto-
rical monuments to carry us any farther, and there
is nothing, I repeat it, but the knowledge of the
primitive languages which is capable of throwing
any light upon thefe clouds of impenetrable dark-
nefs. It is not a little furprifing, that a method fo
natural and practicable has been hitherto neglected
of making difcoveries as interefting at leaft, as the
greateft part of thofe which for thefe two ages paft
have employed the attention of the learned. We
fhould, at leaft, be fatisfied amongft that prodigious
number of various nations inhabiting America, and
differing fo much in language from one another;
which are thofe who fpeak languages totally and
entirely different from thofe of the Old World, and
who, confequently, muft be reckoned to have pafs-
ed over to America in the earlieft ages; and thofe,
who from the analogy of their language, with thefe
ufed in the three other parts of the globe, leave
room to judge that their migration has been more
recent, and ought to be attributed to fhipwrecks, or
to fome accident fimilar to thofe of which I have
fpoken in the courfe of this differtation.

HISTORICAL

HISTORICAL JOURNAL

OF A

VOYAGE to AMERICA;

Addreſſed to the

DUCHESS OF LESGUIERES.

LETTER FIRST.

MADAM,   *Rochefort, June* 30th, **1720.**

YOU were pleaſed to expreſs a deſire I ſhould write you regularly by every opportunity I could find, and I have accordingly given you my promiſe, becauſe I am not capable of refuſing you any thing; but I am greatly afraid you will ſoon grow weary of receiving my letters : for I can hardly perſuade myſelf you will find them near ſo intereſt-ing as you may imagine they ought to be. In a word, you have laid your account with a continued journal; but in the firſt place, I foreſee that the meſſengers, by whoſe hands I muſt tranſmit my letters to you, will never be over and above exact in conveying them, and may poſſibly ſometimes fail in delivering them altogether ; in which caſe, you can only have a mutilated and imperfect journal :

befides,

befides, I am as yet at a lofs where I am to find materials to fill it. For you muft certainly know, that I am fent into a country, where I fhall often be obliged to travel a hundred leagues and upwards, without fo much as meeting with one human creature, or indeed any thing elfe but one continued profpect of rivers, lakes, woods, and mountains. And befides, what fort of men fhall I meet with ? With favages, whofe language I do not underftand, and who are equally unacquainted with mine. Befides, what can men, who live in the moft barbarous ignorance, fay to me, that can affect me; or what can I find to fay to them, who are full as indifferent and unconcerned as to what paffes in Europe, and as little affected with it, as you and I Madam are, with what relates to their private concerns.

In the fecond place, fhould I make ufe of the priviledge of a traveller, I know you too well to venture upon taking that liberty with you, or to flatter myfelf I fhould find any credit with you, fhould I attempt it. You may therefore lay afide all fuch apprehenfions in myfelf, for I feel no manner of inclination to forge adventures : I have already had an experimental proof of the truth of what is faid by an ancient author, that men carry their own peculiar genius and manners about with them crofs all feas, and through all changes of climate, let them go where they will ; and I, for my part, hope to preferve that fincerity, for which you know me, crofs the vaft regions of America, and through thofe feas, which feparate that New World from ours. You are pleafed to exprefs fome concern for my health, which you do not think fufficiently confirmed to undertake fo long and fatiguing a voyage ; but thank God, I gather ftrength daily,

and

and I wifh I could promife myfelf with the fame
certainty, or at leaft probability, every other quali-
fication neceffary to acquit myfelf, as I ought, of
the commiffion, with which I have been entrufted.
But would you believe it, Madam, I thought I
fhould have loft my life about half way between
Paris and Rochefort. Perhaps you ftill remember
what you have often heard me fay, that our rivers in
France were no more than rivulets, compared with
thofe of America: I can affure you, the Loire was
very near taking a fevere revenge on me for this
outrage and affront done to the dignity of that
river.

I had taken boat at Orleans with four or five
officers belonging to Conti's regiment of infantry.
On the fixteenth, being over-againft *Langets*, and
being unable to advance any farther, on account of
a ftrong wind blowing directly in our teeth, we
wanted to gain that village, to make fure of
good lodgings, in cafe of being obliged to pafs
the night there. For this purpofe, it was neceffary
to crofs the river, which we accordingly propofed
to our boatmen, who fhowed great reluctance to
undertake it; but being young people, and we in-
fifting on it, they durft not contradict us. We had
hardly got to the middle of the channel, when we
could have wifhed to have been back again; but it
was now too late, and what troubled me moft of
all, it was I who propofed the advice we fo heartily
repented of. We were really in great danger, which
was evident from the countenances of our conduc-
tors; however, they were not difcouraged, and
managed fo well, that they extricated us out of this
difficulty.

The

The danger being over, one of the company who had frequently been on the point of ftripping, in order to betake himfelf to fwimming, took upon him to cry out with all his force, but with a tone which fhowed there was ftill a palpitation at his heart, that I had been in a great fright. Perhaps he fpoke truer than he thought of; all this was, however, nothing but guefs-work; and efpecially to ward off the reproaches they were beginning to make me, and in order to perfuade others there was no danger, I had always preferved a tolerable good countenance. We frequently meet with thofe falfe bravos, who, to conceal their own apprehenfions, endeavour to make a diverfion by rallying thofe who have much better courage than themfelves. In the mean time, Madam, were I to believe in omens, here was fufficient to form a bad augury of a voyage I was going to undertake for above three thoufand leagues by fea, and to fail in a canoe of bark on two of the greateft rivers in the world, and on lakes almoft as large, and at leaft full as tempeltuous as the Pontus Euxinus, or the Cafpian fea.

The Loire continued to be full as untractable all the reft of the day, fo we flept at *Largets*; our officers, who had their *Lieutenant de Roy* at their head, were civil men enough, and extremely agreeable company. They were, moreover, very religious, and they gave one proof of it, which was far from being doubtful. There was a kind of adventurer that had joined them at Paris, who was half wit, half *petit Maitre :* as far as Orleans he had kept tolerably within bounds, but the moment we were embarked, he began to break out a little, and by degrees, came to talk on religious matters in a very libertine manner. I had the fatisfaction to fee
that

that all our officers were so much offended at it, that at Langets none of them would lodge in the same house with him. A young lieutenant took it upon him to tell him of it, and obliged him to seek a lodging elsewhere.

I arrived here the 19th; I was expected as I was charged with packets from the court; but they looked for somewhat besides, that is to say, some money, which arrived not till to-day. To-morrow I embark on board the Camel, a large and fine frigate belonging to the king, now in the road below the Isle of Aix, where I shall find myself in the midst of my acquaintances. I have already been at sea with M. de Voutron, who is captain of her, and with Chaviteau the first pilot; and I have lived with several of the officers and passengers in Canada. We are told, that we are extremely well-manned, and there is not a sea-officer who is better acquainted with the voyage we are going to make than our captain. Thus I have nothing to desire, whether with regard to the safety or agreeableness of the passage.

I am, &c.

F   L E T T E R

L E T T E R II.

Voyage from Rochelle *to* Quebec ; *some Remarks on that passage, on the great Bank of* Newfoundland, *and on the River* St. Lawrence.

Quebec, Sept. 24, 1720.

Madam,

YEsterday I arrived in this city, after a tedious and troublesome passage of eleven weeks and six days ; we had, however, only a thousand leagues to sail ; thus you see that at sea we do not always travel as M. l'Abbé de Choisy used to say *per la via delle poste*. I have kept no journal of this voyage, as I suffered greatly from the sea-sickness which lasted with me for more than a month. I had flattered myself with being quit this time, having already paid tribute twice before ; but there are constitutions which are absolutely incapable of enduring that element, of which sort mine is one. Now in the condition, to which we are reduced by this indisposition, it is absolutely impossible to give any attention to what passes in the ship. And besides, nothing can be more barren than such a navigation as this ; for we are generally taken up with enquiring how the wind blows, at what rate we advance, and whether it be in the right course ; and during two thirds of the way you see nothing but

F 2

the

the feas and fkies. I am going, however, to give you what my memory can furnifh moft likely to contribute to your amufement for a quarter of an hour, in order to acquit myfelf as much as is poffible of the promife I made you.

We continued in the road the firft of July the whole day, and the fecond we fet fail by the favour of a gentle breeze at north-eaft. The three firft days the wind continued favourable, though in very light breezes, which, from the calmnefs of the fea, were fufficiently acceptable. It feemed as if it wanted to lull us afleep before it fhowed itfelf in all its fury. The fourth or fifth, the wind changed, fo that we were obliged to lie clofe-haul'd *. The fea grew high, and for near fix weeks we were much toffed. The winds fhifted continually, but were much oftener againft us than favourable, fo that we were obliged almoft continually to ply to windward.

On the ninth of Auguft our pilots believed themfelves on the great bank of Newfoundland, and they were not much miftaken; they were even in the right in reckoning fo, it being the bufinefs of a good navigator to be always fomewhat a-head of his fhip; that is to fay, to fuppofe himfelf farther advanced than he really is; but from the 9th to the 16th, we fcarce made any way at all. What is called the great bank of Newfoundland, is properly a mountain, hid under water, about fix hundred French leagues from the weftern fide of that kingdom. The Sieur Denys, who has given the world an excellent work on North-America, and a very inftructive treatife, gives this mountain an hundred and fifty leagues in extent, from north to fouth;

---

* *To lie clofe-haul'd*, that is, to fail almoft directly againft the wind, or as nearly as poffible.

but

but, according to the moſt exact ſea-charts, the beginning of it on the ſouth-ſide is in 41 deg. north
lat. and its northern extremity is in 49 deg. 25 min.

It is indeed true, that both its extremities are ſo
narrow, that it is very difficult to fix its boundaries
with any exactneſs. Its greateſt breadth from eaſt
to weſt is about 90 ſea leagues of England and
France, between 40 and 49 deg. of long. weſt from
the meridian of Paris. I have heard ſailors ſay,
that they have anchored upon it in five fathom water; which is likewiſe contrary to what the Sieur
Denys advances, who pretends he never found leſs
than five and twenty. But it is certain, that in ſeveral places there is upwards of ſixty. Towards
the middle, on the ſide next Europe, it forms a bay
called *La Foſſe*, or the ditch; and this is the reaſon,
why of two ſhips under the ſame meridian, and
within ſight of one another, the one ſhall find
ground, and the other no ſoundings at all.

Before you arrive at the great bank, you find a
leſſer one called the *Banc Jacquet*, ſituated oppoſite
to the middle of the great one. Some mention a
third bank before this, to which they give a coni-
cal figure; but I have ſeen pilots who make no
more than one of all the three, and anſwer ſuch objections as are made to them, by aſſerting, that
there are cavities in the great bank, and of ſuch a
depth as to deceive thoſe who are led into the falſe
ſuppoſition of three different banks, by not happening to run out a ſufficient length of cable when they
caſt anchor. However, let the ſize and ſhape of
this mountain be as they will, ſince it is impoſſible
to aſcertain them to any degree of exactneſs; you
find on it a prodigious quantity of ſhell-fiſh, with
ſeveral ſorts of other fiſhes of all ſizes, moſt part

of

of which ferve for the common nourifhment of the
cod, the number of which feems to equal that of
the grains of fand which cover this bank. For
more than two centuries fince, there have been loaded with them from two to three hundred fhips an-
nually, notwithftanding the diminution is not perceivable. It might not, however, be amifs, to dif-
continue this fifhery from time to time, and the
more fo, as the gulph of St. Lawrence, and even
the river, for more than fixty leagues, the coafts of
Acadia, thofe of the *Ifle Royale*, or Cape Breton,
and of Newfoundland, are no lefs replenifhed with
this fifh, than the great bank. Thefe, Madam,
are true mines, which are more valuable, and require much lefs expence than thofe of Peru and
Mexico.

We fuffered a great deal during the whole time
that the contrary winds detained us on the frontiers
of the empire of the cod-fifh ; this being by much
the moft difagreeable and inconvenient place in all
the ocean to fail in. The fun fcarce ever fhows
himfelf here, and for moft part of the time the air
is impregnated with a cold thick fog, which indi-
cates your approach to the bank, fo as to render it
impoffible to be miftaken. Now what can poffibly
be the caufe of fo conftant and remarkable a phenomenon ! Can it be the neighbourhood of the land
and of thofe forefts with which it is covered ? But
befides, that Cape Race, which is the neareft land
to the great bank is thirty five leagues diftant, the fame
thing happens not on any other coaft of the ifland ;
and further the ifland of Newfoundland is not fubject to fogs, except on the fide towards the great
bank ; every where elfe its coafts enjoy a pure air
and a ferene fky. It is, therefore probable, that
the caufe of the mifts, in which Cape Race is ge-

I

nerally

nerally hid, is the proximity of the great bank, and must be sought for on the bank itself. Now this is my conjecture on this head, which I submit to the judgment of the learned. I begin with observing, that we have another sign by which we discover our near approach to the great bank; and it is this, that on all its extremities commonly called its *Ecorres*, there is always a short tumbling sea with violent winds. May we not look upon this as the cause of the mists which prevail here, and say, that the agitation of the water on a bottom, which is a mixture of sand and mud, renders the air thick and heavy, and that the sun can only attract those gross vapours which he is never able sufficiently to rarify? You will ask me, whence this agitation of the sea on the most elevated parts of the great bank proceeds, whilst every where else and even on the bank itself there is a profound calm? If I am not deceived it is this. We daily find in these places currents, which set sometimes one way and sometimes another, the sea being impressed with an irregular motion by those currents, and beating with impetuosity against the sides of the bank, which are almost every where very steep, is repelled from it with the same violence, and is the true cause of the agitation remarked on it.

If the same thing happens not in approaching all steep coasts, it is owing to their not being of equal extent with this; that there are no currents near them, that they are less strong, or that they do not run counter to each other, that they do not meet with so steep a coast, and are not repelled from it with equal violence. It is besides certain, as I have already observed, after those who follow the seafaring life, that the agitation of the sea, and the mud which it stirs up, contribute much to thicken

the

the air, and encreafe the winds : But that thofe winds when they proceed from no other caufe do not extend very far, and that upon the great bank, at any confiderable diftance from the fide of it, you fail with as much tranquillity as in a road, excepting in the cafe of a violent wind proceeding from fome other quarter.

It was on a Friday the 16th of Auguft, we found ourfelves on the great bank in 75 fathom water. To arrive at the great bank is called *Bancquer* or *Banking*; to depart from it is called *Debanquer* or *Debanking*, two expreffions with which the cod-fifhery has enriched our language. It is the cuftom on finding foundings to cry out, *Vive le Roy*, which is generally done with great chearfulnefs. Our crew were longing for frefh cod; but the fun was fet, and the wind favourable, fo we thought proper to take the advantage of it. Towards eleven o'clock at night arofe a ftrong wind at foutheaft, which, with our mizen only, would have carried us three leagues an hour. Had we had this inconvenience alone by furling as we did that inftant all our other fails, we fhould have had no reafon to complain, but there came on at the fame time fuch a plump of rain, that you would have thought all the cataracts of the heavens had been opened. What was ftill worfe, the thunder began at the time when it commonly ends, it fell fo near us, that the rudder was wounded, and all the failors that worked the fhip felt the fhock of it. Then it grew louder, and a hundred pieces of cannon could not have made a greater noife. We could not hear one another, and fo thick were the peals, as to feem one continued roar. Nor could we fee any thing in the midft of the lightning, fo much were we dazzled with it. In a word, for an hour

and

and an half, our deftruction feemed inevitable; the hearts of the braveft amongft us mifgave them; for the thunder continued always directly over our heads, and had it ftruck us a fecond time we might have become food for the cod, at whofe expence we had reckoned very foon to make good cheer. Caftor or Pollux, for I know not which of the two was then upon duty, had forwarned us under the name of *Feu de St. Elme* *, of all this *Fracas*, other-wife we might poffibly have been furprized and overfet.

An hour and a half afterwards the rain ceafed, the thunder feemed at a diftance, and the flafhes of lightning were only feen faintly on the horizon. The wind continued ftill favourable and without bluftering, and the fea became fmooth as glafs. Every one was then for going to bed, but the beds were all wet, the rain having penetrated through the moft imperceptible chinks, a circumftance which is inevitable when a fhip is much toffed. They, how-ever did the beft they could, and thought themfelves extremely happy to be fo eafily quit. Every thing violent is of fhort duration, and above all a fouth-eaft wind at leaft in thefe feas. It never continues but when it grows ftronger by degrees, and often ends in a ftorm. The calm returned with day-light, we made no progrefs, but diverted ourfelves with fifhing.

Every thing is good in the cod, whilft it is frefh; and it lofes nothing of its good relifh, and becomes even firmer after it has been kept two days in falt; but it is the fifhers only who tafte the moft delici-

* Thefe fires never mifs to be obferved on the yards at the approach of a ftorm.

ous parts of this fish, that is to say, the head, the
tongue, and the liver, which, after having been
steeped in oil and vinegar, with a little pepper, make
a most exquisite sauce. Now, in order to preserve
all these parts would require too much salt; so that
whatever they cannot consume whilst the fishing season lasts, is thrown into the sea. • The largest cod I
have ever seen was not quite three feet in length;
notwithstanding those of the great bank are the
largest : but, there is, perhaps, no animal which
has so wide a throat in proportion to its size, or that
is more voracious. All forts of things are found
in the belly of this fish, even pieces of broken
earthen ware, iron, and glass. It was at first believed capable of digesting all this, but the world
has become sensible of this mistake, which was
founded on this circumstance, that some pieces of
iron half worn away, had been found in the belly
of it. It is the received opinion at this day that
the *Gau*, which is the name that the fishers have
given to the stomach of the cod-fish, turns inside
out, like a pocket, and that by means of this action, this fish disburdens itself of whatever incom-
modes it.

What is called in Holland the *Cabelao*, is a fort
of cod which is caught in the channel and some other
places, and which differs from the cod of America
only in that it is of a much smaller size. That of
the great Bank is salted only, and this is what is called
White, or more commonly *Green Cod*. M. Denys
tells us on this head, that he has seen salt made in
Canada equal to what is carried thither from Brouage
in Old France, but that after they had made the
experiment, the salt-pits, which had been dug on
purpose, were filled up. Those who have the most
exclaimed against this country, as being utterly
good

good for nothing, have been the very perfons who have been more than once the caufe why no advantage has been reaped from it. Dried cod, or what is called *la Merluche*, can only be taken on the coafts; which requires great attendance and much experience. M. Denys, who agrees that all thofe he had ever known to follow this commerce in Acadia ruined themfelves by it, fully proves, and makes it extremely plain, that they are in the wrong who conclude from thence that the cod is not in great abundance in thofe parts. But he afferts, that in order to carry on this fifhery there to advantage, the fifhers muft be perfons refiding in the country; and he reafons in this manner. Every feafon is not equally proper for this fifhery; it can only be carried on from the beginning of the month of May, till the end of Auguft. Now if you bring failors from France, either you muft pay them for the whole year, in which cafe your expences will fwallow up the profits, or you muft pay them for the fifhing feafon only, in which they can never find their account. For to fay that they may be employed for the reft of the year in fawing of boards and felling of timber, is certainly a miftake, as they could not poffibly make the expence of their living out of it; fo that thus either they muft needs ruin the undertaker or die of hunger.

But if they are inhabitants of the place, the undertakers will not only be better ferved, but alfo it will be their own faults if they do not prefently get a fortune. By this means they will be able to make choice of the beft hands; they will take their own time to begin the fifhery, they will make choice of proper places, they will make great profits for the fpace of four months; and the reft of the year they may employ in working for themfelves at home.

Had

Had things been settled upon this bottom in thofe parts for a hundred and fifty years laft paft, Acadia muft have become one of the moft powerful colonies in all America. For whilft it was given out in France, and that with a kind of affectation that it was impoffible ever to do any thing in that country, it enriched the people of New-England by the fifhing trade only, though the Englifh were without feveral advantages for carrying it on, which our fituation offered us.

After leaving the great bank, you meet with feveral leffer ones, all of them equally abounding in fifh, nor is the cod the only fpecies found in thofe feas. And though you do not in fact meet with many *Requiems*, fcarce any *Giltheads* and Bonettas, or thofe other fifhes which require warmer feas, yet to make amends they abound with whales, blowers, fword-fifh, porpuffes, threfhers, with many others of lefs value. We had here more than once the pleafure of viewing the combat of the whale and fword-fifh, than which nothing can be more entertaining. The fword-fifh is of the thicknefs of a cow, from feven to eight feet long, the body tapering towards the tail. It derives its name from its weapon, which is a kind of fword three feet in length and four fingers in breadth. It proceeds from his fnout, and from each fide he has a range of teeth an inch long, and placed at equal diftances from each other. This fifh is dreffed with any fort of fauce, and is excellent eating. His head is more delicious than a calf's, and thicker, and of a fquarer form. His eyes are extremely large. The whale and fword-fifh never meet without a battle, and the latter has the fame of being the conftant aggreffor. Sometimes two fword-fifhes join againft one whale, in which cafe the parties are by no means

means equal. The whale, in lieu of arms offenfive and defenfive, has only his tail; in order to ufe it againft his enemy he dives with his head, and if the blow takes place finifhes him at a ftroke; but the other, who is very adroit in fhunning it, immediately falls upon the whale, and buries his weapon in his fides. And as he feldom pierces quite to the bottom of the fat, does him no great damage; when the whale difcovers the other darting upon him he dives, but the fword-fifh purfues him under water, and obliges him to rife again to the furface; then the battle begins anew, and lafts till the fword-fifh lofes fight of the whale, who makes a flying fight of it, and is a better fwimmer than he on the furface of the water.

The *Flettau*, or threfher, refembles a large plaice, and what is called by the French fifhermen *flet*, appears to be the diminutive of this fifh. He is grey on the back and white under the belly. His length is generally from four to five feet, his breadth at leaft two, and his thicknefs one. His head is very thick, all of it exquifite and extremely tender; from the bones is extracted a juice which is preferable to the fineft marrow. His eyes which are almoft as large as thofe of the fwordfifh, and the gills are moft delicious morfels. The body is thrown into the fea, to fatten the cod, to whom the threfher is the moft dangerous enemy, and who makes but one meal of three of thofe fifhes. I fhall not trouble your Grace with a defcription of all the fpecies of birds which live on thofe feas, and that only by fifhing, all of them being naturally fifhers, as feveral travellers have already mentioned them, though their accounts contain nothing worth notice.

On the 18th, the wind favourable; we believe the winds have carried us a little too far to the south-ward, and we are sailing weft-north-weft, in order to recover our latitude. For ten or twelve days paft we have never feen the fun, and on that account have not been able to take an obfervation. This happens pretty often, and is what occafions the greateft danger of this navigation. Towards eight o'clock in the morning, we perceive a fmall veffel, which feems to make towards us, we ftand towards her, and when we are come near enough, afked her, in what latitude we are? This was an Englifhman, the captain of which anfwered in his own language; we imagined, he faid, we were in 45 deg. We had, however, no reafon to rely too much upon his account, as he might poffibly be in the fame miftake with ourfelves. We take heart not-withftanding, and as the wind continues favourable, we flatter ourfelves if it ftands, with the hopes of paffing the gulph in two days.

Towards four o'clock in the evening the wind fell, which amazed us all; this was, notwithftand-ing, what preferved us. At 11 o'clock at night, the horizon appeared very black a-head of us, tho' every where elfe the heavens were extremely ferene. The failors of the watch did not hefitate to fay, that it was the land we faw, the officer of the watch laugh-ed at them, but on feeing that they perfifted in their opinion, he began to think they might poffi-bly be in the right. Luckily for us, there was fo little wind, that it was with difficulty the fhip would fteer; fo that he hoped day-light would appear be-fore we approached too near the land. At midnight the watch was changed; the failors, who fucceed-ed thofe on the former watch, were immediately of their opinion; but their officer undertook to prove

to

to them that what they faw could not poffibly be
the land, but was a fog which would vanifh as
daylight came on. He was not able to perfuade
them of it, and they perfifted in maintaining that
the heavens were too ferene for any mift to be on
the oppofite fide, except the land lay that way likewife.

At day-break, they all fell a crying out that
they faw the land. The officer, without even deign-
ing to look that way, fhrugged up his fhoulders,
and at four o'clock went to fleep, affuring them,
that when he fhould awake he fhould find this pretended land vanifhed. His fucceffor who was the
Count de Vaudreuil, being more cautious, immediately ordered fome of the fails to be furled, and
was not long before he faw the neceffity of this precaution. As foon as day appeared, we difcovered
the horizon all fet round with land, and at the
fame time a fmall Englifh veffel at anchor within
two cannon fhot of us. M. de Voutron being informed of it caufed the incredulous officer to be called up that inftant, whom they had much to do to
get out of his cabbin, where he maintained that it
was impoffible we could have land fo near us. He
came, however, after two or three fummonfes, and
at fight of the danger to which his obftinacy had
expofed us, he was feized with aftonifhment.. He
is, notwithftanding the moft expert man in France
for navigating on thefe feas, but too great a fhare
of abilities is fometimes of prejudice when we place
too much confidence in them.

Notwithftanding, Madam, if the wind had not
fallen at four o'clock in the evening before, we had
certainly gone to the bottom in the night; for we
were running full fail upon breakers, from whence
it

it was impoſſible we could ever be got off. The difficulty was to know where we were. We were, however, certain that we were not in 45 deg. the evening before. The queſtion was, were we more to the north or ſouth ? And on this there were different opinions. One of our officers aſſured us, that the land which appeared before us was Acadia ; that he had formerly made a voyage thither, and that he knew it again ; another maintained that it was the iſlands of St. Peter. But what reaſon is there to think, ſaid others to him, we are ſo far advanced ? It is not yet twenty-four hours ſince we were upon the great bank, and it is more than an hundred leagues from the great bank, to the iſlands of St. Peter. The pilot Chaviteau pretended, that it was Cape Race. That there is ſome error in our reckoning, ſaid he, there is not the leaſt doubt, and we ought not to wonder at it, it being impoſſible to keep an exact account in the way of currents which we are not acquainted with, and which are continually changing, and eſpecially as we had not the benefit of taking the latitude to ſet us to rights. But it is paſt the bounds of all probability that we ſhould either be on the coaſt of Acadia, or at the iſlands of St. Peter *,

His reaſoning appeared juſt to us, we could, however, have wiſhed he had been miſtaken, for we knew how diſagreeable a thing it was to be en-

---

* In 1725, the ſame Chaviteau committed a blunder much more fatal. He was then likewiſe king's pilot on board the *Camel*, and having been ſeveral days without taking the latitude in the night of the 25th of Auguſt, this ſhip ſtruck upon a rock near Louiſburgh in the iſland of Cape-Breton, and every ſoul on board periſhed. It appeared by the journals that had been kept on board, and which were found afterwards, that they believed themſelves ſtill ſeventy leagues from that iſland.

tangled

tangled with the land under Cape Race. In this uncertainty we refolved to confult the captain of the Englifhman that lay a-head of us, and Chaviteau was charged with this commiffion. He reflected at his return, that the Englifh had been as much fur-prized at finding themfelves in this bay as we were, but with this difference, that this was the place whi-ther their bufinefs led them ; that Cape Race was before us, and Cape du Brole ten leagues below ; that from the midft of thofe breakers, on which we had like to have been caft away, there iffued a ri-ver, at the entry of which there was an Englifh fettlement, whither this fmall veffel was bound with provifions.

About fifteen years ago, there happened to us a very fingular adventure in this very paffage, and which expofed us to, perhaps, as great danger as that which I have been relating. This was a few days after the 15th of Auguft, and till then we had been much incommoded with exceffive heats. One morning, as we were getting up we were feized with fo intenfe a cold as to be obliged to have re-courfe to our winter garments. We could, by no means imagine the caufe of this, as the weather was extremely fine, and as the wind did not blow from the north. At laft, on the third day there-after, at four o'clock in the morning, one of the failors cried out with all his might, Luff, luff, that is, place the helm fo as to bring the fhip nearer to the wind. He was obeyed, and the moment there-after, we perceived an enormous piece of ice which glanced along the fide of the veffel, and againft which fhe muft infallibly have been ftove to pieces, if the failor had not been endued with mariner's eyes, for we could fcarce fee it, and if the man at the helm had been lefs alert in fhifting the tiller.

I

I did not, however, fee this piece of ice, as I was not then got up ; but all who were then upon deck, affured us, that it feemed as high as the towers of *Notre Dame* at Paris, and that it was a great deal higher than the mafts of the fhip. I have often heard it maintained that this was impoffible, becaufe, befides its extraordinary height above the fea, it muft alfo reach to a confiderable depth under water, and that it was not poffible in the nature of things, that fuch a piece of ice could be formed. To this I anfwer, in the firft place, that in order to deny the fact, we muft give the lie to a number of perfons, for it is not the firft time that fuch floating iflands have been feen at fea. The Mother of the Incarnation being upon the fame paffage, run the fame hazard in broad day-light. The piece of ice which for want of wind to carry her out of its way, had like to have fent her to the bottom, was feen by the whole crew, and was reckoned much larger than that which we met with. She adds, that the general abfolution was given as is ufual in cafes of extreme danger.

It is moreover certain, that in Hudfon's bay there are pieces of ice formed by the fall of torrents, which tumble from the top of mountains, and which breaking off in the fummer with a hideous noife, are afterwards carried different ways by the current. The Sieur Jeremie, who paffed feveral years in this bay, tells us, that he had the curiofity to caufe found clofe to one of thefe pieces of ice which had been ftranded, and that after running out a hundred fathom of line, they found no bottom. I return to our adventure. Cape Race, Madam, is the fouth-eaft point of the ifland of Newfoundland ; it is fituated in 46 deg. and about 30 min. north latitude. The coaft runs from hence weftward,

ward, a little inclining to the north for the space of a hundred leagues, and terminates at Cape Ray in 47 deg. Almoſt half-way, is the great bay of Placentia, one of the fineſt ports in all America. Weſt-ſouth-weſt from this is a Hummock, which is ſeen from far, and ſerves to make it known. This is called the *Red Hat*, from its appearing in this form at a diſtance, and from its being of a reddiſh colour. On the 23d at noon, we were abreaſt of it, and in the evening we ſailed along the iſlands of St. Peter, which lay on the ſtarboard ſide, that is to ſay on our right-hand.

Theſe are three iſlands, the two firſt of which are exceeding high, and from the ſide on which we were, could be ſeen nothing but mountains covered with moſs. It is pretended that this moſs in ſome places covers very fine porphyry. On the ſide towards Newfoundland, there is ſome arable land, with an indifferent good port, where we formerly had ſome ſettlements. The largeſt and moſt weſtern of the three, which is more commonly called Maguelon iſland, is not ſo high as the two others, and the land of it appears to be very level. It is about three quarters of a league in length. On the 24th, at day-break, we had left it only five or ſix leagues behind us, but after midnight we had had no wind. Towards five o'clock in the morning, there aroſe a light breeze at ſouth-eaſt. Whilſt we were waiting till it ſhould grow ſtrong enough to fill our ſails, we diverted ourſelves with fiſhing, and caught a conſiderable quantity of cod. We ſpent two hours more than we ought to have done in this diverſion, and we had very ſoon ſufficient reaſon to repent it.

It

It was eight o'clock when we made fail, and we run the whole night in hopes of difcovering Cape Ray which lay upon our right, or the little ifland of St. Paul, which we ought to leave on our left, and which is almoft oppofite to Cape Ray, but night came on without our having had fight of either. We would then have been very glad that we had made ufe of the time we had loft. What was moft difagreeable in this, was, that towards midnight we were overtaken by a ftorm, much fuch another as that which we had met with on the great bank, and as we had no room to doubt of our being near one or other of the two lands between which our courfe lay, we durft not take the benefit of the wind which would have advanced us a good deal in our courfe. Thus, in fpite of Chaviteau's advice, who undertook to carry us thorough in fafety, we lay too. At day-break we perceived Cape Ray, on which the currents were driving us, and to compleat our misfortune, we had not wind enough to get clear of the coaft. We were almoft afhore, when about half an hour paft five in the morning, a light breath of wind at north-weft came in the nick of time to our affiftance; we loft nothing by it, and we were extricated from the danger in which we were. The north-weft, after doing us this good office, would have obliged us extremely had it made way for fome other wind; it did not, however, comply with our wifhes, and for two whole days detained us in the mouth of the gulph of St. Laurence. On the third day we paffed between the ifland of St. Paul and Cape St. Laurence, which is the moft northerly point of the *Ifle Royale*, or ifland of Cape Breton. This paffage is very narrow, and is never ventured upon in foggy weather, becaufe the ifland of St. Paul is fo fmall as to be eafily hid by the mift. That which lies between this ifland and Cape Ray

is

is much broader; but our fails were fet to take the other when the wind fhifted; accordingly we took advantage of it The gulph of St. Laurence is fourfcore leagues in length, which a good wind at fouth-eaft, with the affiftance of the currents, carried us through in twenty-four hours. About halfway you meet the *Ifles aux Oifeaux*, or Bird Iflands, which we failed along at the diftance of a fmall cannon fhot, and which muft not be confounded with thofe which were difcovered by *James Cartier*, near the Ifland of Newfoundland. Thefe of which we are now fpeaking, are two rocks which appeared to me to rife up tapering to a fharp point about fixty feet above the furface of the water, the largeft of which was between two and three hundred feet in circumference. They are very near one another, and I do not believe there is water enough between them for a large fhallop. It is hard to fay what colour they are of, the mute, or dung of fea-fowl, covering entirely both the furface and banks. There are to be feen, however, in fome places veins of a reddifh colour.

They have been vifited feveral times; and whole fhalops have been loaded with eggs of all forts, and the ftench is affirmed to be utterly infupportable. And fome add, that befides the fea-gulls and the cormorants, which come thither from all the neighbouring lands, there are found a number of other fowl that cannot fly. What is wonderful, is, that in fo prodigious a multitude of nefts every one finds his own. We fired one cnnon-fhot, which fpread the alarm over all this feathered commonwealth, when there arofe over the two iflands a thick cloud of thofe fowl of at leaft two or three leagues in circuit. On the morrow, about daybreak the wind fell all at once: Two hours after that we doubled Cape Rofe, and entered the river St.

Lau-

Laurence, which runs north-eaſt and ſouth-weſt; and the northweſt wind, which immediately roſe, would have ſerved us well enough, but as we had loſt two hours on the twenty-fourth in fiſhing, and in conſequence thereof, two whole days at the entry of the gulph, we were obliged to wait here till the north-weſt ſhould fall, that is to ſay, five days, in which we did not make five leagues. This delay was not even the greateſt miſchief which it occaſioned us; it was beſides very cold, and there was a great ſwell which toſſed us exceedingly, and when the gale was about to fall it was very near being the cauſe of our deſtruction in the manner you are preſently going to ſee. But I muſt firſt give you a map of the country where we were. Cape Roſe is properly the mouth of the river St. Laurence, and it is here we muſt meaſure its breadth at its opening, which is about thirty leagues. Somewhat below this, and more to the ſouthward, are the bay and point of Gaſpey or Gachepé. Thoſe who pretend that the river St. Laurence is forty leagues over at its mouth, probably meaſure it from the eaſtern point of Gaſpey. Below the bay you perceive a ſort of iſland, which is in fact, no more than a ſteep rock, of about thirty fathoms in length, ten high, and four broad. One would take it for a fragment of an old wall, and it has been aſſerted that it formerly joined *Mont Joli*, which ſtands over-againſt it on the Continent. This rock has in the middle an opening in the form of an arch, through which a Biſcàyan ſhalop might paſs under ſail, and hence it has got the name of *Iſle Percée*, or the bored Iſland. Navigators know that they are near it when they diſcover a flat mountain, riſing above ſeveral others, called *Roland's Table*. The iſland Bonaventure is a league from Bored Iſland, and almoſt at the ſame diſtance lies the iſland *Miſcon*, eight

leagues

leagues in circuit, which has an excellent harbour. In the offing, at a small distance from this island, is a spring of fresh water, which boils up and jets to a considerable height.

All these parts are excellent for the fishery, and there is every where exceeding good anchoring ground. It would even be easy to erect magazines or warehouses, which would serve by way of store-houses, or repositories for Quebec. But an infinite deal of time which ought to have been employed in making sure of the cod, and several other fisheries, with which this sea abounds, and in fortifying ourselves in those posts, the importance of which we have been too long in discovering, has been lost in carrying on the fur trade. It was natural for us, having near us so sure and commodious sheltering to have gone thither to wait the return of a favourable wind, but we expected it to return every moment, and we thought to make the most of it the moment it sprung up.

At last, on Tuesday the 10th of September, towards noon, the northwest fell ; then finding ourselves without being able to advance, nor even almost to work the ship, we amused ourselves in fishing, and this too cost us very dear. For the man at the helm being more attentive to the fishing than to his rudder, let the ship go up into the wind, which occasioned the sails to lie aback. During the calm, we had already driven considerably on the island of Anticosti, and the accident I have been speaking of caused us come so near it. As the current carried us that way, that we already could distinctly discern the breakers, with which the island is lined on this side ; to compleat our misfortune,

the

the fmall breath of wind which had juft rifen failed us in our greateft need.

Had the calm continued for ever fo fhort a while, there had been an end of us. A moment after our fails filled a little, and we had a mind to bring the fhip about ; but fhe, contrary to cuftom, refufed to ftay, and that twice running ; a certain proof that the current which acted upon her was very ftrong. We now thought ourfelves paft all hope, becaufe we were too near the rocks to rifk wearing her ; but after all we had no other method left. We therefore fet hand to the work, more that we might have nothing to reproach ourfelves with, than from any hope of faving our lives ; and in that very inftant we experienced the truth of this maxim, that God helps thofe who help themfelves. The wind fhifted to the north, and frefhned by little and little, fo that towards feven o'clock in the evening we had quite cleared the point of Anticofti, which had filled us with fo much apprehenfion.

This ifland extends for about forty leagues from north-eaft to fouth-weft, almoft in the middle of the river St. Laurence, being at the fame time extremely narrow. It had been granted to the Sieur Joliet, on his return from the difcovery of the Mifliffippi, a prefent of no great value ; this ifland is abfolutely good for nothing. It is ill wooded, its foil barren, and without a fingle harbour where any veffel can lie in fafety. There was a rumour fome years fince, that a filver mine had been difcovered on it, and for want of miners a goldfmith was fent from Quebec, where I then was, to make an effay of it ; but he made no great progrefs. He foon perceived by the difcourfe of him who had given information of it, that the mine exifted only in the

brain

brain of this perſon, who was inceſſantly recommending to him to put his truſt in the Lord. He was of opinion, that if truſt in God was ſufficient to make him diſcover a mine there was no neceſſity of going to Anticoſti to find it, ſo that he returned as he came. The coaſts of this iſland are abundantly well ſtocked with fiſh; I am notwithſtanding of opinion, that the heirs of the Sieur Joliet, would willingly exchange their immenſe lordſhip for the ſmalleſt fief in France.

After having paſſed this iſland you have the pleaſure of always being between two ſhores, and to make ſure of the progreſs you have made; but there is a neceſſity of uſing much precaution in ſailing on this great river. On Thurſday the third, we left on the larboard ſide the *Mounts Notre Dame* and *Mount Louys*; this is a chain of very high mountains; between which there are ſeveral vallies, which were formerly inhabited by Indians. In the neighbourhood of Mount Lewis, there are even very good lands, and on them ſeveral French plantations. A very advantageous ſettlement might be made here for the fiſhery, eſpecially the whale-fiſhery, and it would alſo be of uſe to the ſhips which come from France; they might there find refreſhments of which they are ſometimes in extreme want. In the night following, the wind encreaſed, and had very near done us an ill turn. We were no great way from Trinity-point, which we were to leave on our left, but our pilots did not believe themſelves ſo near it; and they even imagined they had given it a ſufficient birth ſo as to have nothing to fear from it. Monſieur de Voutron ſtarting up from his ſleep called out to bear away. Had this order been poſtponed but for one quarter of an hour, the ſhip muſt have been daſhed to pieces up-

on

on the point, which appeared some moments afterwards. On the fourth in the evening we came to anchor, for the first time, a little above what is called the *Paps of Matane*. These are two summits of the same mountain, situated at the distance of two leagues from the river. I do not believe that a wilder country can any where be seen. Nothing appears on all hands but impenetrable thickets, rocks, and sands, without one inch of good land. There are, it is true, fine springs, excellent game, and that in great plenty, but hunting is here almost utterly impracticable to any except Indians and Canadians.

We remained here four days, as on the other side of the river we had to avoid the shoal of *Manicouagau*, famous for shipwrecks, and which advances two leagues into the river. It takes its name from a river proceeding from the mountains of Labrador, which forms a pretty large lake of the same name, but more commonly known by that of St. Barnabas, and which empties itself across this shoal. Some of our maps call it *la riviere Noire*, or Black River.

On the eighth we made sail; though, for any way we made it was hardly worth while; but variety serves to divert one, and exercise is of use to the sailors. In the night, between the 10th and 11th, we made fifteen leagues; had we got half a league further we should have got over the most critical part of the whole river. We should, besides, have got up as high as the strong tides, for hitherto they are scarce perceptible, except near the shore; but the wind shifted of a sudden to the south-west, so that we were obliged to look out for a place of shelter which we found under *L'Isle Verte*, or Green-Island,

Iſland, where we remained five days. Here we wanted for nothing, but at the expiration of this time we had a mind to try whether we ſhould be able to find, as we had been made to hope, land-winds on the north ſhore, which might carry us into the high tides.

We therefore came to an anchor at *Moulin Baude*; this traverſe is five leagues. On my arrival I aſked to ſee this mill, and was ſhewn ſome rocks from which iſſues a ſmall rill of chryſtal water, ſufficient at leaſt to make a mill go ; there is, however, no likelihood of a mill ever being built here. There is not, perhaps, in the whole world a more uninhabitable country than this. The Saguenay lies ſomewhat higher ; this is a river capable of carrying the largeſt ſhips twenty-five leagues above its mouth. Entering this river you leave on the right hand the port of Tadouſſac, where moſt part of our geographers have placed a city ; but there never was more than one French houſe in it, with ſome huts of Indians that came here in trading time, and who afterwards carried their huts away with them as they do with the booths of a fair. This is what conſtituted the whole of the city.

It is true that this port was for a long time the reſort of all the Indian nations of the north and eaſt ; that the French repaired thither as ſoon as the navigation was open, whether from France or from Canada ; and laſtly, that the miſſionaries profiting of this opportunity, came thither to negociate in quality of factors for the kingdom of heaven. The fair being ended, the merchants returned to their own homes, the Indians took the road of their foreſts or villages, and the labourers in the harveſt of the goſpel followed theſe latter to culti-

vate

vate the divine feed fown in their minds. Notwithftanding both the relations which have been
publifhed, and thofe who have travelled thither
have faid a great deal on the fubject of Tadouffac,
and our geographers have fuppofed it to be a city;
and fome authors have even advanced that it had
a jurifdiction belonging to it.

In other refpects Tadouffac is an excellent harbour, and I have been affured, that five and twenty
fhips of war might be fheltered in it from all winds,
that the anchorage is fure in it, and that its entry
is extreamly eafy. Its form is almoft round, and
it is furrounded on all fides by fteep rocks of a
prodigious height, from whence iffues a fmall rivulet capable of fupplying all the fhips with water. This whole country is full of marble, but its
greateft riches would be that of the whale-fifhery.
In 1705, being at anchor with the fhip Hero in the
fame place, I faw at the fame time four of thefe
fifhes, which from head to tail were almoft as long
as our fhip. The Bafques formerly carried on this
fifhery with fuccefs; and there are, on a fmall
ifland which bears their name, and which lies a little below Green-Ifland, the remains of furnaces and
the ribs of whales. What a mighty difference muft
there be between a fedentary and domeftic fifhery,
which might be carried on at one's eafe in a river,
and that which is followed on the coafts of Greenland with fo much rifk and at fo vaft an expence.

The two following days no land-wind, and we
regret extremely our former anchoring-place, at
which there were French plantations, whereas here
there are neither men nor beafts to be feen. At
length, on the third day at noon, we anchor, and
we

we clear the paffage of *Ifle Rouge*, or Red-Ifland, which is no eafy matter. You muft firft fteer right upon this ifland, as if you had a mind to land on it; this is done to fhun the point *aux Allouettes*, which lies at the entrance into the Saguenay on the left, and advances a good way into the river; this done, you ftand the direct contrary way. The paffage to the fouthward of Red-ifland is much fafer; but in order to make this we muft have returned directly back, and the wind might have come to have failed us. The *Red Ifland* is no more than a rock almoft level with the furface of the water which appears of a true red colour, and on which many a fhip has been caft away.

Next day with little wind and the help of the tide we come to an anchor above the Ifle *aux Coudres*, which lies at fifteen leagues diftance both from Quebec and Tadouffac. You leave this on the left, and this paffage is dangerous when you have not the wind to your liking; it is rapid, narrow, and a good quarter of a league in length. In Champlain's time it was much eafier; but in 1663, an earthquake plucked up a mountain by the roots, and whirled it upon the *Ifle aux Coudres*, which it encreafed in dimenfions more than one half, and in the place where this mountain ftood appeared a whirlpool, which it is dangerous to approach. One might pafs to the fouthward of the *Ifle aux Coudres*, and this paffage would be both eafy and without danger. It bears the name of Monf. D' Iberville who attempted it with fuccefs; but the general way is to pafs on the north fide of it, and cuftom you know is a fovereign law for the common run of mankind.

Above

Above this whirlpool, which I have juft now been mentioning, is the bay of St. Paul, where begins the plantations on the north fhore, and where there are woods of pine-trees which are much valued ; here are found red pinés of an extreme beauty, and which are never known to break. The fuperiors of the feminary of Quebec are lords of this bay. A fine lead mine has been lately difcovéred in this place. Six leagues farther up the river is an exceeding high promontory, at which terminates a chain of mountains, ftretching more than four hundred leagues to the weftward ; this is called Cape *Tourmente*, probably becaufe he who thus chriftened it had met with fome hard gales of wind under it. There is good anchoring here, where you are furrounded with iflands of all fizes which afford excellent fhelter. The moft confiderable of thefe is the Ifle of Orleans, whofe fertile fields appear in form of an amphitheatre, and agreeably terminate the profpeét. This ifland is about fourteen leagues in circuit, and was erected into an earldom in 1676, under the name of St. Lawrence, in favour of Francis Berthelot, fecretary-general of the artillery, who had purchafed it of Francis de Laval, firft bifhop of Quebec. It had then four villages in it, and now has pretty populous parifhes.

Of the two channels which this ifland forms, that to the fouth only is navigable for fhips. Even fhallops cannot pafs through that to the north, except at high-water. Thus from Cape Tourmente, you muft traverfe the river to get to Quebec, and even this is not without its difficulties ; it is incommoded with fhifting fands, on which there is not at all times water fufficient for the largeft fhips, which obliges thofe who pafs this way not to attempt it, except in the time of flood. This difficulty might

be

be fhunned by taking the channel of M. d' Iberville. Cape Tourmente from whence this traverfe is beft made, is a hundred and ten leagues from the fea, the water near it ftill continuing brackifh. It does not become drinkable till the entrance into the two channels, which are formed by the Ifle of Orleans. This is a phenomenon pretty difficult to explain, and efpecially, if we confider the great rapidity of the river notwithftanding its breadth.

The tides flow regularly in this place five hours, and ebb feven. At Tadouffac they flow and ebb fix hours, and the higher you afcend the river the more the flux diminifhes, and the reflux encreafes. At the diftance of twenty leagues above Quebec, the flux is three hours, and the reflux nine. Beyond this there is no fenfible tide ; when it is half flood in the port of Tadouffac and at the mouth of the Saguenay, it only begins to flow at *Checoutimi* twenty five leagues up this laft river, notwithftanding it is high water at all thefe three places at the fame time. This is no doubt owing to this circumftance, that the rapidity of the Saguenay, which is ftill greater than that of the St. Lawrence, driving back the tide, occafions for fome time a kind of equilibrium of the tides at *Checoutimi*, and at the entrance of this river into the St. Lawrence. This rapidity has befides come to the pitch, in which we now fee it, only fince the earthquake in 1663. This earthquake overturned a mountain, and threw it into the river, which confined its channel, forming a peninfula called *Checoutimi*, beyond which is a rapid ftream impaffable even to canoes. The depth of the Saguenay from its mouth as high as *Checoutimi*, is equal to its rapidity. Thus it would be impoffible to come to an anchor in it, were it not for the convenience

venience of making faſt to the trees, with which its banks are covered.

It has been moreover obſerved, that in the gulph of St. Lawrence, at the diſtance of eight or ten leagues from the ſhore, the tides vary according to the different poſitions of the land, or the difference of ſeaſons; that in ſome places they follow the courſes of the winds, and that in others they go quite contrary to the wind; that at the mouth of the river in certain months of the year the currents bear conſtantly out to ſea, and in other places ſet right in ſhore; laſtly, that in the great river itſelf, as high up as the Seven Iſlands, that is to ſay, for the ſpace of ſixty leagues it never flows on the ſouth ſide, nor ebbs on the north. It is not eaſy to give ſolid reaſons for all this, but what is moſt likely, is, that there are certain motions under water which produce thoſe irregularities, or that there are cur-rents which ſet from the ſurface to the bottom, and from the bottom to the ſurface in the manner of a pump.

Another obſervation we may make in this place, is, that the variation of the compaſs, which in ſome ports of France is only two or three degrees north-weſt, conſtantly diminiſhes as you approach the me-ridian of the Azores, or weſtern Iſlands, where it is no longer ſenſible; but that beyond this it en-creaſes after ſuch a rate that on the great Bank of Newfoundland, it is twenty-two degrees and upwards; that afterwards it begins to diminiſh but ſlowly, ſince it is ſtill ſixteen degrees at Quebec, and twelve in the country of the Hurons, where the ſun ſets thirty three minutes later than at that ca-pital.

On

On Sunday the 22d, we came to an anchor in the traverfe of the Ifle of Orleans, where we went afhore whilft we waited the return of the tide. I found the country here pleafant, the lands good, and the planters in tolerable good circumftances. They have the character of being fomething addicted to witchcraft, and they are applied to, in order to know what is to happen, or what paffes in diftant places. As for inftance, when the fhips expected from France are later than ordinary, they are confulted for intelligence concerning them, and it has been afferted that their anfwers have been fometimes pretty juft; that is to fay, that having gueffed once or twice right enough, and having for their own diverfion made it be believed that they fpoke from certain knowledge, it has been imagined that they confulted with the devil.

When James Cartier difcovered this ifland he found it entirely covered with vines, from whence he called it the Ifle of Bacchus. This navigator was of Brittany; after him came certain Normans, who grubbed up the vines, and in the place of Bacchus fubftituted Pomona and Ceres. In effect, it produces good wheat and excellent fruits. They begin alfo to cultivate tobacco on it, which is far from being bad. At length on Monday the 23d, the Camel anchored before Quebec, whither I had gone two hours before in a canoe of bark. I have a voyage of a thoufand leagues to make in thefe frail vehicles, I muft therefore accuftom myfelf to them by degrees. And now, Madam, thefe are the circumftances of my voyage, which I have been able to recollect; they are, as you fee, trifles, which at moft might be good enough to amufe perfons, who have nothing to do on board fhip. I fhall, perhaps, afterwards have fomething more intereft-

H ing

ing to communicate to you, but shall add nothing to this letter, as I would not miss the opportunity of a merchant ship just ready to set sail. I shall also have the honour to write to you by the king's ship.

I am, &c.

LETTER

L E T T E R III.

Defcription of Quebec; *character of its inhabitants, and the manner of living in the*
French *colony.*

Quebec, Oct. 28, 1720.

Madam,

I AM now going to write you fome particulars
concerning Quebec; all the defcriptions I have
hitherto feen of it are fo faulty, that I imagined I
fhould do you a pleafure in drawing you a true portrait of this capital of New France. It is truly
worthy of being known, were it only for the fingu-
larity of its fituation; there being no other city befides this in the known world that can boaft of a
frefh water harbour a hundred and twenty leagues
from the fea, and that capable of containing a hundred
fhips of the line. It certainly ftands on the moft
navigable river in the univerfe.

This great river as high as the ifland of Orleans,
that is to fay, at the diftance of a hundred and ten
or twelve leagues from the fea, is never lefs than
four or five leagues in breadth; but above this
ifland it fuddenly narrows, and that at fuch a rate
as to be no more than a mile broad at Quebec;
from which circumftance this place has been called

H 2

Quebeio or Quebec, which in the Algonquin language signifies a strait, or narrowing. The Abenaquis, whose language is a dialect of the Algonquin, call it Quelibec, that is to say, shut up, because from the entry of the little river *de la Chaudiere*, by which these Indians usually came to Quebec, from the neighbourhood of Acadia; the point of Levi, which projects towards the Isle of Orleans, entirely hides the south channel, as the Isle of Orleans does that of the north, so that the port of Quebec appears from thence like a great bay.

The first object you perceive on your arrival in the road is a fine sheet of water, about thirty feet in breadth, and forty high. This is situated close by the entry of the lesser channel of the Isle of Orleans, and is seen from a long point on the south-side of the river, which as I have already observed seems to join to the Isle of Orleans. This cascade is called the Falls of Montmorency, and the other Point Levi. The reason of which is, that the admiral de Montmorency, and the Duc de Ventadour his nephew, were successively viceroys of New France. There is no person, who would not imagine, that so plentiful a fall of water, and which never dries up must proceed from some fine river; it is, however, no more than a puny stream, in which in some places there is hardly water up to the ankle; it flows, however, constantly, and derives its source from a pleasant lake twelve leagues distant from the falls.

The city stands a league higher, on the same side and at the place where the river is narrowest. But between it and the Isle of Orleans, is a bason a large league, over every way into which discharges itself the little river St. Charles, flowing from the

north-

north-weſt. Quebec ſtands between the mouth of
this river and Cape Diamond, which projects a little into the river. The anchoring place is oppoſite
to it, in five and twenty fathoms water good ground.
Notwithſtanding when it blows hard at north-eaſt,
ſhips drag their anchors ſometimes but with ſcarce
any danger.

When Samuel Champlain founded this city in
1608, the tide uſually roſe to the foot of the rock.
Since that time the river has retired by little
and little, and has at laſt left dry a large piece of
ground, on which the lower town has ſince been
built, and which is now ſufficiently elevated above
the water's edge, to ſecure its inhabitants againſt the
inundations of the river. The firſt thing you meet
with on landing is a pretty large ſquare, and of an
irregular form, having in front a row of well built
houſes, the back part of which leans againſt the
rock, ſo that they have no great depth. Theſe
form a ſtreet of a conſiderable length, occupying
the whole breadth of the ſquare, and extending on
the right and left as far as the two ways which lead
to the upper town. The ſquare is bounded towards
the left by a ſmall church, and towards the right
by two rows of houſes placed in a parallel direction.
There is alſo another ſtreet on the other ſide between
the church and the harbour, and at the turning of
the river under Cape Diamond, there is likewiſe
another pretty long flight of houſes on the banks
of a creek called *the Bay of Mothers*. This quarter may be reckoned properly enough a ſort of ſub-
urbs to the lower town.

Between this ſuburb and the great ſtreet, you go
up to the higher town by ſo ſteep an aſcent, that it
has been found neceſſary to cut it into ſteps. Thus

it

it is impoffible to afcend it except on foot. But
in going from the fquare towards the right a way
has been made, the declivity of which is much
more gentle, which is lined with houfes. At the
place where thefe two ways meet begins that part of
the upper town which faces the river, there being
another lower town on the fide towards the little river St. Charles. The firft building worthy of notice you meet with on your right hand in the former of thofe fides, is the bifhop's palace; the left
being entirely occupied with private houfes. When
you are got about twenty paces farther, you find
yourfelf between two tolerably large fquares; that
towards the left is the place of arms, fronting which,
is the fort or citadel, where the governor-general
refides; on the oppofite fide ftands the convent of
the Recollects, the other fides of the fquare being
lined with handfome houfes.

In the fquare towards your right you come firft
of all to the cathedral, which ferves alfo for a parifh
church to the whole city. Near this, and on the
angle formed by the river St. Lawrence, and that
of St. Charles ftands the feminary. Oppofite to the
cathedral is the college of the jefuits, and on the
fides between them are fome very handfome houfes.
From the place of arms run two ftreets which are
croffed by a third, and which form a large ifle entirely occupied by the church and convent of the
Recollects. From the fecond fquare to the river
St. Charles, are two defcents, one on the fouth towards the feminary, which is very fteep and with
very few houfes on it; the other near the enclofure
of the jefuits, which is very winding, has the *Hotel
Dieu*, or Hofpital, and half-way down is lined with
fmall houfes, and terminates at the palace where the
intendant refides. On the other fide of the Jefuit's
col-

college, where their church ſtands, is a pretty long
ſtreet, in which is the convent of the Urſuline nuns.
The whole of the upper town is built on a bottom
partly of marble and partly of ſlate.

Such, Madam, is the topographical deſcription
of Quebec, which as you ſee is of a conſiderable
large extent, and in which almoſt all the houſes are
built of ſtone, though for all that they do not reckon above ſeven thouſand ſouls in it *. But in order to give you a compleat idea of this city, I muſt
give you a particular account of its principal edifices, and ſhall afterwards ſpeak of its fortifications.
The church of the lower town was built in conſequence of a vow made during the ſiege of Quebec,
in 1690. It is dedicated to our Lady of Victory,
and ſerves as a chapel of eaſe for the conveniency
of the inhabitants of the lower town. Its ſtructure
is extremely ſimple, a modeſt neatneſs forming all
its ornament. Some ſiſters of the congregation,
whom I ſhall have occaſion to mention in the ſequel,
are eſtabliſhed to the number of four or five, between this church and the port, where they teach a
ſchool.

In the epiſcopal palace there is nothing finiſhed
but the chapel, and one half of the building pro-
jected by the plan, according to which it is to be an
oblong ſquare. If it is ever compleated, it will be
a magnificent edifice. The garden extends to the
brow of the rock, and commands the proſpect of
all the road. When the capital of New France,
ſhall have become as flouriſhing as that of Old
France (and we ſhould not deſpair of any thing,

* One may eaſily ſee by the plan of this city that it has
conſiderably encreaſed within theſe twenty years laſt paſt.

Paris

Paris having been for a long time much inferior to
what Quebec is at this day) as far as the sight can
reach, nothing will be seen but towns, villas, pleasure houses, and all this is already chalked out;
when the great river St. Lawrence, who rowls ma-
jestically his waters which he brings from the extremities of the north or west shall be covered with
ships; when the isle of Orleans and both shores of
each of the rivers which form this port, shall difcover fine meadows, fruitful hills, and fertile fields,
and in order to accomplish this, there wants only
more inhabitants; when part of the river St. Charles,
which agreeably meanders through a charming valley, shall be joined to the city, the most beautiful
quarter of which it will undoubtedly form; when
the whole road shall have been faced with magnificent quays, and the port surrounded with superb
edifices; and when we shall see three or four hundred ships lying in it loaden with riches, of which
we have hitherto been unable to avail ourselves,
and bringing in exchange those of both worlds, you
will then acknowledge, Madam, that this terras
must afford a prospect which nothing can equal, and
that even now it ought to be something singularly
striking.

The cathedral would make but an indifferent pa-
rish church in one of the smallest towns in France;
judge then whether it deserves to be the seat of the
sole bishoprick in all the French empire in America, which is much more extensive than that of
the Romans ever was. No architecture, the choir,
the great altar, and chapels, have all the air of a
country church. What is most passable in it, is a
very high tower, solidly built, and which, at a diftance, has no bad effect. The seminary which ad-
joins to this church is a large square, the buildings
of

of which are not yet finished, what is already compleated is well executed, and has all the conveniencies neceffary in this country. This houfe is now
rebuilding for the third time, it was burnt down to
the ground in 1703, and in the month of October,
in the year 1705, when it was near compleatly
rebuilt, it was again almoft entirely confumed by
the flames. From the garden you difcover the
whole of the road and the river St. Charles, as far
as the eye can reach.

The fort or citadel is a fine building, with two
pavilions by way of wings; you enter it through
a fpacious and regular court, but it has no garden
belonging to it, the fort being built on the brink of
the rock. This defect is fupplied in fome meafure
with a beautiful gallery, with a balcony, which
reaches the whole length of the building; it commands the road, to the middle of which one may
be eafily heard by means of a fpeaking trumpet;
and hence too you fee the whole lower town under
your feet. On leaving the fort, and turning to the
left, you enter a pretty large efplanade, and by a
gentle declivity you reach the fummit of Cape Diamond, which makes a very fine platform. Befides
the beauty of the profpect, you breathe in this place
the pureft air; you fee from it a number of porpoifes as white as fnow playing on the furface of
the water, and you fometimes find a fort of dia-
monds on it finer than thofe of Alençon. I have
feen fome of them full as well cut as if they had
come from the hand of the moft expert workman.
They were formerly found here in great plenty,
and hence this cape has the name it bears. At prefent they are very fcarce. The defcent towards the
country is ftill more gentle than that towards the
efplanade.

The

The Fathers Recollects have a large and beautiful church, which might do them honour even at Versailles. It is very neatly wainscotted, and is adorned with a large *Tribune* or gallery somewhat heavy, but the wainscotting of which is extremely well carved, which goes quite round, and in which are included the confession seats. This is the work of one of their brother converts. In a word, nothing is wanting to render it compleat, except the taking away some pictures very coarsely daubed ; brother Luke has put up some of his hand which have no need of those foils. Their house is answerable to the church; it is large, solid, and commodious, and adorned with a spacious and well-cultivated garden. The Ursiline nuns have suffered by two fires as well as the seminary ; and besides, their funds are so small, and the dowries they receive with the girls in this country are so moderate, that after their house was burnt down for the first time, it was resolved to send them back to France. They have, however, had the good fortune to recover themselves both times, and their church is now actually finished. They are neatly and commodiously lodged, which is the fruit of the good example they set the rest of the colony by their oeconomy, their sobriety and industry; they gild, embroider, and are all usefully employed, and what comes out of their hands is generally of a good taste.

You have no doubt read in some relations, that the college of the jesuits was a very fine building. It is certain, that when this city was no more than an unseemly heap of French barracks, and huts of Indians, this house, which with the fort, were the only edifices built with stone, made some appearance; the first travellers, who judged of it by comparison, represented it as a very fine structure, those

who

who followed them, and who, according to cuftom copied from them, expreffed themfelves in the fame manner. Notwithftanding the huts having fince difappeared, and the barracks having been changed into houfes moft of them well-built, the college in fome fort disfigures the city, and threatens falling to ruin every day.

Its fituation is far from being advantageous, it being deprived of the greateft beauty it could poffibly have had, which is that of the profpect. It had at firft a diftant view of the road, and its founders were fimple enough to imagine they would always be allowed to enjoy it; but they were deceived. The cathedral and feminary now hide it, leaving them only the profpect of the fquare, which is far from being a fufficient compenfation for what they loft. The court of this college is little and ill-kept, and refembles more than any thing elfe a farmer's yard. The garden is large and well-kept, being terminated by a fmall wood, the remains of the ancient foreft which formerly covered this whole mountain *.

The church has nothing worth notice on the outfide except a handfome fteeple; it is entirely roofed with flate, and is the only one in all Canada which has this advantage; all the buildings here being generally covered with fhingles. It is very much ornamented in the infide; the gallery is bold, light, and well-wrought, and is furrounded with an iron baluftrade, painted and gilt, and of excellent workmanfhip; the pulpit is all gilt, and the work both in iron and wood excellent; there are three altars

* The college has fince been rebuilt from the foundation, and is at prefent a noble building.

hand-

handfomely defigned, fome good pictures, and is
without any dome or cupola, but a flat cieling handfomely ornamented ; it has no ftone pavement, in
place of which it is floored with ftrong planks, which
makes this church fupportable in winter, whilft you
are pierced with cold in the others. I make no
mention of *four large maffy cylindrical columns, each
of a fingle block of a certain fort of porphyry, black
as jet, and without either fpots or veins,* with which
the baron de la Hontan has thought fit to enrich the
great altar; they would certainly do better than
thofe actually there, which are hollow and coarfely
daubed in imitation of marble. One might, however, have forgiven this author, if he had never dif-
figured the truth, except to add luftre to churches.

The *Hotel Dieu,* or hofpital has two large wards,
one for men and the other for women. The beds
here are kept exceeding clean, the fick are well attended, and every thing is commodious and extremely neat. The church ftands behind the women's
ward, and has nothing worth notice except the great
altar. The houfe is ferved by the nuns Hofpitallers of
St. Auguftine, of the congregation of the Mercy of
Jefus ; the firft of whom come originally from
Dieppe. They have begun to build themfelves a
commodious apartment, but will not, in all likelihood, foon finifh it for want of funds. As their
houfe is fituated on the defcent, half-way down the
hill, on a flat place, which extends a little towards
the river St. Charles, they enjoy a very pleafant
profpect.

The intendant's houfe is called the palace, becaufe
the fuperior council affembles in it. This is a large
pavilion the two extremities of which project fome
feet,

feet, and to which you afcend by a double flight of ftairs. The garden front which faces the little river, which ftands very near upon á level with it, is much more agreeable than that by which you enter. The king's magazines face the court on the right fide, and behind that is the prifon. The gate by which you enter is hid by the mountain, on which the upper town ftands, and which on this fide affords no profpect, except that of a fteep rock, extremely difagreeable to the fight. It was ftill worfe before the fire, which reduced fome years ago this whole palace to afhes; it having at that time no outer court, and the buildings then facing the ftreet which was very narrow. As you go along this ftreet, or to fpeak more properly, this road, you come firft of all into the country, and at the diftance of half a quarter of a league you find the Hofpital-General. This is the fineft houfe in all Canada, and would be no difparagement to our largeft cities in France; the Fathers Recollects formerly owned the ground on which it ftands. M. de St. Vallier, bifhop of Quebec, removed them into the city, bought their fettlement, and expended a hundred thoufand crowns in buildings, furniture, and in foundations. The only fault of this hofpital is its being built in a marfh; they hope to be able to remedy it by draining this marfh; but the river St. Charles makes a winding in this place, into which the waters do not eafily flow, fo that this inconvenience can never be effectually removed.

The prelate, who is the founder, has his apartment in the houfe, which he makes his ordinary refidence; having let his palace, which is alfo his own building, for the benefit of the poor. He even is not above ferving as chaplain to the hofpital, as well as to the nuns, the functions of which office,

he

he fills with a zeal and application which would be admired in a simple prieft who got his bread by it. The artizans, or others, who on account of their great age, are without the means of getting their fubfiftence, are received into this hofpital till all the beds in it are full, and thirty nuns are employed in ferving them. Thefe are a Scion or Colony from the hofpital of Quebec; but in order to diftinguifh them, the bifhop has given them certain peculiar regulations, and obliges them to wear a filver crofs on their breaft. Moft part of them are young women of condition, and as they are not thofe of the eafieft circumftances in the country the bifhop has portioned feveral of them.

Quebec is not regularly fortified, but they have been long employed in rendering it a place of ftrength. This city would not be eafily taken even in the condition in which it now is. The harbour is flanked by two baftions, which in high tides are almoft level with the furface of the water, that is to fay, they are elevated five and twenty feet from the ground, for fo high do the tides flow in the time of the equinox. A little above the baftion on the right, has been built a half baftion, which is cut out of the rock, and a little higher, on the fide towards the gallery of the fort is a battery of twenty-five pieces of cannon. Higher ftill is a fmall fquare fort, called the citadel, and the ways which communicate from one fortification to another are extremely fteep. To the left of the harbour quite along the road, as far as the river St. Charles, are good batteries of cannon with feveral mortars.

From the angle of the citadel, which fronts the city has been built an oreillon of a baftion, from whence has been drawn a curtain at right angles, which

which communicates with a very elevated cavalier, on which ftands a windmill fortified. As you defcend from this cavalier, and at the diftance of a mufket fhot from it, you meet firft a tower fortified with a baftion, and at the fame diftance from this a fecond. The defign was to line all this with ftone, which was to have had the fame angles with the baftions, and to have terminated at the extremity of the rock, oppofite to the palace, where there is already a fmall redoubt, as well as on Cape Diamond. Why this has not been put in execution I have not learned. Such, Madam, was the condition of the place nearly in 1711, when the Englifh fitted out a great armament for the conqueft of Canada, which was caft away through the temerity of the admiral, who, contrary to the advice of his pilot, went too near to the Seven Iflands, where he loft all his largeft fhips, and three thoufand of his beft troops.

Quebec is ftill at this day in the fame fituation, which you may affure yourfelf of by the plan in relievo, which M. de Chauffegros de Leri, chief engineer, fends into France this year, to be placed with the other plans of fortified places in the Louvre. After having informed you of what relates to the exterior of our capital, I muft now fay a word or two with refpect to its principal inhabitants; this is its beft fide, and if by confidering only its houfes, fquares, ftreets, churches, and publick buildings, we might reduce it to the rank of our fmalleft cities in France, yet the quality of thofe who inhabit it, will fufficiently vindicate us in beftowing upon it the title of a capital.

I have already faid, that they reckon no more than feven thoufand fouls at Quebec; yet you find

in

in it a fmall number of the beft company, where
nothing is wanting that can poffibly contribute to
form an agreeable fociety. A governor-general,
with an etat-major, a nobleffe, officers, and troops,
an intendant, with a fuperior council, and fubaltern
jurifdictions, a commiffary of the marine, a grand
provoft, and furveyor of the highways, with a grand
mafter of the waters and forefts, whofe jurifdiction
is certainly the moft extenfive in the world; rich
merchants, or fuch as live as if they were fo.; a
bifhop and numerous feminary; the recollects and
jefuits, three communities of women well educated,
affemblies, full as brilliant as any where, at the lady
Governefs's, and lady Intendants. Enough, in my
opinion, to enable all forts of perfons whatever to
pafs their time very agreeably.

They accordingly do fo, every one contributing
all in his power to make life agreeable and chear-
ful. They play at cards, or go abroad on parties
of pleafure in the fummer-time in calafhes or canoes,
in winter, in fledges upon the fnow, or on fkaits upon the ice. Hunting is a great exercife amongft
them, and there are a number of gentlemen who
have no other way of providing handfomely for
their fubfiftence. The current news confift of a
a very few articles, and thofe of Europe arrive all
at once, though they fupply matter of difcourfe for
great part of the year. They reafon like politicians on what is paft, and form conjectures on what
is likely to happen; the fciences and fine arts have
alfo their part, fo that the converfation never flags
for want of matter. The Canadians, that is to
fay, the Creoles of Canada draw in with their native
breath an air of freedom, which renders them very
agreeable in the commerce of life, and no where
in the world is our language fpoken in greater purity.

rity. There is not even the smallest foreign accent remarked in their pronunciation.

You meet with no rich men in this country, and it is really great pity, every one endeavouring to put as good a face on it as possible, and nobody scarce thinking of laying up wealth. They make good cheer, provided they are also able to be at the expence of fine cloaths ; if not, they retrench in the article of the table to be able to appear well dressed. And indeed, we must allow, that dress becomes our Creolians extremely well. They are all here of very advantageous stature, and both sexes have the finest complexion in the world ; a gay and sprightly behaviour, with great sweetness and politeness of manners are common to all of them ; and the least rusticity, either in language or behaviour, is utterly unknown even in the remotest and most distant parts.

The case is very different as I am informed with respect to our English neighbours, and to judge of the two colonies by the way of life, behaviour, and speech of the inhabitants, nobody would hesitate to say that ours were the most flourishing. In New-England and the other provinces of the continent of America, subject to the British empire, there prevails an opulence which they are utterly at a loss how to use ; and in New France, a poverty hid by an air of being in easy circumstances, which seems not at all studied. Trade, and the cultivation of their plantations strengthen the first, whereas the second is supported by the industry of its inhabitants; and the taste of the nation diffuses over it something infinitely pleasing. The English planter a-masses wealth, and never makes any superfluous expence ; the French inhabitant again enjoys what he

I   has

has acquired, and often makes a parade of what he is not poffeffed of. That labours for his pofterity; this again leaves his offspring involved in the fame neceffities he was in himfelf at his firft fetting out, and to extricate themfelves as they can. The Englifh Americans are averfe to war, becaufe they have a great deal to lofe; they take no care to manage the Indians from a belief that they ftand in no need of them. The French youth, for very different reafons, abominate the thoughts of peace, and live well with the natives, whofe efteem they eafily gain in time of war, and their friendfhip at all times. I might carry the parallel a great way farther, but I am obliged to conclude; the King's fhip is juft going to fet fail, and the merchantmen are making ready to follow her, fo that, perhaps, in three days time, there will not be fo much as a fingle veffel of any fort in the road.

I am, &c.

LETTER

L E T T E R   IV.

Of the Huron *village of* Loretto. *The çaufes
which have prevented the progrefs of the* French
colony of Canada. *Of the current money.*

Madam,   *Quebec, Feb,* 15, 1721.

I AM juft returned from a little journey or pilgrimage of devotion, of which I fhall give you an
account; but I muft in the firft place inform you,
that I was miftaken when in the conclufion of my
laft letter I had told you, that before three days
were over, the road of Quebec would be empty. A
fhip belonging to Marfeilles is ftill there, and has
even found the means of being fo under the pro-
tection of the ice with which the river is covered.
This is a fecret which may have its ufe. It is good to
have refources againft all accidents that can happen.

The captain of this veffel had taken up his anchors on the fecond of September towards evening,
and after falling down the river about a league, he
came to anchor again, in order to wait for fome of
his paffengers, who came on board after it was quite
dark. He gave orders to have every thing ready
as foon as it fhould be ebb water, and went early to
bed. About midnight, he was wakened with the
news that the veffel was filling with water; he cau-

fed

fed all the pumps to be fet a going but to no purpofe. The water continued to encreafe inftead of diminifhing; at laft, every one thought upon faving
his life, and it was time, for the laft of them had
hardly got a-fhore when the veffel funk and entirely
difappeared. A bark loaded with merchant goods
for Montreal, had the fame fate at the entrance into
lake St. Peter, but they are in hopes of getting
them both up, as foon as the good weather comes
in. Some even flatter themfelves with being able
to recover the greateft part of the effects with which
thefe two veffels are loaded; others believe they will
not, and I am of the fame opinion; however, I
fhall not be here to give you an account of it. In
the mean time, this affair of the Provençall veffel
may be attended with fome confequences, for the
captain fufpects that fomebody or other has played
him a trick. But to return to our pilgrimage.

About three leagues from this place, towards the
North-eaft, is a fmall village of the Indians, called
Hurons, who are chriftians, and who have a chapel built on the fame model, and with the fame dimenfions as the Santa Cafa of Italy, from whence
an Image of the virgin, a copy of that which is in
this famous fanctuary, has been fent to our Neophytes. A wilder place than this could not have
been chofen for the fituation of this miffion. In
the mean time, the concourfe of the faithful to this
place is very great; and whether it be the effect of
imagination, devotion, prejudice, or of any other
caufe, many perfons have affured me, that upon
their arrival they have been feized with an inward
and facred horror, of which they can give no account. But the folid piety of the inhabitants of
this defert, makes an impreffion upon all, which
is

is so much the greater, as it is assisted by thought and reflection.

The inhabitants are savages, or Indians, but who derive nothing from their birth and original but what is really estimable, that is to say, the simplicity and openness of the first ages of the world, together with those improvements which Grace has made upon them; a patriarchal faith, a sincere piety, that rectitude and docility of heart which constitute a true saint; an incredible innocence of manners; and lastly, pure Christianity, on which the world has not yet breathed that contagious air which corrupts it; and that frequently attended with acts of the most heroick virtue. Nothing can be more affecting than to hear them sing in two choirs, the men on one side, and the women on the other, the prayers and hymns of the church in their own language. Nor is there any thing which can be compared to that fervour and modesty which they display in all their religious exercises; and I have never seen any one, who was not touched with it to the bottom of his heart.

This village has been formerly much better peopled than at present, but distempers, and I know not what cause, which insensibly reduces to nothing all the nations of this continent, have greatly diminished the number of its inhabitants. The old age and infirmities of some of their ancient pastors had likewise occasioned the falling off of some from their primitive zeal, but it has been no difficult matter to bring them back to it again; and he who directs them at present has nothing to do but to keep things on the same footing in which he found them. It is true, that it is impossible to carry to a farther length than has been done the precautions they use

to

to prevent the introducing any new relaxation of manners. Intoxicating liquors, the moſt common and almoſt the ſole ſtumbling block, which is able to cauſe the ſavages to fall off, are prohibited by a ſolemn vow, the breach of which is ſubmitted to a publick penance, as well as every other fault which occaſions ſcandal; and a relapſe is generally ſufficient to baniſh the criminal without any hopes of return from a place, which ought to be the impregnable fortreſs and the ſacred aſylum of piety and innocence. Peace and ſubordination reign here in a perfect manner; and this village ſeems to conſtitute but one family, which is regulated by the pureſt maxims of the goſpel. This muſt always occaſion matter of ſurprize to every one, who conſiders to what a height theſe people, particularly the Hurons, uſually carry their natural fierceneſs and the love of independance.

The greateſt, and perhaps the only trouble which the miſſionary has, is to find wherewithal to ſubſiſt his flock; the territory which he poſſeſſes, not being ſufficient for that purpoſe, and there are very good reaſons againſt abandoning it; however, Providence ſupplies this defect. Monſieur and Madame Begon were of our pilgrimage, and were received by our good Neophytes as perſons of their rank ought to be, who, at the ſame time, never ſuffered them to want the neceſſaries of life. After a reception, entirely military on the part of the warriors, and the acclamations of the multitude, they began with exerciſes of piety, which contributed to the mutual edification of all preſent. This was followed with a general feſtival at the expence of Madam Begon, who received all the honours of it. The men, according to cuſtom, eat in one houſe, and the women with the little children in another. I

all

call it a house and not a cabin, for these Indians
have for some time lived after the French manner.

The women on such occasions testify their gratitude only by their silence and modesty ; but because
this was the first lady in the colony, who had ever
regaled the whole village, an orator was granted to
the Huron women, by whose mouth they displayed
all the grateful sentiments of their hearts towards
their illustrious benefactress. As for the men, after
their chief had harangued the Intendant, they danced
and sung as much as they thought fit. Nothing,
Madam, can be less entertaining than those songs
and dances. At first, they seat themselves on the
ground, like so many apes without any order ; from
time to time one man rises, and advances slowly to
the middle of the place, always as they say in cadence, turning his head from one side to the other,
and singing an air, containing not the smallest melody
to any ear but that of a savage or Indian, and pro-
nouncing a few words which are of no signification.
Sometimes it is a war-song, sometimes a death-song,
sometimes an attack, or a surprize ; for as these
people drink nothing but water, they have no drink-
ing songs, and they have not as yet thought of
making any on their amours. Whilst this person
is singing, the pit or audience never cease beating
time, by drawing from the bottom of their breast
a *Hé*, being a note which never varies. The con-
noisseurs, to whom I refer the matter, pretend that
they are never once out in keeping time.

As soon as one person has given over, another
takes his place, and this continues till the spectators
thank them for their entertainment, which they
would not be long of doing were it not convenient

to

to fhew a little complaifance to thofe people. Their
mufick is indeed very far from being agreeable, at
leaft, if I may form a judgment of it from what I
have heard of it.

It is however quite another thing at church; the
women particularly having a furprizing foftnefs of
voice, and at the fame time a confiderable fhare of
tafte as well as genius for mufick.

On fuch occafions their harangue or oration is extremely worthy of attention; they explain, in a few
words, and almoft always in a very ingenious manner, the occafion of the feftival, which they never
fail to afcribe to very generous motives. The
praifes of him who is at the expence are not forgotten, and they fometimes take the opportunity,
when certain perfonages, particularly when the Governor-general or Intendant are prefent, to afk a favour, or to reprefent their grievances. The orator
of the Huron women faid that day in his harangue
fome things fo very extraordinary, that we could
not help fufpecting that the interpreter, then Peter
Daniel Ricker, the miffionary, had lent him fome of
his wit and politenefs; but he protefted he had added nothing of his own; which we believed, becaufe
we knew him to be one of the openeft and fin-
cereft men in the world.

Before this little journey, I had made fome fmall
excurfions in the neighbourhood of this city, but as
the ground was every where covered with fnow to
the depth of five or fix feet, I have not thereby been
enabled to fpeak much of the nature of the country. Notwithftanding, having before travelled over
it at all feafons of the year, I can affure you that
you very rarely meet any where elfe with a more fertile

tile country, or a better soil. I have applied myself particularly this winter to learn what advantages
may be drawn from this colony, and I shall now
communicate to you the fruit of my enquiries. It
is a complaint as old as the colony itself, and not
without foundation, that Canada does not enrich
France. It is likewise true that none of the inhabitants are rich; but is this the fault of the country
itself, or rather of its first settlers? I shall endeavour to put you in the way of forming a judgment
on this article.

The original source of the misfortune of these
provinces, which they have honoured with the fine
name of *New France*, is the report which was at
first spread in the kingdom, that there were no mines
in them, and their not paying sufficient attention to
a much greater advantage which may be drawn from
this colony, which is the augmentation of trade;
that in order to bring this about settlements must
be made; that this is done by little and little, and
without being sensibly felt in such a kingdom as
France; that the two only objects which present
themselves at first view in *Canada* and *Acadia*, I mean
the fishery and fur trade, absolutely require that
these two countries should be well peopled; and that
if they had been so, perhaps, they would have sent
greater returns to France, than Spain has drawn
from the richest provinces of the New World, especially, if they had added to these articles the building of ships; but the splendor of the gold and silver which came from Peru and Mexico, dazzled
the eyes of all Europe in such a manner, that any
country which did not produce these precious metals
was looked upon as absolutely good for nothing.
Let us see what a sensible author who has been on
the spot says upon this head.

The

The common queftions they afk us, fays Mark Lefcarbot, are, " Are there any treafures to be found in that country ? Any gold and filver ? But nobody enquires whether the people are difpofed to hear and relifh the doctrines of Chriftianity. It is, however, certain, that there are mines here, but thefe muft be wrought with induftry, labour, and patience. The beft mine I know is corn and wine, together with the raifing of cattle ; he who poffeffes thefe things has money ; but we do not live by mines. The mariners who come in queft of fifh from all parts of Europe, above eight or nine hundred leagues from their own country, find the beft of mines, without blowing up rocks, digging into the entrails of the earth, or living in the obfcurity of the infernal regions.—They find, I fay, the beft of mines in the bottom of the waters, and in the trade of furs and fkins, by which they make good money."

Not only a bad character has been given to New France without knowing it ; but even thofe who imagined they fhould draw advantages from it, have not purfued the meafures proper for that purpofe. In the firft place, they were a very long time in fixing themfelves ; they cleared lands without having well examined them, they fowed them, and built houfes on them, and afterwards frequently deferted them, without knowing why, and went to fettle elfewhere. This inconftancy has contributed more than any thing to make us lofe Acadia, and prevent us from drawing any advantage from it, during the time we were in poffeffion of that fine peninfula. The author, already cited, who was a witnefs of this our wavering and irrefolute conduct, fcruples not to upbraid thofe with it who were the moft culpable. " It is thus," fays he, " that we
have

have made levies of armed men, that we have hurried with ardour into new undertakings, that we have laid down and begun the fineft projects, and in the end have deferted them all. . . . . Indeed to be fuccefsful in fuch enterprizes we ought to be well fupported ; but we ought likewife to have men of refolution, who will not retract, but carry this point of honour always in their eyes, *to conquer or die*, it being a great and a glorious thing to die in the execution of a noble defign, fuch as laying the foundations of a new kingdom, or eftablifhing the Chriftian faith among a people unacquainted with the true God." I could pufh thefe reflections a great deal farther, but am cautious of engaging in a difpute, into which I neither can nor ought to enter with the knowledge I have of it at prefent.

I come now to the commerce of Canada. This has turned for a long time folely upon the fifhery and fur-trade. The cod-fifhery had been carried on upon the great bank, and the coafts of Newfoundland, long before the difcovery of the river St. Laurence, but we were too late in making a fettlement on that ifland, and fuffered the Englifh to get the ftart of us. At laft we got poffeffion of the harbour and bay of Placentia, where our royal fquadrons have been at anchor oftener than once ; we have withftood fieges there, and the Canadian militia have performed warlike exploits in that place which are not inferior to thofe of the braveft bucaneers of St. Domingo. They have frequently laid wafte the fettlements, and ruined the trade of the Englifh in that ifland ; but that people, from whom we eafily took their ftrongeft places, were too well acquainted with their enemies to be difconcerted in their meafures. Accuftomed to behold the Canadian fire kindle in the frozen regions of the

north,

north, and go out of its own accord, when it ought to have difplayed itfelf with the greateft activity, they have behaved at the approach of our people, as an experienced pilot does at the fight of an unavoidable tempeft. They wifely gave way to the ftorm, and afterwards, without interruption, repaired the damages their fettlements had received from it; and by this conduct, though continually worfted in Newfoundland, whether they acted on the offenfive or defenfive, they have always carried on an incomparably greater trade than their conquerors, and have at laft remained the fole mafters and peaceable poffeffors of that ifland.

We have behaved ftill worfe in Canada; this great and rich province has been for a long time divided amongft feveral private perfons, none of whom have enriched themfelves, whilft the Englifh have made immenfe profits by the fifhery on its coafts. The fettlements which thefe proprietors have made, wanting folidity, and they themfelves being deftitute of a regular plan, and the one deftroying the other, they have left the country nearly in the fame condition in which they found it, and in a ftate of contempt and neglect from which it has not recovered till the moment we loft it. Our enemies were the firft who made us fenfible of its value.

The only trade to which this colony has been long reduced, is that of furs; and the faults committed in it are paft number. Perhaps, our national character never fhowed itfelf in a ftronger light than in this affair. When we difcovered this vaft Continent, it was full of wild beafts. A handful of Frenchmen has made them almoft entirely difappear in lefs than an age, and there are fome the fpecies of which is entirely deftroyed. They killed
the

the elks and moufe-deer merely for the pleafure of kil-
ling them, and to fhew their dexterity. They had
not even the precaution to interpofe the authority of
the prince to ftop fuch a flagrant diforder. But the
greateft mifchiefs arofe from the infatiable avidity of
private perfons, who applied themfelves folely to
this commerce.

They arrived for the moft part from France, with
nothing but what they had on their backs, and they
were impatient to appear in a better fituation. At
firft this was an eafy matter; the Indians knew not
what riches were contained in their woods, till the
rapacioufnefs with which their furs were bought up
made them acquainted with it; prodigious quantities were got from them for trifles, which many
would not have been at the trouble to gather together. Even fince they have had their eyes opened
with refpect to the value of this commodity, and
have acquired a tafte for fomething more folid, it
was for a long time very eafy to fatisfy them at a
fmall expence; and with a little prudence this trade
might have been continued on a tolerable good footing.

Neverthelefs, we fhould be puzzled to name but
one family at this day which has grown rich by this
traffick. We have feen fortunes equally immenfe
and fudden, rife up, and difappear almoft at the fame
time, not unlike to thofe moving mountains mentioned by travellers, which the wind raifes or throws down
in the fandy defarts of Africa. Nothing has been
more common in this country than to fee people
dragging out a languifhing old age in mifery and
difgrace, after having been in a condition to fettle
themfelves on an honourable footing. After all,
Madam, thofe fortunes which private perfons, who

never deferved them, have failed of acquiring, are not worthy of the publick's regret, if the bad confequences had not fallen upon the colony, which, in a fhort time, was reduced to the condition of feeing a fpring, from whence fo much riches might have flowed into its bofom, entirely dried up or diverted into another channel.

Its great plenty was the beginning of its ruin. By means of accumulating beaver fkins, which has always been the principal object of this commerce, fo great a quantity were heaped up in the warehoufes that no vent could be found for them, whence it happened, that the merchants declining to buy any more, our adventurers, called here *Coureurs de Rois*, or hunters, took the refolution of carrying them to the Englifh, and many of them fettled in the province of New-York. Several attempts were made to put a ftop to the progrefs of thefe defertions, but to little effect; on the contrary, thofe who had been led by motives of intereft, to take refuge among their neighbours, were kept there by the fear of punifhment; and the vagabonds, who had acquired a tafte for a wandering and independant life, remained amongft the favages or Indians, from whom they were no longer diftinguifhable but by their vices. They frequently had recourfe to amnefties to recal thofe fugitives, which were at firft of little confequence; but in the end being managed with prudence, they produced part of the effect promifed from them.

Another method was made ufe of which was ftill more efficacious; but thofe people who were zealous for good order and the advancement of religion, found the remedy worfe than the difeafe. This was to grant permiffion to thofe in whom they thought
they

they could repofe confidence to trade in the Indian countries, and to prohibit all others from going out of the colony. The number of thefe licences was limited, and they were diftributed amongft poor widows and orphans, who might fell them to the *Traders* for more or lefs, according as the trade was good or bad, or according to the nature of the places to which the licences granted the liberty of trading; for they ufed the precaution to fpecify thofe places, to prevent too great a number from going the fame way.

Befides thofe licences, the number of which was regulated by the court, and the diftribution of which belonged to the governor-general, there were others for the commandants of forts, and for extraordinary occafions, which the governor ftill grants under the name of fimple *Permiffions.* Thus one part of our youth is continually rambling and roving about; and though thofe diforders, which formerly fo much difgraced this profeffion, are no longer committed, at leaft not fo openly, yet it infects them with a habit of libertinifm, of which they never entirely get rid; at leaft, it gives them a diftafte for labour, it exhaufts their ftrength, they become incapable of the leaft conftraint, and when they are no longer able to undergo the fatigues of travelling, which foon happens, for thefe fatigues are exceffive, they remain without the leaft refource, and are no longer good for any thing. Hence it comes to pafs, that arts have been a long time neglected, a great quantity of good land remains ftill uncultivated, and the country is but very indifferently peopled.

It has been often propofed to abolifh thofe pernicious licences, not with a view of hurting the trade, but

but even of rendering it more flourishing, and for that purpose to make some French settlements in proper places, where it would be easy to assemble the Indians, at least for certain seasons of the year. By this means, this vast country would be insensibly filled with inhabitants, and perhaps, this is the only method by which that project which the court has so long had at heart of *Frenchifying* the Indians, that is the term they make use of, could be brought about. I believe, I may at least affirm, that if this method had been followed, Canada would have been at present much better peopled than it is ; that the Indians drawn and kept together by the comforts and conveniencies of life, which they would have found in our settlements, would not have been so miserable, nor so much addicted to a wandering life, and consequently their numbers would have encreased, whereas they have diminished at a surprising rate, and would have attached themselves to us in such a manner that we might now have disposed of them as of the subjects of the crown ; besides, that the missionaries would have had fewer obstacles to encounter with in their conversion. What we now see at Loretto, and amongst a small proportion of the Iroquoise, Algonquins, and Abenaquis, settled in the colony, leaves no room to doubt the truth of what I have advanced, and there are none of those who have had the greatest intercourse with the Indians, who do not agree, that these people are not to be depended on, when they are not Christians. I want no other example, but that of the Abenaquis, who, though far from being numerous, have been during the two last wars the chief bulwark of New France against New England.

Besides

Befides this project, Madam, which I have been juft now explaining to you, is as old as the colony; it was formed by M. de Champlain its founder, and has been approved of by almoft all the miffionaries I have known, whofe painful labours in the fituation things have long been in, produce no great good effects, at leaft in the diftant miffions. It would be now, indeed, too late to refume this defign with refpect to the Indians, who difappear in a manner as fenfible as it is inconceivable. But what hinders its being followed with refpect to the French, and enlarging the colony by degrees, till it fhould join to that of Louifiana, and thus ftrengthen the one by the other? It has been in this manner, that the Englifh, in lefs than a century and a half have peopled above five hundred leagues of the country, and formed a power upon this Continent, which when we view it nearly we cannot but behold with terror.

Canada is capable of furnifhing many articles for a trade with the Weft-India iflands, and fometimes actually fends thither no mean quantity of flour, planks, and other timber proper for building. As there is, perhaps, no country in the whole world, which produces more forts of wood nor of better kinds, you may judge what immenfe riches may be one day drawn from it. It appears that very few perfons are well informed with refpect to this point. Nor am I, as yet, fufficiently informed myfelf, to be able to enter into a more minute detail; I am fomewhat better acquainted with what relates to the oil-trade, and fhall have occafion to fpeak of it very foon: As I am in a hurry to finifh this letter, I have only time to conclude what relates to the commerce of this country in general.

Nothing has in all appearance contributed more
to its decay, than the frequent changes which have
been made in the coin. I will give you the hiſtory
of it in a few words. In 1670, the company of
the Weſt-Indies, to whom the king had ceded the
right to the property of the French iſlands on the
Continent of America, had leave given to export
to the Weſt-India iſlands, to the amount of one
hundred thouſand livres, in ſmall pieces, marked
with a particular ſtamp and inſcription. The king's
edict is dated in the month of February, and bore
that thoſe pieces ſhould only paſs current in the iſles.
But in ſome difficulties which fell out, the council
iſſued on the 18th of November of the year 1672,
an *Arret*, by which it was ordained, that the above-
mentioned, as well as all other coin which ſhould
paſs current in France, ſhould alſo paſs current not
only in the French iſlands, but alſo in thoſe parts
of the continent of America, which are ſubject to
the crown, at the rate of thirty-three and one third
per cent. advance ; that is to ſay, the pieces of fifteen
ſols for twenty, and the others in proportion.

The ſame *Arret* ordained, that all contracts, bills,
accounts, bargains, and payments, between all ſorts
of perſons whatſoever, ſhould be made at a certain
price in current money, without making uſe of any
exchange or reckoning in ſugar, or any other commodity, on pain of nullity of the act. And with
reſpect to tranſactions by-paſt, it was ordered, that
all ſtipulations of contracts, bills, debts, quit-rents,
leaſes, or farms of ſugar, or other commodities,
ſhould be made payable in money, according to the
current value of the above coin. In conſequence
of this arret, the coin encreaſed one fourth in value
in New France, which very ſoon occaſioned many
difficulties. In effect, M. de Champigny Noroy,
who

who was appointed intendant of Quebec, in 1684, and who is now in the fame employ at Havre de Grace, found himfelf foon embarraffed as well with refpeƈt to the payment of the troops, as to the other expences the king muft be at in this colony.

And befides the funds which were fent from France, arrived almoft always too late, the firft of January being the day on which it was abfolutely neceffary to pay the officers and foldiers, as well as to defray other charges equally indifpenfable. To obviate the moft preffing demands, M. de Champigny thought proper to iffue certain bills, which fhould ftand in place of coin, taking care, however, conftantly to obferve the augmentation of the value of the money. A verbal procefs was drawn up of this proceeding, and, by virtue of an ordinance of the governor-general and intendant, every piece of this money, which was made of cards, had its value, with the mark of the treafury, and the arms of France, ftamped upon it, as were thofe of the governor and intendant in Spanifh wax. Afterwards paper money was ftruck in France, and ftamped with the fame impreffion as the current-money of the realm, and it was ordained, that the bills fhould be returned into the treafury of Canada every year, before the arrival of the fhips from France, in order to receive an additional mark to prevent the introducing of counterfeits.

This paper-money was of no long continuance, fo that they returned to the ufe of card-money, on which new impreffions were ftamped. The intendant figned fuch bills as were of four livres and upwards value, only marking the others. In latter times, the governor-general figned alfo fuch as were of fix livres and above. In the beginning of the Autumn,

all

all the bills were carried back to the treasurer, who gave bills of exchange for the value on the treasurer-general of the marine at Rochefort, or his clerk, to be charged to the account of the expences of the following year. Such as were spoiled were no longer suffered to pass current, and were burned after having first drawn up a verbal process of it.

Whilst these bills of exchange were faithfully paid, those money-bills were preferred to real specie; as soon as they ceased to be honoured, they gave over carrying the money-bills to the treasurer, so that in 1702, M. de Champigny was at a great deal of pains to no purpose in endeavouring to retire all those he had made. His successors were under the necessity of making new ones every year, for paying of salaries, which multiplied them to such a degree, that at last they became of no value at all, and nobody would receive them in payment. The consequence of this was an entire stagnation of trade, and the disorder went so far, that in 1713, the inhabitants proposed to lose one half, on condition that the king should take them up and pay the other half.

This proposal was agreed to the year following, but the orders given, in consequence thereof, were not fully executed till 1717. A declaration was then published, abolishing these money-bills, when they begun paying the salaries of the officers of the colony in silver. The augmentation of one fourth advance, was abrogated at the same time: Experience having made it appear, that the augmentation of the species in a colony does not keep the money from going out of it as had been pretended, and that money could never have a free and proper circulation, but by paying in commodities whatever

was

was imported from France. In effect, in this case, the colony keeps her money at home, whereas in the suppofition that she has not merchandize sufficient to pay for all that she receives, she is obliged to pay the balance in filver, and how should it be otherwife?

In a word, Madam, you will be furprized when I tell you, that in 1706, the trade of the most ancient of all our colonies was carried on in a bottom, or capital of no more than 650,000 livres, and things have fince been pretty much in the fame fituation. Now this fum divided amongft thirty thoufand inhabitants is neither capable of enriching them, nor of enabling them to purchafe the commodities of France. For this reafon, most part of them go ftark naked, efpecially thofe that live in remote habitations. They have not even fo much as the advantage of felling the furplus of their commodities to the inhabitants of cities, thefe being obliged, in order to fubfift, to have lands in the country, and to cultivate them themfelves for their own account.

After the king had taken Canada back again out of the hands of the companies, his majefty expended confiderably more on it for feveral years than he has done fince; and the colony in thofe times fent into France to the value of near one million livres in beaver yearly, notwithftanding it was not fo populous as at prefent: But she has always drawn more from France than she has been able to pay, doing juft as a private perfon would, who with a revenue of thirty thoufand livres, fhould fpend at the rate of upwards of forty thoufand. By this means, her credit has funk, and fo has brought on the ruin of her trade, which, fince the year 1706,

K 3 con-

confifted of fcarce any thing befides what is called the leffer peltry. Every merchant would be con-cerned in it which has occafioned its ruin, as they often paid more for them to the Indians than they were able to fell them for in France.

I am, &c.

LETTER V.

Of the beavers of Canada ; *in what they differ
from those of* Europe ; *of their manner of
building* ; *of the advantage which may accrue
to the colony from them* ; *of the hunting of the
beaver and musk-rat.*

Quebec, March 1, 1721.

Madam,

I Ought to have set out within a day or two after
writing my last letter; but I am still detained
for want of a carriage. In the mean-time, I cannot
do better than entertain you with an account of the
curiosities of this country. I shall begin with the
most singular article of all, that is to say, the beaver. The spoil of this animal has hitherto been
the principal article in the commerce of New France.
It is itself one of the greatest wonders in nature,
and may very well afford many a striking lesson of
industry, foresight, dexterity, and perseverance in
labour.

The beaver was not unknown in France before
the discovery of America; we find in the ancient
books of the Hatters of Paris, regulations for the
K 4

manu-

manufacture of beaver-hats; now the beaver of
America and Europe are abfolutely the fame animal;
but whether it is, that the European beavers are become extremely rare; or that their fur is not equally
good in quality with that of the beavers of America, there is no longer mention made of any, befides this latter, except it is with refpect to the Caftoreum, of which I fhall fay a word or two in the
end of this letter. I do not even know that any
author has mentioned this animal, as an object of
curiofity, perhaps, for want of having obferved it
clofely enough; perhaps too, becaufe the European beavers are of the nature of land beavers,
the difference of which from the others I fhall prefently fhew you.

However this be, the beaver of Canada is an
amphibious quadruped, which cannot live for any
long time in the water, and which is able to live
entirely without it, provided it have the conveniency
of bathing itfelf fometimes. The largeft beavers
are fomewhat lefs than four feet in length and fifteen
inches in breadth over the haunches, weighing about
fixty pounds. Its colour is different according to
the different climates, in which it is found. In the
moft diftant northern parts they are generally quite
black, though there are fometimes found beavers
entirely white. In the moft temperate countries they
are brown, their colour becoming lighter and lighter
in proportion as they approach toward the fouth.
In the country of the Illinois, they are almoft yellow, and fome are even feen of a ftraw-colour. It
has alfo been obferved, that in proportion as their
colour is lighter they yield a lefs quantity of fur,
and confequently are lefs valuable. This is plainly
the work of Providence, which fecures them from
the cold in proportion as they are expofed to it.

The

The fur is of two forts all the body over, excepting at the feet, where it is very fhort. The longeft of it is from eight to ten lines in length, and it even goes fometimes on the back as far as two inches, diminifhing gradually towards the head and tail. This part of the fur is harfh, courfe, and fhining, and is properly that which gives the animal its colour. In viewing it through a microfcope, you obferve the middle lefs opake, which proves it to be hollow, for which caufe no ufe is ever made of it. The other part of the fur is a very thick and fine down, of an inch in length at moft, and is what is commonly manufactured. In Europe, it was formerly known by the name of Mufcovia wool. This is properly the coat of the beaver, the firft ferving only for ornament, and perhaps to affift him in fwimming.

It is pretended that the beaver lives fifteen or twenty years; that the female carries her young four months, and that her ordinary litter is four, though fome travellers have raifed it to eight, which as I believe happens but rarely. She has four teats, two on the great pectoral mufcle between the fecond and third of the true ribs, and two about four fingers higher. The mufcles of this animal are exceeding ftrong, and thicker in appearance than its fize requires. Its inteftines on the contrary are extremely flender, its bones very hard, and its two jaws which are almoft equal, furprizingly ftrong; each of thefe is furnifhed with ten teeth, two incifive and eight molar. The fuperior incifives are two inches and a half long, the inferior upwards of three, following the bending of the jaw, which gives them a prodigious and furprifing force for fo fmall an animal. It has been further obferved, that the two jaws do not exactly correfpond, but that the fuperior

rior advances confiderably over the inferior, fo that they crofs like the two blades of a pair of fciffars: Laftly, that the length of both the one and the other is precifely the third part of their root.

The head of the beaver is very near like that of a mountain rat. Its fnout is pretty long, the eyes little, the ears fhort, round, hairy on the outfide, and fmooth within. Its legs are fhort, particularly the forelegs, which are only four or five inches long, and pretty much like thofe of the badger. The nails are made obliquely and hollow like quills, the hind feet are quite different, being flat and furnifh-ed with membranes between the toes ; thus the bea-ver can walk though flowly, and fwims with the fame eafe as any other aquatick animal. Befides, in refpect of its tail, it is altogether a fifh, having been juridically declared fuch by the faculty of medicine of Paris, in confequence of which declaration, the faculty of theology have decided that it might be lawfully eaten on meagre days. M. Lemery was miftaken in faying, that this decifion regarded only the hinder part of the beaver. It has been placed all of it in the fame clafs with mackrel.

It is true, that hitherto we have not been able to profit much by this toleration ; the beavers are at prefent fo far from our habitations, that it is rare to meet with any that are eatable. Our Indians who live among us keep it after having dried it in the fmoke, and I give you my word, Madam, it is the worft eating I ever tafted. It is alfo neceffary when you have got frefh beaver, to give it a boiling in order to take away a very difagreeable relifh. With this precaution, it is exceeding good eating, there be-ing no fort of meat either lighter, more wholefome, or more delicious, it is even affirmed to be as nourifhing

rifhing as veal; when boiled it ftands in need of some feafoning to give it a relifh, but roafted has no need of any thing. What is moft remarkable in this amphibious animal is its tail. This is almoft oval, four inches broad at the root, five in the middle, and three at the extremity, I mean, however, in large beavers only. It is an inch thick, and a foot in length. Its fubftance is a firm fat, or tender cartilage, much like the flefh of the porpoife, but which grows harder when it is kept for any confiderable time. It is covered with a fcaly fkin, the fcales of which are hexagonal, half a line in thicknefs, from three to four lines long, and refting upon each other like thofe of fifhes. An extream flender pellicle ferves to fupport them, and they are indented fo as to be eafily feparated after the death of the animal.

This is in brief the defcription of this curious creature. If you would have a ftill greater detail of it, you may fatisfy yourfelf by looking into the memoirs of the royal academy of fciences for the year 1704. The anatomical defcription of the beaver has been inferted in it, done by M. Sarrafin correfpondent of the academy, king's phyfician in this country, and expert in medicine, anatomy, furgery, and botany; and a man of very fine accomplifhments, who diftinguifhes himfelf no lefs in the fuperior council of which he is member, than by his abilities in every point relating to his profeffion. It is really matter of furprize to find a man of fuch univerfal merit in a colony. But to return to the beaver.

The true tefticles of this amphibious animal were not known to the antients, probably, becaufe they were very little, and lay concealed in the loins.
They

They had given this name to the bags in which the caftoreum is contained, which are very different, and in number four in the lower belly of the beaver. The two firft, which are called fuperior, from their being more elevated than the reft, are of the form of a pear, and communicate with each other like the two pockets of a knapfack. The other two which are called inferior are roundifh towards the bottom. The former contain a foft, refinous, adhefive matter, mixed with fmall fibres, greyifh without, and yellow within, of a ftrong difagreeable and penetrating fcent, and very inflammable, which is the true caftoreum. It hardens in the air in a month's time, and becomes brown, brittle, and friable. When they have a mind to caufe it harden fooner than ordinary, 'tis only placing it in a chimney.

It is pretended that the caftoreum which comes from Dantzick is better than that of Canada; I refer it to the Druggifts. It is certain that the bags which contain this latter are fmaller, and that even here the largeft are the moft efteemed. Befides their thicknefs, they muft alfo be heavy, brown, of a ftrong penetrating fcent, full of a hard, bitter, and friable matter, of the fame colour, or yellowifh interwoven with a delicate membrane, and of an acrid tafte. The properties of caftoreum are to attenuate vifcous matter, fortify the brain, cure the vapours, provoke the menfes in women, prevent corruption, and caufe ill humours to evaporate by perfpiration. It is alfo ufed with fuccefs againft the epilepfy, or falling-ficknefs, the palfy, apoplexy, and deafnefs.

The inferior bags contain an unctuous and fattifh liquor like honey. Its colour is of a pale yellow, its odour fetid, little different from that of the caftoreum,

reum, but somewhat weaker and more disagreeable.
It thickens as it grows older, and takes the consistence of tallow. This liquor is a resolvent, and a
fortifier of the nerves, for which purpose it must
be applied upon the part. It is besides a folly to
say with some authors on the faith of the antient
naturalists, that when the beaver finds himself pursued, to save his life he bites off these pretended testicles which he abandons to the hunters. It is his
fur he ought then to strip himself of, in comparison of which all the rest is of little value. It is,
however, owing to this fable that this animal got
the name of Castor. Its skin, after being stript of
the fur, is not to be neglected; of it are made gloves
and stockings, as might several other things, but it
being difficult to take off all the fur without cutting
it they make use of the skin of the land beaver.

You have, perhaps, heard of green and dry
beaver, and you may also be desirous to know the
difference; which is this. The dry beaver is its
skin before it has been employed in any use: the
green beaver are such as have been worn by the Indians, who, after having well tawed them on the
inside, and rubbed them with the marrow of certain
animals, with which I am not acquainted, in order
to render them more pliant, sew several of them together, making a sort of garment, which they call
a robe, and in which they wrap themselves with the
fur inwards. They never put it off in winter, day
nor night; the long hair soon falls off, the down
remaining and becoming more oily, in which condition it is much fitter to be worked up by the hatters; who cannot make any use of the dry, without a mixture of this fat fur along with it. They
pretend it ought to have been worn from fifteen to
eighteen months to be in its perfection. I leave you

to judge whether our firſt traders were ſimple enough
to let the Indians know what a valuable commodity
their old cloaths were. It was, however, impoſſible to keep a ſecret of this nature for any conſiderable time, being entruſted to a paſſion which immediately betrays itſelf. About thirty years ago one
Guigues, who had had the farm of the beaver, finding a prodigious quantity of this fur upon his hands,
bethought himſelf, in order to create a vent for it,
of having it ſpun and carded with wool, and of this
compoſition he cauſed make cloths, flannels, ſtock-
ing, and other ſuch like manufactures, but with ſmall
ſucceſs. This trial ſhewed that the fur of the beaver was only fit for making hats. It is too ſhort to
be capable of being ſpun alone, and a great deal
more than one half muſt conſiſt of wool, ſo that
there is very little profit to be made by this manufacture. There is, however, one of this ſort ſtill
kept up in Holland, where you meet with cloaths
and druggets of it ; but theſe ſtuffs come dear, and
beſides do not wear well. The beaver wool very
ſoon leaves it, forming on the ſurface a ſort of nap
which deſtroys all its luſtre. The ſtockings which
have been made of it in France had the ſame defect.

Theſe, Madam, are all the advantages the beavers are capable of affording the commerce of this
colony : their foreſight, their unanimity, and that
wonderful ſubordination we ſo much admire in them,
their attention to provide conveniencies, of which
we could not before imagine brutes capable of perceiving the advantages, afford mankind ſtill more
important leſſons, than the ant to whom the holy
ſcripture ſends the ſluggard. They are at leaſt a-
mongſt the quadrupeds, what the bees are amongſt
winged inſects. I have not heard perſons well informed

formed fay, that they have a king or queen, and it
is not true, that when they are at work in a body,
there is a chief or a leader who gives orders and
punifhes the flothful ; but by virtue of that inftinct
which this animal has from him, whofe Providence
governs them, every one knows his own proper
office, and every thing is done without confufion,
and in the moft admirable order. Perhaps, after
all, the reafon why we are fo ftruck with it is for
want of having recourfe to that fovereign intelligence, who makes ufe of creatures void of reafon,
the better to difplay his wifdom and power, and to
make us fenfible that our reafon itfelf is almoft always, through our prefumption, the caufe of our
miftakes.

The firft thing which our ingenious brutes do,
when they are about to chufe a habitation, is to call
an affembly if you pleafe, of the ftates of the province. However this be, there are fometimes three
or four hundred of them together in one place,
forming a town which might properly enough be
called a little Venice. Firft of all they pitch upon
a fpot where there are plenty of provifions, with
all the materials neceffary for building. Above all
things water is abfolutely neceffary, and in cafe they
can find neither lake nor pool, they fupply that
defect by ftopping the courfe of fome rivulet, or of
fome fmall river, by means of a dyke, or to fpeak
in the language of this country, of a caufeway.
For this purpofe, they fet about felling of trees,
but higher than the place where they have refolved
to build ; three or four beavers place themfelves
round fome great tree, and find ways and means to
lay it along the ground with their teeth. This is
not all ; they take their meafures fo well, that it
always falls towards the water, to the end they may
have

have lefs way to drag it, after cutting it into proper lengths. They have afterwards only to roll thofe pieces fo cut towards the water, where, after they have been launched, they navigate them towards the place where they are to be employed.

Thefe pieces are more or lefs thick or long, according as the nature and fituation of the place require, for thefe architects forefee every thing. Sometimes they make ufe of the trunks of great trees, which they place in a flat direction; fometimes the caufeway confifts of piles nearly as thick as one's thigh, fupported by ftrong ftakes, and interwoven with fmall branches; and every where the vacant fpaces are filled with a fat earth fo well applied, that not a drop of water paffes through. The beavers prepare this earth with their feet; and their tail not only ferves inftead of a trowel for building; but alfo ferves them inftead of a wheelbarrow for tranfporting this mortar, which is performed by trailing themfelves along on their hinder feet. When they have arrived at the water-fide, they take it up with their teeth, and apply it firft with their feet, and then plaifter it with their tail. The foundations of thefe dykes are commonly ten or twelve feet thick, diminifhing always upward, till at laft they come to two or three; the ftricteft proportion is always exactly obferved; the rule and the compafs are in the eye of the great mafter of arts and fciences. Laftly, it has been obferved, that the fide towards the current of the water is always made floping, and the other fide quite upright. In a word, it would be difficult for our beft workmen to build any thing either more folid or more regular.

The conftruction of the cabins is no lefs wonderful. Thefe are generally built on piles in the
mid-

middle of thofe fmall lakes formed by the dykes :
fometimes on the bank of a river, or at the extremity of fome point advancing into the water. Their
figure is round or oval, and their roofs are arched
like the bottom of a bafket. Their partitions are
two feet thick, the materials of them being the
fame, though lefs fubftantial, than thofe in the caufeways ; and all is fo well plaiftered with clay in the
infide, that not the fmalleft breath of air can enter.
Two thirds of the edifice ftands above water, and
in this part each beaver has his place affigned him;
which he takes care to floor with leaves or fmall
branches of pine-trees. There is never any ordure
to be feen here, and to this end, befides the common gate of the cabin and another iffue by which
thefe animals go out to bathe, there are feveral
openings by which they difcharge their excrements
into the water. The common cabins lodge eight
or ten beavers, and fome have been known to contain thirty, but this is rarely feen. All of them
are near enough to have an eafy communication
with each other.

The winter never furprizes the beavers. All the
works I have been mentioning are finifhed by the
end of September, when every one lays in his win-
ter-ftock of provifions. Whilft their bufinefs leads
them abroad into the country or woods, they live
upon the fruit, bark, and leaves of trees ; they fifh
alfo for crawfifh and fome other kinds ; every thing
is then at the beft. But when the bufinefs is to lay
in a ftore, fufficient to laft them, whilft the earth
is hid under the fnow, they put up with wood of a
foft texture, fuch as poplars, afpens, and other fuch
like trees. Thefe they lay up in piles, and difpofe
in fuch wife, as to be always able to come at the
pieces which have been foftened in the water. It has

been

been conftantly remarked, that thefe piles are more or lefs large, according as the winter is to be longer or fhorter, which ferves as an Almanack to the Indians, who are never miftaken with refpect to the duration of the cold. The beavers before they eat the wood, cut it into fmall flender pieces, and carry it into their apartment; each cabin having only one ftore-room for the whole family.

When the melting of the fnow is at its greateft height as it never fails to occafion great inundations, the beavers quit their cabins which are no longer habitable, every one fhifting for himfelf as well as he can. The females return thither as foon as the waters are fallen, and it is then they bring forth their young. The males keep abroad till towards the month of July, when they re-affemble, in order to repair the breaches which the fwelling of the waters may have made in their cabbins or dykes. In cafe thefe have been deftroyed by the hunters, or provided they are not worth the trouble of repairing them, they fet about building of others; but they are often obliged to change the place of their abode, and that for many reafons. The moft common is for want of provifions; they are alfo driven out by the hunters, or by carnivorous animals, againft whom they have no other defence than flight alone. One might reafonably wonder, that the author of nature fhould have given a lefs fhare of ftrength to the moft part of ufeful animals than to fuch as are not fo; if this very thing did not make a brighter difplay of his power and wifdom, in caufing the former, notwithftanding their weaknefs to multiply much fafter than the latter.

There are places to which the beavers feem to have fo ftrong a liking that they can never leave
them

them though they are conftantly difturbed in them.
On the way from Montreal to Lake Huron, by
way of the great river, is conftantly found every
year a neft which thofe animals build or repair every
fummer ; for the firft thing which thofe travellers,
who arrive firft do, is to break down the cabin and
dyke which fupplies it with water. Had not this
caufeway dammed up the water, there would not
have been fufficient to continue their voyages, fo
that of neceffity there muft have been a carrying-
place ; fo that it feems thofe officious beavers poft
themfelves there entirely for the conveniency of
paffengers.

The Indians were formerly of opinion, if we
may believe fome accounts, that the beavers were a
fpecies of animals endued with reafon, which had
a government, laws, and language of their own ;
that this amphibious commonwealth chofe chiefs or
officers, who in the publick works affigned to each
his tafk, placed fentries to give the alarm at the
approach of an enemy, and who punifhed the lazy
corporally, or with exile. Thofe pretended exiles
are fuch as are probably called land beavers, who
actually live feparate from the others, never work,
and live under-ground, where their fole bufinefs is
to make themfelves a covered way to the water.
They are known by the fmall quantity of fur on
their backs, proceeding, without doubt from their
rubbing themfelves continually againft the ground.
And befides, they are lean, which is the confequence
of their lazinefs ; they are found in much greater
plenty in warm than in cold countries. I have already taken notice that our European beavers are much
liker thefe laft than the others ; and Lemery actually
fays, that they retire into holes and caverns on the
banks of rivers, and efpecially in Poland. There are

L 2   alfo

also some of them in Germany, along the shores of
the Ebro in Spain, and on the Rhone, the Iser, and
the Oise in France. What is certain is, that we
see not so much of the marvellous in the European
beavers, for which those of Canada are so highly
distinguished. Your ladyship will certainly agree
with me, that it is great pity, none of these wonderful creatures were ever found either on the Tiber
or on Parnassus ; how many fine things would they
have given occasion to the Greek and Roman poets
to say on that subject.

It appears, that the Indians of Canada did not
give them much disturbance before our arrival in
their country. The skins of the beaver were not
used by those people by way of garments, and the
flesh of bears, elks, and some other wild beasts,
seemed, in all probability, preferable to that of the
beaver. They were, however, in use to hunt them,
and this hunting had both its season and ceremonial
fixed ; but when people hunt only out of necessity,
and when this is confined to pure necessaries, there
is no great havock made ; thus when we arrived in
Canada we found a prodigious number of these
creatures in it.

The hunting of the beaver is not difficult ; this
animal shewing not near so much strength in defend-
ing himself, or dexterity in shunning the snares of
his enemies, as he discovers industry in providing
himself good lodgings, and foresight in getting all
the necessaries of life. It is during the winter that
war is carried on against him in form ; that is to
say, from the beginning of November to the month
of April. At that time, like most other animals,
he has the greatest quantity of fur, and his skin is
thinnest. This hunting is performed four ways,
                                                    with

with nets, by lying upon the watch, by opening
the ice, and with gins. The firſt and third are generally joined together; the ſecond way is ſeldom
made uſe of; the little eyes of this animal being ſo
ſharp, and its hearing ſo acute, that it is difficult
to get within ſhot of it, before it gains the water-
ſide, from which it never goes far at this time of
the year, and in which it dives immediately. It
would even be loſt after being wounded, in caſe
it is able to reach the water, for when mortally
wounded it never comes up again. The two laſt
manners are therefore moſt generally practiſed.

Though the beavers lay up their winter proviſion,
they notwithſtanding from time to time make ſome
excurſions into the woods in queſt of freſher and
more tender food, which delicacy of theirs ſometimes coſts them their lives. The Indians lay traps
in their way made nearly in the form of the figure
4, and for a bait place ſmall bits of tender wood
newly cut. The beaver no ſooner touches it, than
a large log falls upon his body, which breaks his
back, when the hunter, coming up, eaſily diſpatches
him. The method by opening the ice requires
more precaution, and is done in this manner. When
the ice is yet but half a foot in thickneſs, an opening is made with a hatchet; thither the beavers
come for a ſupply of freſh air; the hunters watch
for them at the hole, and perceive them coming at
a great diſtance, their breath occaſioning a conſiderable motion in the water; thus it is eaſy for them
to take their meaſures for knocking them in the
head the moment they raiſe it above water. In order to make ſure of their game, and to prevent
their being perceived by the beavers, they cover the
hole with the leaves of reeds, and of the plant *Ty-
pha*, and after they underſtand that the animal is

within

within reach, they feize him by one of his legs, throw him upon the ice, and difpatch him before he recovers from his confternation.

When their cabin happens to be near fome rivulet, the hunting of the beaver is ftill more eafy. They cut the ice crofs-wife, in order to fpread a net under it; they afterwards break down the cabin. The beavers that are within it, never fail to make towards the rivulet, where they are taken in the net. But they muft not be fuffered to remain in it for any time, as they would very foon extricate themfelves, by cutting it with their teeth. Thofe whofe cabins are in lakes, have, at the diftance of three or four hundred paces from the water-fide, a kind of country houfe for the benefit of the air; in hunting of thefe the huntfmen divide into two bodies, one breaks the houfe in the country, whilft the other falls upon that in the lake; the beavers which are in this laft, and they pitch upon the time when they are all at home, run for fanctuary to the other, where they find themfelves bewildered in a cloud of duft, which has been raifed on purpofe, and which blinds them fo, that they are fubdued with eafe. Laftly, in fome places, they content themfelves with making an opening in their caufeways; by this means, the beavers find themfelves foon on dry ground; fo that they remain without defence; or elfe they run to put fome remedy to the diforder, the caufe of which is as yet unknown to them; and as the hunters are ready to receive them, it is rare that they fail, or at leaft that they return empty-handed.

There are feveral other particularities with refpect to the beavers, which I find in fome memoirs, the truth of which I will not take upon me to maintain.

tain. It is pretended, that when these animals have discovered hunters, or any of those beasts of prey which make war on them, they dive to the bottom, beating the water with their tails with so prodigious a noise, as to be heard at the distance of half a league. This is probably to warn the rest to be upon their guard. It is said also, that they are of so quick a scent, that when they are in the water they will perceive a canoe at a great distance. But they add, that they see only side-ways like the hares, which defect often delivers them into the hands of the hunters, whom they would endeavour to avoid. Lastly, it is asserted, that when the beaver has lost his mate, he never couples with another, as is related of the turtle.

The Indians take great care to hinder their dogs from touching the bones of the beaver, they being so very hard as to spoil their teeth. The same thing is said of the bones of the porcupine. The common run of these barbarians give another reason for this precaution, which is, say they, for fear of irritating the spirits of those animals, which might render their hunting unprosperous another time. But I am inclined to be of opinion, that this reason was found out after the practice was established; for thus has superstition usurped the place of natural causes to the shame of human understanding. I moreover wonder, Madam, that no attempt has hitherto been made to transport to France some of these wonderful creatures; we have many places where they might find every thing proper for building and subsistence, and I am of opinion they would multiply greatly in a short time.

We

We have alfo in this country a little animal of much the fame nature with the beaver, and which on many accounts appears to be a diminutive of it, called the *Mufk-rat*. This has almoft all the properties of the beaver; the ftructure of the body, and efpecially of the head, is fo very like, that we fhould be apt to take the mufk-rat for a fmall beaver, were his tail only cut off, in which he differs little from the common European rat; and were it not for his tefticles, which contain a moft exquifite mufk. This animal, which weighs about four pounds, is pretty like that which Ray fpeaks of under the name of the *Mus Alpinus*. He takes the field in March, at which time his food confifts of bits of wood, which he peels before he eats them. After the diffolving of the fnows he lives upon the roots of nettles, and afterwards on the ftalks and leaves of that plant. In fummer he lives on ftraw-berries and rafberries, which fucceed the other fruits of the Autumn. During all this time you rarely fee the male and female afunder.

At the approach of winter they feparate, when each takes up his lodgings apart by himfelf in fome hole, or in the hollow of a tree, without any provifion, and the Indians affure us, that they eat not the leaft morfel of any thing whilft the cold continues. They likewife build cabins nearly in the form of thofe of the beavers, but far from being fo well executed. As to their place of abode, it is always by the water-fide, fo that they have no need to build caufeways. It is faid, that the fur of the mufk-rat is ufed in the manufacture of hats, along with that of the beaver, without any difadvantage. Its flefh is tolerable good eating, except in time of rut, at which feafon it is impoffible to cure it of a

relifh

relish of musk, which is far from being as agreeable to the taste, as it is to the scent. I was very much disposed to give your Grace an account of the other kinds of hunting practised amongst our Indians, and of the animals which are peculiar to this country; but I am obliged to refer this part to some other opportunity, as I am this moment told that my carriage is ready.

I am, &c.

LETTER

L E T T E R VI.

Voyage from Quebec *to the* Three Rivers. *Of riding poſt on the ſnow. Of the lordſhips of* New France. *Deſcription of* Beckancourt. *Tradition with reſpect to the origin of the name of the* Stinking River. *Deſcription of the* Three Rivers. *Sequel of the huntings of the* Indians.

Three Rivers, March 6, 1721.

Madam,

I Arrived yeſterday in this town, after a journey of two days, and though it is twenty-five leagues diſtant from Quebec, I could very eaſily have travelled the whole of it in twelve hours, as I took the way of a *Combiature,* which the ſnow and ice render exceeding eaſy in this country in the winter feaſon, and as it is full as cheap as the common way of travelling. They make uſe of a ſledge for this purpoſe, or of what the French here call a *Cariole,* which glides ſo ſmoothly, that one horſe is enough to draw it at full gallop, which is their ordinary pace. They frequently change horſes and have them very cheap. In caſe of neceſſity, one might travel this way ſixty leagues in twenty-four

hours

hours, and much more commodiously than in the best post-chaise in the world.

I lay the first night at *Pointe aux Trembles*, seven leagues from the capital, from whence I set out at eleven at night. This is one of the better sort of parishes in this country. The church is large and well-built, and the inhabitants are in very good circumstances. In several the ancient planters are richer than the lords of the manors, the reason of which is this : Canada was only a vast forest when the French first settled in it. Those to whom lordships were given, were not proper persons to cultivate them themselves. They were officers, gentlemen, or communities, who had not funds sufficient to procure and maintain the necessary number of workmen upon them. It was therefore necessary to settle and plant them with inhabitants, who, before they could raise what was sufficient to maintain them, were obliged to labour hard, and even to lay out all the advances of money. Thus they held of the lords at a very slender quit-rent, so that with fines of alienation, which were here very small, and what is called the *Droit du moulin & Metairie*, a lordship of two leagues in front, and of an unlimited depth, yields no great revenue in a country so thinly peopled, and with so little inland trade.

This was no doubt one reason, which induced the late King Lewis XIV. to permit all noblemen and gentlemen, settled in Canada, to exercise commerce as well by sea as land, without question, interruption, or derogating from their quality and rights. These are the terms of the arrêt, passed by the council on the 10th of March, 1685. Moreover, there are in this country, no lordships, even amongst those which give titles, who have right of

pa-

patronage ; for on the pretenfion of fome lords, founded on their having built the parifh church, his majefty in council, pronounced the fame year 1685, that this right belonged to the bifhop alone, as well becaufe he ought to be better able to judge of the capacity of the candidates, than any other perfon, as becaufe the falaries of the curates are paid out of the tithes, which belong to the bifhop. The king in the fame arrêt further declares, that the right of patronage is not deemed honorary.

I fet out from *Pointe aux Trembles* on the fourth, before day-break, with a horfe blind of an eye, which I afterwards exchanged for a lame one, and this again for one that was broken-winded. With thefe three relays, I travelled feventeen leagues in feven or eight hours, and arrived early at the houfe of the baron de Beckancourt, grand-mafter, or in-fpector of the highways of Canada, who would not fuffer me to go any farther. This gentleman too has a village of Abenaquife Indians on his lands, which is governed in fpiritual matters by a Jefuit, to whom I gladly paid my refpects as I paffed. The baron lives at the mouth of a little river which comes from the fouth, and whofe whole courfe is within his eftate, which is alfo known by his own name. It is not however this large tract which has been erected into a barony, but that on the other fide of the river.

The life M. de Beckancourt leads in this defart, there being as yet no inhabitant in it befides the lord, recalls naturally enough the way of living of the ancient patriarchs to our memory, who were not above putting their hands to work with their fervants in country-work, and lived almoft in the fame fobriety and temperance with them. The pro-fit to be made by trading with the Indians in his neigh-

neighbourhood, by buying furs at the firft-hand, is well worth all the quit-rents he could receive from any planters to whom he could have parcelled out his lands. In time it will be in his own option to have vaffals, when he may have much better terms, after having firft cleared all his eftate. The river of Beckancourt was formerly called the Stinking-River: I acquainted myfelf with the occafion of this name, as the water of it appeared to be clear and excellent in other refpects, which was alfo confirmed by others, and that there was no fuch thing as a difagreeable fcent in the whole country, I was however, told by others, that this name was owing to the bad quality of the waters; others again attributed it to the great quantity of mufk-rats found on it, the fmell of which is intolerable to an Indian; a third account, and which is related by fuch as have made deeper refearches into the ancient hiftory of the country, and which is therefore pretended to be the true one, is as follows.

Some Algonquins, being at war with the Onnontcharonnons, better known by the name of the nation of the Iroquet, and whofe ancient abode was, fay they, in the ifland of Montreal. The name they bear proves them to be of the Huron language; notwithftanding, it is pretended that the Hurons were they who drove them from their ancient refidence, and who have even in part deftroyed them. Be this as it will, they were, at the time I have been mentioning, at war with the Algonquins, who, to put an end to the war, they began to be weary of, at one blow, bethought themfelves of a ftratagem which fucceeded according to their wifhes. They took the field, by occupying both fides of the little river, now called the river of Beckancourt. They afterwards detached fome canoes, the crews of which
feigned

feigned as if they were fishing in the river. They knew their enemies were at no great distance, and made no doubt they would immediately fall upon the pretended fishers ; in fact, they soon fell upon them with a large fleet of canoes, when they again counterfeiting fear, took to flight and gained the banks of the river. They were followed close by the enemy, who made sure of destroying an handful of men, who to draw them the deeper into the snare, affected an extraordinary panick. This feint succeeded ; the pursuers continued to advance, and as the custom is of those barbarians raising a most horrible shouting, they imagined they had now nothing to do, but to launch forth and seize their prey.

At the same instant, a shower of arrows discharged from behind the bushes, which lined the river, threw them into a confusion, from which they were not suffered to recover. A second discharge, which followed close upon the first, compleated the rout. They wanted to fly in their turn, but could no longer make use of their canoes, which were bored on all sides. They plunged into the water, in hopes of escaping that way, but besides, that most of them were wounded, they found, on reaching the shore, the fate they sought to shun, so that not a soul escaped the Algonquins, who gave no quarter, nor made any prisoners. The nation of the Iroquet have never recovered this check, and though some of these Indians have been seen since the arrival ofthe French in Canada, there is now no doubt of their having been entirely destroyed long since. However, the number of dead bodies, which remained in the water, and on the banks of the river, infected it to such a degree, that it has kept the name of the Stinking-River ever since.

The

The Abenaquife town of Beckancourt is not now fo populous as formerly. They would, certainly, for all that, be of great fervice to us in cafe a war fhould happen to break out. Thefe Indians are the beft partifans in the whole country, and are always very ready to make inroads into New-England, where the name of them has thrown terror even into Bofton itfelf. They would be equally ferviceable to us againft the Iroquois, to whom they are nothing inferior in bravery, and whom they much furpafs in point of difcipline. They are all Chriftians, and an handfome chapel has been built for them, where they practife with much edification, all the duties of Chriftian devotion. It muft, however, be acknowledged, that their fervour is not fo confpicuous as formerly when they firft fettled among us. Since that time, they have been made acquainted with the ufe of fpirituous liquors, which they have taken a tafte to, and of which no Indian ever drinks but on purpofe to intoxicate himfelf; notwithftanding, fatal experience has taught us, that in proportion as men deviate from their duty to God, the lefs regard do they entertain for their perfons, and the nearer do they draw to the Englifh. It is much to be feared the Lord fhould permit them to become enemies to us, to punifh us for having contributed thereto, from motives of fordid intereft, and for having helped to make them vicious as has already happened to fome nations.

After embracing the miffionary at Beckancourt, vifiting his canton, and making with him melancholy reflections on the inevitable confequences of this diforder I have been mentioning, and for which he is often under the neceffity of making his moan before the Lord; I croffed the river St. Lawrence, in order to get to this town. Nothing, Madam, can

pof-

poffibly exceed the delightfulnefs of its fituation. It is built on a fandy declivity, on which there is juft barren ground fufficient to contain the town, if ever it come to be a large place; for at prefent it is far from being confiderable. It is, moreover, furrounded with every thing that can contribute to render a place at once rich and pleafant. The river, which is near half a league over, wafhes its foundations. Beyond this you fee nothing but cultivated lands, and thofe extremely fertile, and crowned with the nobleft forefts in the univerfe. A little below, and on the fame fide with the town, the St. Lawrence receives a fine river, which juft before it pays the tribute of its own waters, receives thofe of two others, one on the right, and the other on the left, from whence this place has the name of the Three Rivers.

Above, and almoft at an equal diftance, lake St. Peter begins, which is about three leagues broad and feven long. Thus there is nothing to confine the profpect on that fide, and the fun feems to fet in the water. This lake, which is no more than a widening of the river, receives feveral rivers. It is probable enough that thefe rivers have, in a courfe of years, worn away the low moving earth on which they flowed; this is very fenfible with refpect to lake St. Francis, in the mouth of which are feveral iflands, which might have formerly been joined to the Continent. Befides, over all the lake, except in the middle of the channel, which is kept at its full depth by the force of the current, there is no failing except in canoes, and there are even fome places, where large canoes, ever fo little loaded, cannot eafily pafs; to make amends, it is every where well ftored with fifh, and that too of the moft excellent forts.

They reckon but about feven or eight hundred fouls on the Three Rivers; but it has in its neighbourhood fufficient wherewithal to enrich a great city. There is exceeding plentiful iron mines, which may be made to turn to account whenever it is judged proper *. However, notwithftanding the fmall number of inhabitants in this place, its fituation renders it of vaft importance, and it is alfo one of the moft ancient eftablifhments in the colony. This poft has always, even from the moft early times, had a governor. He has a thoufand crowns falary, with an *Etat Major*. Here is a convent of Recollets; a very fine parifh church, where the fame fathers officiate, and a noble hofpital adjoining to a convent of Urfuline nuns, to the number of forty, who ferve the hofpital. This is alfo a foundation of M. de St. Vallier. As early as the year 1650, the fenefchal or high fteward of New France, whofe jurifdiction was abforbed in that of the fupreme council of Quebec, and of the intendant, had a lieutenant at the Three Rivers; at this day this city has an ordinary tribunal for criminal matters, the chief of which is a lieutenant general.

This city owes its origin to the great concourfe of Indians, of different nations, at this place in the beginning of the colony. There reforted to it chiefly feveral from the moft diftant quarters of the north by way of the Three Rivers, which have given this city its name, and which are navigable a great way upwards. The fituation of the place joined to the great trade carried on at it, induced fome French to fettle here, and the nearnefs of the river Sorel, then called the Iroquois river, and of which I fhall foon take notice, obliged the governors general to

* They are now actually working them, and they produce fome of the beft iron in the world.

build

build a Fort here, where they kept a good garrifon, and which at firft had a governor of its own. Thus this poft was henceforwards looked upon as one of the moft important places in New France. After fome years the Indians, weary of the continual ravages of the Iroquois, and from whom the French themfelves had enough to do to defend themfelves, and the paffes being no longer free in which thofe Indians lay in ambufh, and finding themfelves hardly fecure, even under the cannon of our fort, they left off bringing their furs. The jefuits, with all the new converts they could gather, retired to a place three leagues below, which had been given them by the Abbé de la Madeleine, one of the members of the company of the Hundred Affociates, erected by cardinal Richelieu, from whence this fpot had the name of Cap de la Madeleine, which it ftill bears *.

The miffion tranfported thither did not however fubfift long. This is partly the effect of the levity natural to the Indians, but chiefly to a feries of wars and difeafes, which have almoft wholly deftroyed this infant church. You find, however, in the neighbourhood a company of Algonquins, moft of whom have been baptifed in their infancy, but have no outward exercife of religion. The members of the Weft-India Company, who have at prefent the farm of the beaver-trade, have in vain attempted to draw them to Checontini, where they have already re-affembled feveral families of the fame nation, and of the Montagnez, under the direction of a jefuit miffionary. Some others were for uniting them with the Abenaquis of St. Francis. All the anfwer they made to thefe invitations was,

* Befides the iron mines which are pretty rich at Cap de la Madeleine, they have alfo fome years fince difcovered feveral fprings of mineral water, of the fame quality with thofe of Forges.

that

that they could not think of abandoning a place where the bones of their forefathers were depofited ; but fome believe, and not without grounds, that this oppofition is lefs owing to them, than to fome perfons who reap advantages from their nearnefs to them, and who, certainly do not reflect to what a contemptible confideration they poftpone the falvation of thofe Indians.

I have been juft told, that fome days hence there will be an opportunity of fending this letter to Quebec, from whence it may foon reach France by way of the Royal Ifland. I will fill up the remaining fpace with what relates to the huntings of the Indians ; that of the beaver, as I have already remarked, was not confidered as a principal object, till they faw the value we fet upon the fpoils of this animal. Before this, the bear held the firft rank with them, and here too fuperftition had the greateft fhare. The following is what is practifed at this day, among thofe who are not Chriftians, in the hunting of this animal.

It is always fome war-chief who fixes the time of it, and who takes care to invite the hunters. This invitation, which is made with great ceremony, is followed by a faft of ten days continuance, during which it is unlawful to tafte fo much as a drop of water ; and I muft tell your Grace, by the way, that what the Indians call fafting, is wholly abftaining from every fort of food or drink ; nay more, in fpite of the extreme weaknefs to which they are of neceffity reduced by fo fevere a faft, they are always finging the live long day. The reafon of this faft, is to induce the fpirits to difcover the place where a great number of bears may be found. Several even go a great way farther to obtain this
grace.

grace. Some have been feen to cut their flefh in feveral parts of the body, in order to render their
genii propitious. But it is proper to know, that
they never implore their fuccour to enable them to
conquer thofe furious animals, but are contented
with knowing where they lie. Thus Ajax did not
pray to Jupiter to enable him to overcome his enemies, but only day-light enough to compleat the
victory.

The Indians addrefs their vows for the fame reafon to the manes of the beafts they have killed in
their former huntings, and as their minds are wholly
intent on fuch thoughts whilft they are awake, it is
but natural they fhould often dream of bears in
their fleep, which can never be very found with
fuch empty ftomachs ; but neither is this enough to
determine them : it is likewife neceffary, that all,
or at leaft the greateft part of thofe who are to be
of the party, fhould alfo fee bears, and in the fame
canton ; now how is it poffible fo many dreamers
fhould agree in this point ? However, provided
fome expert hunter dream twice or thrice an end of
feeing bears in a certain fixed place, whether it be
the effect of complaifance, for nothing can be more
fo than the Indians, or whether it is by dint of hearing the affair fpoke of, their empty brains at laft
take the impreffion, every one foon falls a dream-
ing, or at leaft pretends fo to do, when they determine to fet out for that place. The faft ended,
and the place of hunting fixed, the chief who is
appointed to conduct it, gives a grand repaft to all
who are to be of the party, and no one dares pre-
fume to come to it, till he has firft bathed,
that is to fay, wafhed himfelf in the river, be the
weather ever fo fevere, provided it is not frozen.
This feaft, is not like many others, where they are

ob-

obliged to eat up every thing ; though they have
had a long faft, and perhaps, on this very account,
they obferve great fobriety in eating. He who does
the honours, touches nothing, and his whole employment, whilft the reft are at table, is to rehearfe
his ancient feats of hunting. The feaft concludes
with new invocations of the fpirits of the departed
bears. They afterwards fet out on their march be-
dawbed with black, and equipped as if for war,
amidft the acclamations of the whole village. Thus
hunting is no lefs noble amongft thefe nations than
war ; and the alliance of a good hunter is even
more courted than that of a famous warriour, as
hunting furnifhes the whole family with food and
raiment, beyond which the Indians never extend
their care. But no one, is deemed a great hunter,
except he has killed twelve large beafts in one
day.

Thefe people have two great advantages over us
in refpect to this exercife ; for in the firft place, nothing ftops them, neither thickets, nor ditches, nor
torrents, nor pools, nor rivers. They go always
ftrait forwards in the directeft line poffible. In the
fecond place, there are few or perhaps no animals
which they will not overtake by fpeed of foot.
Some have been feen, fay they, arriving in the village driving a parcel of bears with a fwitch, like a
flock of fheep ; and the nimbleft deer is not more
fo than they. Befides the hunter himfelf reaps very
little benefit by his fuccefs ; he is obliged to make
large prefents, and even if they prevent him by taking it at their own hand from him, he muft fee himfelf robbed without complaining, and remain fatif-
fied with the glory of having laboured for the publick. It is, however, allowed him in the diftribution of what he has caught, to begin with his own

fa-

family. But it muſt be acknowledged, that thoſe with whom we have the moſt commerce, have already loſt ſomewhat of this ancient generoſity, and of this admirable diſintereſtedneſs. Nothing is more contagious than a ſelfiſh and intereſted ſpirit, and nothing is more capable of corrupting the morals.

The ſeaſon of hunting the bear is in winter. Theſe animals are then concealed in the hollow trunks of trees, in which if they happen to fall they make themſelves a den with their roots, the entry of which they ſtop with pine branches, by which means they are perfectly well ſheltered from all the inclemencies of the weather. If all this is ſtill inſufficient, they make a hole in the ground, taking great care to ſtop the mouth well when once they are entered. Some have been ſeen couched in the bottom of their dens, ſo as to be hardly perceivable, even when examined very nearly. But in whatever manner the bear is lodged, he never once quits his apartments all the winter; this is a circumſtance paſt all manner of doubt. It is no leſs certain, that he lays up no manner of proviſion, and conſequently that he muſt of neceſſity live all that while without taſting food or drink, and that as ſome have advanced his ſole nouriſhment is the licking his paws; but with reſpect to this particular, every one is at liberty to believe as he pleaſes. What is certain, is, that ſome of them have been kept chained for a whole winter, without having the leaſt morſel of food, or any drink given them, and at the end of ſix months, they have been found as fat as in the beginning. It is no doubt ſurpriſing enough, that an animal, provided of ſo warm a fur, and which is far from having a delicate appearance, ſhould take more precautions againſt the cold than any other. This may ſerve to convince

M 4   us,

us, that we ought never to form our judgment of things by appearance, and that every one is the beſt judge of his own wants.

There is therefore but little courſing neceſſary to catch the bear ; the point is only to find his burrow, and the places which they haunt. When the huntſ-men imagine they have come near ſuch a place, they form themſelves into a large circle, a quarter of a league in circumference, more or leſs, accord-ing to the number of ſportſmen ; they then move onwards, drawing nearer and nearer, every one trying as he advances to diſcover the retreat of ſome bear. By this means, if there are any at all in this ſpace, they are certain of diſcovering them, for our Indians are excellent ferrets. Next day they go to work in the ſame manner, and continue ſo to do all the time the hunting laſts.

As ſoon as a bear is killed, the huntſman places his lighted pipe in his mouth, and blows the beaſts throat and windpipe full of the ſmoke, at the ſame time conjuring his ſpirit to hold no reſentment for the inſult done his body, and to be propitious to him in his future huntings. But as the ſpirit makes no anſwer, the huntſmen to know whether his pray-ers have been heard, cuts off the membrane under his tongue, which he keeps till his return to the vil-lage, when every one throws his own membranes into the fire, after many invocations, and abundance of ceremony. If theſe happen to crackle and ſhri-vel up, and it can hardly be otherwiſe, it is looked upon as a certain ſign, that the manes of the bears are appeaſed ; if otherwiſe, they imagine the de-parted bears are wroth with them, and that next year's hunting will be unproſperous, at leaſt till ſome

means

means are found of reconciling them, for they have a remedy for every thing.

The hunters make good cheer whilſt the hunting laſts, and, if it is ever ſo little ſuccefsful, bring home ſufficient to regale their friends, and to maintain their families a long time. To ſee the reception given them, the praiſes with which they are loaded, and their own air of ſelf-ſatisfaction and applauſe, you would imagine them returning from ſome important expedition, loaden with the ſpoils of a conquered enemy. One muſt be a man indeed, ſay they to them, and they even ſpeak ſo of themſelves, thus to combat and overcome bears. Another particular, which occaſions them no leſs eulogiums, and which adds equally to their vanity, is the circumſtance of devouring all, without leaving a morſel uneaten, at a grand repaſt given them at their return by the perſon who commanded the hunting-party. The firſt diſh ſerved up is the largeſt bear that has been killed, and that too whole, and with all his entrails. He is not even ſo much as flead, they being ſatisfied with having ſinged off the hair as is done to a hog. This feaſt is ſacred to I know not what genius, whoſe indignation they apprehend, ſhould they leave a morſel uneaten. They muſt not ſo much as leave any of the broth in which the meat has been boiled, which is nothing but a quantity of oil, or of liquid fat. Nothing can be more execrable food, and there never happens a feaſt of this ſort, but ſome one eats himſelf to death, and ſeveral ſuffer ſeverely.

The bear is never dangerous in this country, but when he is hungry, or after being wounded. They, however, uſe abundance of precautions in approaching him. They ſeldom attack the men, on the
con-

contrary, they take to flight at the firft fight of one, and a dog will drive them a great way before him ; if therefore they are every where fuch as they are in Canada, one might eafily anfwer the queftion of M. Defpreaux, that the bear dreads the traveller, and not the traveller the bear. The bear is in rut in the month of July ; he then grows fo lean, and his flefh of fo fickly and difagreeable a relifh, that even the Indians, who have not the moft delicate fto-machs, and who often eat fuch things as would make an European fhudder, will hardly touch it. Who could imagine that an animal of this nature, and of fo unlovely an appearance, fhould grow leaner in one month by the *belle paffion*, than after an abftinence of fix ! It is not fo furprifing he fhould be at this feafon fo fierce, and in fo ill an humour, that it fhould be dangerous to meet him. This is the effect of jealoufy.

This feafon once over, he recovers his former *embompoint*, and to which nothing more contributes, than the fruits he finds every where in the woods, and of which he is extreme greedy. He is parti-cularly fond of grapes, and as all the forefts are full of vines which rife to the tops of the higheft trees, he makes no difficulty of climbing up in queft of them. But fhould an hunter difcover him, his toothfomnefs would coft him dear. After having thus fed a good while on fruits, his flefh becomes exceedingly delicious, and continues fo till the fpring. It is, however, conftantly attended with one very great fault, that of being too oily, fo that except great moderation is ufed in eating it, it cer-tainly occafions a dyfentery. It is, moreover, very nourifhing, and a bear's cub is at leaft nothing in-ferior to lamb.

I for-

I forgot to inform your Grace, that the Indians always carry a great number of dogs with them in their huntings; thefe are the only domeftick animals they breed, and that too only for hunting: they appear to be all of one fpecies, with upright ears, and a long fnout like that of a wolf; they are remarkable for their fidelity to their mafters, who feed them however but very ill, and never make much of them. They are very early bred to that kind of hunting for which they are intended, and excellent hunters they make. I have no more time to write you, being this moment called on to go on board.

I am, &c.

L E T T E R VII.

Defcription of the Country and Iflands of Richelieu *and of* St. Francis. *Of the* Abenaquis *village. Of the ancient fort of* Richelieu, *and of fuch as were formerly in each
parifh. Shining actions of two* Canadian
Ladies. Of the other huntings of the Indians.

St. Francis, March 11, 1721.

Madam,

I Set out on the 9th from the Three Rivers. I
did no more than crofs lake St. Peter, inclining
towards the fouth. I performed this journey in a
fledge, or as it is called here a cariole, the ice being ftill ftrong enough for all forts of carriages,
and I arrived towards noon at St. Francis. I employed the afternoon, and yefterday the whole day,
in vifiting this canton, and am now going to give
you an account of what I faw.

At the extremity of Lake St. Peter is a prodigious number of iflands of all fizes, called *les Ifles
de Richelieu,* or Richelieu Iflands, and turning towards the left coming from Quebec, you find fix
more, which lie towards the fhore of a creek of a
toler-

tolerable depth, into which a pretty large river difcharges itfelf, which takes its rife in the neighbourhood of New-York. The iflands, river, and whole
country bear the name of St. Francis. Each of the
iflands is above a quarter of a league long; their
breadth is unequal; moft of thofe of Richelieu are
fmaller. All were formerly full of deer, does, roebucks, and elks; game fwarmed in a furprifing
manner, as it is ftill far from fcarce; but the large
beafts have difappeared. There are alfo caught
excellent fifh in the river St. Francis, and at its
mouth. In winter they make holes in the ice,
through which they let down nets five or fix fathoms long, which are never drawn up empty.
The fifhes moft commonly taken here are bars, achi-
gans, and efpecially mafquinongez, a fort of pikes,
which have the head larger than ours, and the mouth
placed under a fort of crooked fnout, which gives
them a fingular figure. The lands of St. Francis,
to judge of them by the trees they produce, and
by the little which has yet been cultivated of them
are very good. The planters are, however, poor
enough, and feveral of them would be reduced to
a ftate of indigence, did not the trade they carry on
with the Indians, their neighbours, help to fupport
them. But may not this trade, likewife, be a means
of hindering them from growing rich, by rendering them lazy?

The Indians I am now fpeaking of, are, Abe-
naquies, amongft whom are fome Algonquins, So-
kokies, and Mahingans, better known by the name
of Wolfs. This nation was formerly fettled on
the banks of the river Mantat, in New-York, of
which country they feem to be natives. The Abe-
naquies came to St. Francis, from the fouthern
fhores of New France, in the neighbourhood of
New-

New-England. Their firft fettlement, after leaving their own country to live amongft us, was on a little river which difcharges itfelf into the St. Lawrence, almoft oppofite to Sillery, that is to fay, about a league and a half above Quebec, on the fouth fhore. They fettled here near a fall of water, called *le Sault de la Claudiere*, or the fall of the kettle. They now live on the banks of the St. Francis, two leagues from its difcharge into lake St. Peter. This fpot is very delightful, which is pity, thefe people having no relifh for the beauties of a fine fituation, and the huts of Indians contributing but little to the embellifhment of a profpect. This village is extremely populous, all the inhabitants of which are Chriftians. The nation is docile, and always much attached to the French. But the miffionary has the fame inquietudes on their account with him at Beckancourt, and for the fame reafons.

I was regaled here with the juice of the maple; this is the feafon of its flowing. It is extremely delicious, has a moft pleafing coolnefs, and is exceeding wholfome; the manner of extracting it is very fimple. When the fap begins to afcend, they pierce the trunk of the tree, and by means of a bit of wood, which is inferted in it, and along which it flows, as through a pipe, the liquor is conveyed into a veffel placed under it. In order to produce an abundant flow, there muft be much fnow on the ground, with frofty nights, a ferene fky, and the wind not too cool. Our maples might poffibly have the fame virtue, had we as much fnow in France as there is in Canada, and were they to laft as long. In proportion as the fap thickens the flow abates, and in a little time after, wholly ceafes. It is eafy to guefs, that after fuch a difcharge of what

may

may be called its blood, the tree ſhould be far from being bettered: we are told, however, they will endure it for ſeveral years running. They would, perhaps, do better to let them reſt for two or three years, to give them time to recover their ſtrength. But at length, after it has been entirely drained, it is ſentenced to be cut down, and is extremely proper for many uſes, as well the wood as the roots and boughs. This tree muſt needs be very common, as great numbers of them are burnt.

The liquor of the maple is tolerably clear, tho' ſomewhat whitiſh. It is exceeding cooling and refreſhing, and leaves on the palate a certain flavour of ſugar, which is very agreeable. It is a great friend to the breaſt, and let the quantity drank be ever ſo great, or the party ever ſo much heated, it is perfectly harmleſs. The reaſon is, that it is entirely free from that crudity which occaſions pleuriſies, but has on the contrary a balſamick quality which ſweetens the blood, and a certain ſalt which preſerves its warmth. They add, that it never chryſtallizes, but that if it is kept for a certain ſpace of time, it becomes an excellent vinegar. I do not pretend to vouch this for fact, and I know a traveller ought not ſlightly to adopt every thing that is told him.

It is very probable the Indians, who are perfectly well-acquainted with all the virtues of their plants, have at all times, as well as at this day, made conſtant uſe of this liquor. But it is certain, they were ignorant of the art of making a ſugar from it, which we have ſince learnt them. They were ſatisfied with giving it two or three boilings, in order to thicken it a little, and to make a kind of ſyrup from it, which is pleaſant enough. They further

ther method they use to make sugar of is to let it
boil, till it takes a sufficient consistence, when it
purifies of its own accord, without the mixture of
any foreign ingredient. Only they must be very
careful that the sugar be not over-boiled, and to
skim it well. The greatest fault in this process is
to let the syrup harden too much, which renders it
too fat, so that it never loses a relish of honey,
which renders it not so agreeable to the taste, at
least till such time as it is clarified.

This sugar when made with care, which it certainly requires, is a natural pectoral, and does not
burn the stomach. Besides the manufacturing, it
is done at a trifling expence. It has been commonly believed, that it is impossible to refine it in
the same manner with the sugar extracted from
canes. I own, I see no reason to think so, and it
is very certain that when it comes out of the hands
of the Indians, it is purer and much better than
that of the islands, which has had no more done
to it. In fine, I gave some of it to a refiner of
Orleans, who found no other fault to it, than that
I have mentioned, and who attributed this defect
wholly to its not having been left to drip long
enough. He even judged it of a quality preferable to the other sort, and of this it was, he made
those tablets, with which I had the honour to present your Grace, and which you were pleased to
esteem so much. It may be objected, that were
this of of a good quality, it would have been made
a branch of trade; but there is not a sufficient quantity made for this, and perhaps, they are therefore
in the wrong: but there are many things besides
this which are neglected in this country.

The plane-tree, the cherry-tree, the afh, and walnut-trees of feveral kinds, alfo yield a liquor from which fugar is made ; but there is a lefs quantity of it, and the fugar made from it, is not fo good. Some, however, prefer that made from the afh, but there is very little of it made. Would your Grace have thought that there fhould be found in Canada what Virgil mentions, whilft he is predicting the golden age, *Et dura quercus fudabunt rofcida Mella*, That honey fhould diftil from the oak ?

This whole country has long been the fcene of many a bloody battle, as, during the war with the Iroquois, it was moft expofed to the incurfions of thofe barbarians. They ufually came down by way of a river, which falls into the St. Lawrence, a little above lake St. Peter, and on the fame fide with St. Francis, and which for this reafon bore their name ; it has fince gone by the name of *la Riviere de Sorel*. The iflands of Richelieu which they firft met with, ferved both for a retreat and place of ambufh ; but after this pafs was fhut up to them by a fort, built at the mouth of the river, they came down by land both above and below, and efpecially made their inroads on the fide of St. Francis, where they found the fame conveniencies for pillaging, and where they committed cruelties horrible to relate.

Thence they fpread themfelves over all the colony, fo that in order to defend the inhabitants from their fury, there was a neceffity of building in every parifh a kind of fort, where the planters and other perfons might take fanctuary on the firft alarm. In thefe there were two centinels kept night and day, and in every one of them fome field-pieces, or at

leaft

leaft patereroes, as well to keep the enemy at a diftance, as to advertife the inhabitants to be on their
guard, or to give the fignal for fuccour. Thefe
forts were no more than fo many large enclofures
fenced with palifadoes with fome redoubts. ʼ The
church and manor houfe of the lord were alfo within thefe places, in which there was alfo a fpace for
women, children, and cattle, in cafe of neceffity.
Thefe were fufficient to protect the people from any
infult, none of them having ever, as I know, been
taken by the Iroquois.

They have even feldom taken the trouble to
block them up, and ftill more rarely to attack them
with open force. The one is too dangerous an
enterprize for Indians, who have no defenfive arms,
and who are not fond of victories bought with blood-
fhed. The other is altogether remote from their
way of making war. There are, however, two
attacks of the fort de Vercheres, which are famous
in the Canadian annals, and it feems the Iroquois
fet their hearts here upon reducing them contrary to
their cuftom, only to fhew the valour and intrepi-
dity of two Amazons.

In 1690, thefe barbarians having learnt that Madam de Vercheres was almoft left alone in the fort, approached it without being difcovered, and put themfelves in a pofture for fcaling the palifado. Some
mufket-fhot which were fired at them very feafonably, drove them to a diftance ; but they inftantly
returned : they were again repulfed, and what occafioned their utter aftonifhment, they could only
difcover a woman, whom they met wherever they
went. This was Madam de Vercheres, who appeared as undifmayed as if fhe had had a numerous garrifon. The hopes of the befiegers in the

begin-

beginning of reducing with eafe a place unprovided with men to defend it, made them return feveral times to the charge; but the lady always repulfed them. She continued to defend herfelf for two days, with a valour and prefence of mind which would have done honour to an old warriour; and fhe at laft compelled the enemy to retire, for fear of having their retreat cut off, full of fhame of having been repulfed by a woman.

Two years afterwards, another party of the fame nation, but much more numerous than the firft, appeared in fight of the fort, whilft all the inhabitants were abroad, and generally at work in the field. The Iroquois finding them fcattered in this manner and void of all diftruft, feized them all one after another, and then marched towards the fort. The daughter of the lord of the land, fourteen years old, was at the diftance of two hundred paces from it. At the firft cry fhe heard, fhe run to get into it; the Indians purfued her, and one of them came up with her juft as fhe had her foot upon the threfhold; but having laid hold of her by the handkerchief fhe wore about her neck, fhe loofed it, and fhut the gate on herfelf.

There was not a foul in the fort, befides a young foldier and a number of women, who, at the fight of their hufbands, who were faft bound, and led prifoners, raifed moft lamentable cries; the young lady loft neither her courage nor prefence of mind. She begun with taking of her head-drefs, bound up her hair, put on a hat and coat, locked up all the women, whofe groans and weeping could not fail of giving new courage to the enemy. Afterwards fhe fixed a piece of cannon, and feveral mufket-fhot, and fhewing herfelf with her foldier, fometime in

one

one redoubt, fometimes in another, and changing her drefs from time to time, and always firing very feafonably, on feeing the Iraquoife approach the breaft-work, thefe Indians thought there were many men in the garrifon, and when the chevalier de Crifafy, informed by the firing of the cannon, appeared to fuccour the place, the men were already decamped.

Let us now return to our hunting; that of the elk would be no lefs advantagious to us at this day than that of the beaver, had our predeceffors in the colony paid due attention to the profits which might have been made by it, and had they not almoft entirely deftroyed the whole fpecies, at leaft in fuch places as are within our reach.

What they call here the orignal, is the fame with the animal, which in Germany, Poland, and Ruffia, is called the elk, or the great beaft. This animal in this country is of the fize of a horfe, or mule of the country of Auvergne; this has a broad crupper, the tail but a finger's length, the hough extremely high, with the feet and legs of a ftag; the neck, withers, and upper part of the hough are covered with long hair; the head is above two feet long, which he ftretches forward, and which gives the animal a very aukward appearance; his muzzle is thick, and bending on the upper-part, like that of a camel; and his noftrils are fo wide, that one may with eafe thruft half his arm into them; laftly, his antlers are full as long as thofe of a ftag, and are much more fpreading; they are branching and flat like thofe of a doe, and are renewed every year; but I do not know whether they receive an increafe which denotes the age of the animal.

It

It has been pretended that the orignal, or elk, is fubject to the epilepfy, and when he is feized with any fit, he cures himfelf by rubbing his ear with his left hind foot till the blood comes; a circum-ftance which has made his hoof be taken for a fpe-cific againft the falling ficknefs. This is applied over the heart of the patient, which is alfo done for a palpitation of the heart; they place in the left hand, and rub the ear with it. But why do not they make the blood come as the elk does? This horny fubftance is alfo believed to be good in the pleurify, in cholic pains, in fluxes, vertigoes, and purples, when pulverifed and taken in water. I have heard fay, that the Algonquins, who formerly fed on the flefh of this animal, were very fubject to the epilepfy, and yet made no ufe of this remedy. They were, perhaps, acquainted with a better.

The colour of the elk's hair is a mixture of light grey, and of a dark red. It grows hollow as the beaft grows older, never lies flat, nor quits its elaftic force; thus it is in vain to beat it, it conftantly rifes again. They make matraffes and hair bottoms of it. Its flefh is of an agreeable relifh, light and nourifhing, and it would be great pity if it gave the falling-ficknefs; but our hunters, who have lived on it for feveral winters running, never per-ceived the leaft ill qualitity in it. The fkin is ftrong, foft, and oily, is made into Chamois leather, and makes excellent buff-coats, which are alfo very light.

The Indians look upon the elk as an animal of good omen, and believe that thofe who dream of them often, may expect a long life; it is quite the contrary with the bear, except on the approach of the feafon for hunting thofe creatures. There is

also

alſo a very diverting tradition among the Indians
of a great elk, of ſuch a monſtrous ſize, that the
reſt are like piſmires in compariſon of him ; his
legs, ſay they, are ſo long, that eight feet of ſnow
are not the leaſt incumbrance to him ; his hide is
proof againſt all manner of weapons, and he has
a ſort of arm proceeding from his ſhoulders, which
he uſes as we do ours. He is always attended by a
vaſt number of elks which form his court, and
which render him all the ſervices he requires.
Thus the antients had their Phenix and Pegaſus, and
the Chineſe and Japoneſe their Kirim, their Foké,
their Water-dragon, and their bird of Paradiſe.
Tutto 'l mondo é Paeſe.

The elk is a lover of cold countries ; he feeds on
graſs in ſummer, and in winter gnaws the bark of
trees. When the ſnow is very deep, theſe animals
aſſemble in ſome pine-wood, to ſhelter themſelves
from the ſeverity of the weather, where they remain
whilſt there is any thing to live upon. This is the
beſt ſeaſon for hunting them, except when the ſun
has ſtrength enough to melt the ſnow. For the
froſt forming a kind of cruſt on the ſurface in the
night, the elk, who is a heavy animal, breaks it
with his forked hoof, and with great difficulty ex-
tricates himſelf except at this time, and above all,
when the ſnow is not deep, it is very difficult to
get near him, at leaſt, without danger, for when he
is wounded he is furious, and will return boldly
on the huntſman and tread him under his feet. The
way to ſhun him is to throw him your coat, on which
he will diſcharge all his vengeance, whilſt the
huntſman concealed behind ſome tree, is at liberty
to take proper meaſures for diſpatching him. The
elk goes always at a hard trot, but ſuch as equals
the ſwifteſt ſpeed of the buffalo, and will hold out

a

a great while. But the Indians are ftill better cour-
fers than he. It is affirmed that he falls down upon
his knees to drink, eat and fleep, and that he has
a bone in his heart, which being reduced to powder, and taken in broth, facilitates delivery, and
foftens the pains of child bearing.

The moft northern nations of Canada have a
way of hunting this animal, very fimple and free
from danger. The hunters divide into two bands,
one embarks on board canoes, which canoes keep
at a fmall diftance from each other, forming a pretty
large femicircle, the two ends of which reach the
fhore. The other body, which remains afhore,
perform pretty much the fame thing, and at firft
furround a large track of ground. Then the huntfmen let loofe their dogs, and raife all the elks within the bounds of this femicircle, and drive them
into the river or lake, which they no fooner enter
than they are fired upon from all the canoes, and
not a fhot miffes, fo that rarely any one efcapes.

Champlain mentions another way of hunting,
not only the elk, but alfo the deer and caribou,
which has fome refemblance to this. They furround a fpace of ground with pofts, interwoven
with branches of trees, leaving a pretty narrow
opening, where they place nets made of thongs of
raw hides. This fpace is of a triangular form, and
from the angle in which the entry is, they form another, but much larger triangle. Thus the two enclofures communicate with each other at the two angles. The two fides of the fecond triangle are alfo
inclofed with pofts, interwoven in the fame manner, and the hunters drawn up in one line form
the bafis of it. They then advance, keeping the
line entire, raifing prodigious cries, and ftriking
against

againſt ſomething which reſounds greatly. The game thus rouſed, and being able to eſcape by none of the ſides, can only fly into the other encloſure, where ſeveral are taken at their firſt entering by the neck or horns. They make great efforts to diſentangle themſelves, and ſometimes carry away or break the thongs. They alſo ſometimes ſtrangle themſelves, or at leaſt give the huntſmen time to diſpatch them at leiſure. Even thoſe that eſcape are not a whit advanced, but find themſelves encloſed in a ſpace too narrow to be able to ſhun the arrows which are ſhot at them from all hands,

The elk has other enemies beſides the Indians, and who carry on full as cruel a war againſt him. The moſt terrible of all theſe is the *Carcajou* or *Quincajou*, a kind of cat, with a tail ſo long that he twiſts it ſeveral times round his body, and with a ſkin of a browniſh red. As ſoon as this hunter comes up with the elk, he leaps upon him, and faſtens upon his neck, about which he twiſts his long tail, and then cuts his jugular. The elk has no means of ſhunning this diſaſter, but by flying to the water the moment he is ſeized by this dangerous enemy. The carcajou, who cannot endure the water, quits his hold immediately ; but, if the water happen to be at too great a diſtance, he will deſtroy the elk before he reaches it. This hunter too as he does not poſſeſs the faculty of ſmelling with the greateſt acuteneſs, carries three foxes a hunting with him, which he ſends on the diſcovery. The moment they have got ſcent of an elk, two of them place themſelves by his ſide, and the third takes poſt behind him ; and all three manage matters ſo well, by haraſſing the prey, that they compel him to go to the place where they have left the carcajou, with whom they afterwards ſettle about the

the dividing the prey. Another wile of the carca-jou, in order to feize his prey is to climb upon a tree, where couched along fome projecting branch, he waits till an elk paffes, and leaps upon him, the moment he fees him within his reach.. There are, many perfons, Madam, who have taken it into their heads to imagine, that the accounts of Cana-da, make the Indians more terrible people than they really are. They are, however, men. But under what climate can we find brute animals, indued with fo ftrong an inftinct, and fo forcibly inclined to induftry, as the fox, the beaver, and the car-cajou.

The ftag in Canada is abfolutely the fame with ours in France, though, perhaps, generally fome-what bigger. It does not appear that the Indians give them much difturbance; at leaft, I do not find they make war upon him in form and with much preparation. It is quite different with refpect to the caribou, an animal differing in nothing from the raindeer, except in the colour of its hair, which is brown a little inclining to red. This crea-ture is not quite fo tall as the elk, and has more of the afs or mule in its fhape, and is at leaft equal in fpeed with the deer. Some years fince, one of them was feen on Cape Diamond, above Quebec; he probably was flying before fome hun-ters, but immediately perceived he was in no place of fafety, and made fcarce any more than one leap from thence into the river. A wild goat on the alps could hardly have done more. He afterwards fwam crofs the river with the fame celerity, but was very little the better for having fo done. Some Canadians who were going out againft an enemy, and lay encamped at point Levi, having perceived him, watched his landing, and fhot him. The

tongue

tongue of this animal is highly efteemed, and his true country feems to be near Hudfon's-Bay. The Sieur Jeremie, who paffed feveral years in thefe northern parts, tells us, that between Danifh river and Port Nelfon, prodigious numbers of them were to be feen, which being driven by the gnats, and a fort of vermine called *Tons*, come to cool and refrefh themfelves by the fea-fhore, and that for the fpace of forty or fifty leagues you are continually meeting herds of ten thoufand in number at the leaft.

It appears that the *Caribou* has not multiplied greatly in the moft frequented parts of Canada; but the elk was every where found in great numbers, on our firft difcovery of this country. And thefe animals were not only capable of becoming a confiderable article in commerce, but alfo a great conveniency of life, had there been more care taken to preferve them. This is what has not been done, and whether it is that the numbers of them have been thinned, and the fpecies in fome fort diminifhed, or that by frighting them, they have grown wilder, and fo have been obliged to retire to other parts, nothing can be more rare than to meet with any of them at prefent.

In the fouthern and weftern parts of New France, on both fides of the Miffiffippi, the kind of hunting moft in vogue, is, that of the buffalo, which is performed in this manner. The huntfmen draw up in four lines, forming a very large fquare, and begin with fetting the grafs on fire, that being dry and very rank at this feafon; they afterwards advance in proportion as the fire gets ground, clofing their ranks as they go. The buffaloes, which are extremely timorous of fire, always fly, till at laft
they

they find themfelves fo hemmed in, and fo clofe to one another, that generally not a fingle beaft efcapes. It is affirmed, that no party ever returns from hunting without having killed fifteen hundred or two thoufand beafts. But left two different companies fhould hurt one another, they take care before they fet out, to fettle the time and place they intend to hunt. There are even penalties for fuch as tranfgrefs this regulation, as well as for thofe who quit their pofts, and fo give the buffaloes an opportunity of efcaping. Thefe pains and penalties are, that the perfons tranfgreffing may be ftripped by any private perfon at will of every thing, and which is the greateft poffible affront to an Indian, their arms not excepted, they may alfo throw down their cabbins. The chief is fubject to this law as well as the reft, and any one who fhould go to rebel againft it, would endanger the kindling a war, which fay they would not be fo eafily extinguifhed.

The buffalo of Canada is larger than ours ; his horns are fhort, black, and low ; there is a great rough beard under the muzzle, and another tuft on the crown of the head, which falling over the eyes, give him a hideous afpect. He has on the back, a hunch or fwelling, which begins over his haunches, encreafing always as it approaches his fhoulders. The firft rib forwards is a whole cubit higher than thofe towards the back, and is three fingers broad, and the whole rifing is covered with a long reddifh hair. The reft of the body is covered with a black wool, in great efteem. It is affirmed, that the fleece of a buffalo weighs eight pounds. This animal has a very broad cheft, the crupper pretty thin, the tail extremely fhort, and fcarce any neck at all ; but the head is larger than that of ours. He commonly flies as foon as he perceives any one, and

one

one dog will make a whole herd of them take to the gallop. He has a very delicate and quick fcent, and in order to approach him without being perceived, near enough to fhoot him, you muft take care not to have the wind of him. But when he is wounded he grows furious and will turn upon the hunters. He is equally dangerous when the cow buffalo has young newly brought forth. His flefh is good, but that of the female only is eaten, that of the male being too hard and tough. As to the hide, there is none better in the known world; it is eafily dreffed, and though exceeding ftrong, becomes as fupple and foft as the beft fhamois leather. The Indians make bucklers of it, which are very light, and which a mufket-ball will hardly pierce.

There is another fort of buffalo found in the neighbourhood of Hudfon's-Bay, the hide and wool of which are equally valuable with thofe of the fort now mentioned. The following is what the *Sieur Jeremie* fays of it. " Fifteen leagues from Danes-River, you find the Sea-wolf-River, there being in fact great numbers of thofe animals in it. Between thofe two rivers, are a kind of buffaloes, called by us *Boeufs mufqués*, or mufk-buffaloes, from their having fo ftrong a fcent of mufk, that, at a certain feafon, it is impoffible to eat them. Thefe animals have a very fine wool, it is longer than that of the Barbary fheep. I had fome of it brought over to France in 1708, of which I caufed ftockings to be made for me, which were finer than filk ftockings." Thefe buffaloes, though fmaller than ours, have, however, much longer and thicker horns; their roots join on the crown of their heads, and reach down by their eyes almoft as low as the throat; the end afterwards bends upwards, forming a fort of crefcent. Some of thefe are fo thick,

that

that I have feen fome, which after being feparated from the fkull weighed fixty pounds a pair. Their legs are very fhort, fo that this wool continually trails along the ground as they walk; which renders them fo deformed, that at a fmall diftance you can hardly diftinguifh on which fide the head ftands. There is no great number of thefe animals, fo that had the Indians been fent out to hunt them, the fpecies had before now been entirely deftroyed. Add to this, that as their legs are very fhort, they are killed when the fnow lies deep, with lances, and are utterly incapable of efcaping.

The moft common animal in Canada at this day is the roe-buck, which differs in nothing from ours. He is faid to fhed tears when he finds himfelf hard preffed by the huntfmen. When young his fkin is ftriped with different colours; afterwards this hair falls off, and other hair of the fame colour with that of the reft of thefe animals grows up in its ftead. This creature is far from being fierce, and is eafily tamed; he appears to be naturally a lover of mankind. The tame female retires to the woods when fhe is in rut, and after fhe has had the male, returns to her mafter's houfe. When the time of bringing forth is come, fhe retires once more to the woods, where fhe remains fome days with her young, and after that fhe returns to fhew herfelf to her mafter; fhe conftantly vifits her young; they follow her when they think it is time, and take the fawns, which fhe continues to nourifh in the houfe. It is furprifing enough any of our habitations fhould be without whole herds of them; the Indians hunt them only occafionally.

There are alfo many wolves in Canada, or rather a kind of cats, for they have nothing of the wolf
but

but a kind of howling; in every other circumſtance
they are, ſays M. Sarraſin, *ex genere felino*, of the
cat kind. Theſe are natural hunters, living only
on the animals they catch, and which they purſue
to the top of the talleſt trees. Their fleſh is white
and very good eating; their fur and ſkin are both well
known in France; this is one of the fineſt furs in
the whole country, and one of the moſt conſiderable articles in its commerce. That of a certain ſpecies of black foxes, which live in the northern
mountains, is ſtill more eſteemed. I have, however
heard, that the black fox of Muſcovy, and of the
northern parts of Europe is ſtill more highly valued. They are, moreover, exceeding rare here,
probably on account of the difficulty of catching
them.

There is a more common ſort, the hair of which
is black or grey, mixed with white; others of them
are quite grey, and others again of a tawny red.
They are found in the Upper Miſſiſſippi, of infinite beauty, and with a fur of an argentine or ſilver grey. We find here likewiſe tygers and wolves
of a ſmaller ſort than ours. The foxes hunt the
water-fowl after a very ingenious manner: they advance a little into the water, and afterwards retire,
playing a thouſand antick tricks on the banks.
The ducks, buſtards, and other ſuch birds, tickled
with the ſport, approach the fox; when he ſees
them within reach, he keeps very quiet for a while
at firſt, that he may not frighten them, moving
only his tail, as if on purpoſe to draw them ſtill
nearer, and the fooliſh creatures are ſuch dupes to
his craftineſs, as to come and peck at his tail;
the fox immediately ſprings upon them, and ſeldom miſſes his aim. Dogs have been bred to the
ſame

fame fport with tolerable fuccefs, and the fame dogs carry on a fierce war againft the foxes.

There is a kind of polecat, which goes by the name of *Enfant du Diable*, or the Child of the Devil; or *Bête puante*; a title derived from his ill fcent, becaufe his urine, which he lets go, when he finds himfelf purfued, infects the air for half a quarter of a league round; this is in other refpects a very beautiful creature. He is of the fize of a fmall cat, but thicker, the fkin or fur fhining, and of a greyifh colour, with white lines, forming a fort of oval on the back from the neck quite to the tail. This tail is bufhy like that of a fox, and turned up like a fquirrel. Its fur, like that of the animal called *Pekan*, another fort of wild-cat, much of the fame fize with ours, and of the otter, the ordinary polecat, the *pitois*, wood-rat, ermine, and martin, are what is called *la menue pelleterie*, or lefter peltry. The ermine is of the fize of our fquirrel, but not quite fo long; his fur is of a moft beautiful white, and his tail is long, and the tip of it black as jet; our martins are not fo red as thofe of France, and have a much finer fur. They commonly keep in the middle of woods, whence they never ftir but once in two or three years, but always in large flocks. The Indians have a notion, that the year in which they leave the woods, will be good for hunting, that is, that there will be a great fall of fnow. Martins fkins fell actually here at a crown a piece, I mean the ordinary fort, for fuch as are brown go as high as four livres and upwards.

The *pitoi* differs from the polecat only in that its fur is longer, blacker, and thicker. Thefe two animals make war on the birds, even of the largeft

forts,

forts, and make great ravages amongst dove-coats and henroofts. The wood-rat is twice the fize of ours; he has a bufhy tail, and is of a beautiful filver grey: there are even fome entirely of a moft beautiful white; the female has a bag under her belly, which fhe opens and fhuts at pleafure; in this fhe places her young when fhe is purfued, and fo faves them with herfelf from their common enemy.

With regard to the fquirrel, this animal enjoys a tolerable degree of tranquillity, fo that there are a prodigious number of them in this country. They are diftinguifhed into three different forts; the red, which are exactly the fame with ours; thofe called *Swiffes* of a fmaller fize, and fo called, becaufe they have long ftripes of red, white and black, much like the liveries of the pope's Swifs guards; and the flying fquirrel, of much the fame fize with the Swiffes, and with a dark grey fur; they are called flying fquirrels, not that they really can fly, but from their leaping from tree to tree, to the diftance of forty paces and more. From a higher place, they will fly or leap double the diftance. What gives them this facility of leaping, is two membranes, one on each fide, reaching between their fore and hind legs, and which when ftretched are two inches broad; they are very thin, and covered over with a fort of cats hair or down. This little animal is eafily tamed, and is very lively except when afleep, which is often the cafe, and he puts up wherever he can find a place, in one's fleeves, pockets, and muffs. He firft pitches upon his mafter; whom he will diftinguifh amongft twenty perfons.

The Canadian porcupine is of the fize of a middling dog, but fhorter and not fo tall; his hair is about

O

four inches long, of the thicknefs of a fmall ftalk of corn, is white, hollow, and very ftrong, efpecially upon the back; thefe are his weapons, offenfive and defenfive. He darts them at once againft any enemy who attempts his life, and if it pierce the flefh ever fo little, it muft be inftantly drawn out, otherwife it finks quite into it; for this reafon people are very cautious of letting their dogs come near him. His flefh is extreme good eating. A porcupine roafted is full as good as a fucking pig.

Hares and rabbits are like thofe of Europe, except that their hind legs are longer. Their fkins are in no great requeft, as the hair is continually falling off; it is pity, for their hair is exceeding fine and might be ufed without detriment in the hat-manufacture. They grow grey in winter, and never ftir from their warrens or holes, where they live on the tendereft branches of the birch-trees. In fummer they are of a carrotty red; the fox makes a continual and a moft cruel war upon them fummer and winter, and the Indians take them in winter on the fnow, with gins, when they go out in fearch of provifions.

I have the honour to be, &c.

LETTER

L E T T E R   VIII.

Description of the country between lake St. Peter *and* Montreal; *in what it differs from that near* Quebec. *Description of the island and city of* Montreal, *and the country adjacent. Of the sea-cow, sea-wolf, porpoise, and whale-fishery.*

Montreal, March 20, 1721.

Madam,

I Set out on the 13th from St. Francis, and next day arrived in this city. In this passage, which is about twenty leagues, I had not the same pleasure as formerly of performing the same journey by water in a canoe, in the finest weather imaginable, and in viewing, as I advanced, channels and pieces of water without end, formed by a multitude of islands, which seemed at a distance part of the Continent, and to stop the river in his course, those delightful scenes which were perpetually varying like the scenes of a theatre, and which one would think had been contrived on purpose for the pleasure of travellers; I had, however, some amends made me by the singular sight of an Archipelago, become, in some sort, a Continent, and by the conveniency of taking the air in my cariole, on channels lying

O 2   be-

between two iflands, which feemed to have been planted by the hand like fo many orangeries.

With refpect to the profpect, it cannot be called beautiful at this feafon. Nothing can be more difmal than that univerfal whitenefs, which takes place in the room of that vaft variety of colours, the greateft charm of the country, than the trees which prefent nothing to the view, but naked tops, and whofe branches are covered with icicles. Further, Madam, the lake of St. Francis is in this country, what the Loire is in France. Towards Quebec the lands are good, though generally without any thing capable of affording pleafure to the fight; in other refpects, this climate is very rude; as the further you go down the river, the nearer you approach to the north, and confequently the colder it becomes. Quebec lies in 47 deg. 56 min. The Three Rivers in 46 deg. and a few minutes; and Montreal between 44 and 45; the river above lake St. Peter making and winding towards the fouth. One would think therefore, after pafling Richelieu iflands, that one were tranfported into another climate. The air becomes fofter and more temperate, the country more level, the river more pleafant, and the banks infinitely more agreeable and delightful. You meet with iflands from time to time, fome of which are inhabited, and others in their natural ftate, which afford the fight the fineft landfkips in the world; in a word, this is the *Touraine* and the *Limagne* of *Auvergne*, compared with the countries of *Maine* and *Normandy*.

The ifland of Montreal, which is, as it were the centre of this fine country, is ten leagues in length from eaft to weft, and near four leagues in its greateft breadth; the mountain whence it derives it name,

and

and which has two summits of unequal height, is situated almost in the middle between its two extremities, and only at the distance of near half a league from the south-shore of it, on which Montreal is built. This city was first called *Ville Marie* by its founders, but this name has never obtained the sanction of custom in conversation, and holds place only in the public acts, and amongst the lords proprietaries, who are exceeding jealous of it. These lords, who are not only lords of the city, but also of the whole island, are the governors of the seminary of St. Sulpicius ; and as almost all the lands on it are excellent, and well cultivated, and the city as populous as Quebec, we may venture to say, this lordship is well worth half a score the best in all Canada. This is the fruit of the industry and wisdom of the lords proprietors of this island, and it is certain, that had it been parcelled out amongst a score of proprietors, it would neither have been in the flourishing state in which we now see it, nor would the inhabitants have been near so happy.

The city of Montreal has a very pleasing aspect, and is besides conveniently situated, the streets well laid out, and the houses well built. The beauty of the country round it, and of its prospects, inspire a certain chearfulness of which every body is perfectly sensible. It is not fortified, only a simple palisado with bastions, and in a very indifferent condition, with a sorry redoubt on a small spot, which serves as a sort of outwork, and terminates in a gentle declivity, at the end of which is a small square, which is all the defence it has. This is the place you first find on your entering the city on the side of Quebec. It is not yet quite forty years since it was entirely without any fortifications, and consequently was every day exposed to the incursions of the English

O 3   and

and Indians, who could easily have burnt it. The Chevalier de Callieres, brother to him who was plenipotentiary at Ryswick, was he who first inclosed it, whilst he was governor of it. There has been some years since a project for walling it round *; but it will be no easy matter to bring the inhabitants to contribute to it. They are brave, but far from rich ; they have been already found very hard to be perswaded to the necessity of this expence, and are fully persuaded that their own courage is more than sufficient to defend their city against all invaders. Our Canadians in general have a good opinion of themselves in this particular, and we must acknowlege, not without good grounds. But by a natural consequence of this self-sufficiency it is much easier to surprise than to defeat them.

Montreal is of a quadrangular form, situated on the bank of the river, which rising gently, divides the city lengthwise into the upper and lower towns, though you can scarce perceive the ascent from the one to the other ; the hospital, royal magazines, and place of arms, are in the lower-town, which is also the quarter in which the merchants for the most part have their houses. The seminary and parish-church, the convent of the Recollets, the jesuits, the daughters of the congregation, the governor, and most of the officers dwell in the high-town. Beyond a small stream coming from the north-west, and which terminates the city on this side, you come to a few houses and the hospital general ; and turning towards the right beyond the Recollets, whose convent is at the extremity of the city, on the same side, there is a kind of suburb beginning to be built, which will in time be a very fine quarter.

* This project has been since put in execution.

The jefuits have only a fmall houfe here, but their church, the roof of which is juft upon the point of being finifhed is large and well built. The convent of the Recollets is more fpacious, and their community more numerous. The feminary is in the centre of the town ; they feem to have thought more of rendering it folid and commodious than magnificent; you may, however, ftill difcover it to be the manor-houfe ; it communicates with the parifh-church, which has much more the air of a cathedral than that of Quebec. Divine worfhip is celebrated here with a modefty and dignity which infpire the fpectators with an awful notion of that God who is worfhipped in it.

The houfe of the daughters of the Congregation, though one of the largeft in the city, is ftill too fmall to lodge fo numerous a community. · This is the head of an order and the noviciate of an inftitute, which ought to be fo much the dearer to New France, and to this city in particular, on account of its taking its rife in it ; and as the whole colony has felt the advantage of fo noble an endowment. The Hotel-Dieu, or Hofpital is ferved by thefe nuns, the firft of whom came from la Flêche in Anjou. They are poor, which, however, neither appears in their hall, or yards, which are fpacious, well-furnifhed, and extremely well provided with beds ; nor in their church, which is handfome, and exceeding richly ornamented ; nor in their houfe, which is well built, neat and commodious ; but they are at the fame time ill-fed, though all of them are indefatigable either in the inftruction of the youth or in taking care of the fick.

The hofpital-general owes its foundation to a private perfon called Charron, who affociated with fe-

veral

veral pious perfons, not only for this good work,
but alfo to provide fchool-mafters for the country-
parifhes, who fhould perform the fame functions
with refpect to the boys, which the fifters of the
congregation did with regard to the fair fex; but
this fociety foon diffolved; fome being called off by
their private concerns, and others by their natural
inconftancy, fo that the Sieur Charron was foon left
alone. He was not however difcouraged, he opened his purfe, and found the fecret to caufe feveral
perfons in power open theirs; he built a houfe, affembled mafters and hofpitallers, and men took a
pleafure in aiding and impowering one who fpared
neither his money nor his labour, and whom no
difficulties were capable of deterring. Laftly, before his death, which happened in the year 1719,
he had the confolation to fee his project beyond all
fear of mifcarrying, at leaft with refpect to the
hofpital-general. The houfe is a fine edifice and
the church a very handfome one. The fchool-
mafters are ftill on no folid foundations in the parifhes, and the prohibition made them by the court
of wearing an uniform drefs, and of taking fimple
vows, may poffibly occafion this project to be dif-
continued.

Between the ifland of Montreal and the Continent on the north fide, is another ifland of about
eight leagues in length, and full two in breadth
where broadeft. This was at firft called *l' Ifle de
Montmafny*, after a governor-general of Canada of
this name; it was afterwards granted to the jefuits,
who gave it the name of *l' Ifle Jefus*, which it ftill
retains, though it has paffed from them to the fuperiors of the feminary of Quebec, who have begun to plant it with inhabitants, and as the foil is

ex-

excellent, there is ground to hope it will very foon be cleared.

The channel which feparates the two iflands, bears the name of *the river of Meadows*, as it runs between very fine ones. Its courfe is interrupted in the middle by a rapid current, called the Fall of the Recollet, in memory of a monk of that order drowned in it. The religious of the feminary of Montreal had, for a great while, an Indian miffion in this place, which they have lately tranfported fomewhere elfe.

The third arm of the river is interfperfed with fo prodigious a multitude of iflands, that there is almoft as much land as water. This channel bears the name of *Milles Ifles*, or *the Thoufand Iflands*, or St. John's River. At the extremity of the *Ifle Jefus*, is the fmall ifland *l'Ifle Bizard*, from the name of a Swifs officer, whofe property it was, and who died a major of Montreal. A little higher towards the fouth, you find the ifland *Perrot*, thus termed from M. Perrot, who was the firft governor of Montreal, and the father of the countefs de la Roche Allard, and of the lady of the prefident Lubert. This ifland is almoft two leagues every way, and the foil is excellent; they are beginning to clear it. The ifland *Bizard* terminates the lake of the two mountains, as the ifland Perrot feparates it from that of *St. Louis*.

The lake of the two mountains is properly the opening of the great river, otherwife called *la Riviere des Outaowais*, into the St. Lawrence. It is two leagues long, and almoft as many broad. That of St. Louis is fomething larger, but is only a widening of the river St. Laurence. Hitherto the
French

French colony reached no further to the weftward; but they begin to make new plantations higher up the river, and the foil is every where excellent.

What has been the prefervation, or at leaft the fafety of Montreal, and all the country round it during the laft wars, is two villages of Iroquois Chriftians, and the fort of *Chambly*. The firft of thefe villages is that of *Sault St. Lewis*, fituated on the Continent, on the fouth-fide of the river, and three leagues above Montreal. It is very populous, and has ever been looked upon as one of our ftrongeft barriers againft the idolatrous Iroquois, and the Englifh of New-York. It has already changed its fituation twice within the fpace of two leagues. Its fecond ftation, when I faw it in 1706, was near a rapid ftream, called *Sault St. Lewis*, which name it ftill retains though at a confiderable diftance from it. It appears to have entirely fixed at laft; for the church which they are juft about to finifh, and the miffionaries houfe are each in their own kind two of the fineft edifices in all Canada; the fituation of them is charming. The river which is very broad in this place is embellifhed with feveral iflands, which have a very pleafant afpect. The ifland of Montreal is well ftocked with inhabitants, forms the view on one hand, and the fight has no bounds on the other fide, except lake St. Louis, which begins a little above this.

The fecond village bears the name of *la Montaigne*, having been for a long time fituated on the double-headed mountain, which has given its name to the ifland. It has fince been tranflated to the fall of the Recollet, as I have already told you; it now ftands on the Terra Firma oppofite to the weftern extremity of the ifland. The ecclefiafticks of the feminary

nary of Montreal govern in it. There have many
brave warriors come from thefe two towns, and
the terror which prevailed here was admirable till
the avarice of our dealers introduced drunkennefs
amongft them, which has made ftill greater favages
here than in the miffions of St. Francis and Becan-
kourt.

The miffionaries have in vain employed all their
induftry and vigilance to put a ftop to the torrent
of this diforder; in vain have they made ufe of the
aid of the fecular arm, threatned them with the
wrath of heaven, made ufe of the moft perfuafive
arguments, all has been to no purpofe, and even
where it was impoffible not to difcover the hand of
God ftretched out againft the authors of this evil,
all have been found infufficient to bring thofe Chriftians back to a fenfe of their duty, who had been
once blindfolded by the fordid and moft contemptible paffion of lucre. Even in the very ftreets of
Montreal, are feen the moft fhocking fpectacles,
the never-failing effects of the drunkennefs of thefe
barbarians; hufbands, wives, fathers, mothers,
children, brothers and fifters, feizing one another
by the throats, tearing of one another by the ears,
and worrying one another with their teeth like fo
many inraged wolves. The air refounded during
the night with their cries and howlings much more
horrible than thofe with which wild beafts affright
the woods.

Thofe, who perhaps have greateft reafon to reproach themfelves with thefe horrors, are the firft
to afk whether they are Chriftians. One might anfwer them, yes, they are Chriftians, and New Converts who know not what they do; but thofe who
in cold blood, and with a perfect knowledge of
what

what they are about, reduce, from fordid motives
of avarice, thofe fimple people to this condition,
can they be imagined to have any religion at all?
We certainly know that an Indian will give all he is
worth for one glafs of brandy, this is ftrong temptation to our dealers, againft which, neither the exclamations of their paftors, nor the zeal and authority of the magiftrate, nor refpect for the laws, nor
the feverity of the divine juftice, nor the dread of
the judgments of the Almighty, nor the thoughts
of a Hell hereafter, of which thefe barbarians ex-
hibit a very ftriking picture, have been able to avail.
But it is time to turn away our eyes from fo difagreeable a fpeculation.

The chief part of the peltry or fur-trade, after
the northern and weftern nations left off frequent-
ing the city of the *Three Rivers*, was for fome time
carried on at Montreal, whither the Indians reforted
at certain feafons from all parts of Canada. This was
a kind of fair, which drew great numbers of French
to this city. The governor general and intendant
came hither likewife, and made ufe of thofe occafions to fettle any differences which might have happened amongft our allies. But fhould your Grace
happen by chance to light on la Hontan's book, where
he treats of this fair, I muft caution you to be on
your guard left you take every thing he fays of it
for matter of fact. He has even forgot to give it
fo much as an air of probability. The women of
Montreal never gave any ground for what this author lays to their charge, and there is no reafon to
fear for their honour with refpect to the Indians. It
is without example that any of them have ever taken the leaft liberty with any French woman, even
when they have been their prifoners. They have
never been fubject to the leaft temptation by them,
and

and it were to be wifhed, that Frenchmen had
the fame diftafte of the Indian women. La Hontan could not be ignorant of what is notorious to
the whole country ; but he had a mind to render
his account entertaining ; on which account every
thing true or falfe was the fame to him. One is always fure of pleafing fome people of a certain caft,
by obferving no meafure in the liberty one affumes
of inventing, calumniating, and in our way of ex-
preffing ourfelves on certain topicks.

There are ftill now and then companies or rather
flotillas of Indians arriving at Montreal, but nothing in comparifon of what ufed to refort hither
in time paft. The war of the Iroquois is what has
interrupted the great concourfe of Indians in the
colony. In order to provide againft this evil, ftore-
houfes have been erected in the countries of moft
Indian nations, together with forts, in which there
is always a governor and a garrifon, ftrong enough
to fecure the merchandize in them. The Indians
are above all things defirous there fhould be a gun-
fmith amongft them, and in feveral there are miffionaries, who would generally do more good there,
were there no other Frenchmen with them befides
themfelves. It would one would think have been proper to have reftored things upon the old footing, efpecially as there is an univerfal peace and tranquillity
all over the colony. This would have been a good
means of reftraining the *Couriers de Bois*, whofe avidity, without mentioning all the diforders introduced by libertinifm, which occafions a thoufand mean-
neffes, which render us contemptible to the barbarians, has lowered the price of our commodities, and
raifed that of their peltry. Befides that, the Indians, who are by nature haughty, have grown info-
lent

lent fince they have feen themfelves courted by us.

The fifhery is much more likely and proper to enrich Canada than the fur-trade ; which is alfo entirely independent of the Indians. There are two reafons for applying to this, which, however, have not been able to induce our planters to make it the principal object of their commerce. I have nothing to add, to what I have already had the honour to tell you with refpect to the cod-fifhery, which is alone worth more than a Peru, had the founders of New France taken proper meafures to fecure the poffeffion of it to us. I begin with that of the fea-wolf, fea-cow, and porpoife, which may be carried on over all the gulf of St. Lawrence, and even a great way up that river.

The fea-wolf owes its name to its cry, which is a fort of howling, for as to its figure it has nothing of the wolf, nor of any known land animal. Lefcarbot affirms, that he has heard fome of them, whofe cry refembled that of a fcreech-owl ; but this might poffibly have been the cry of young ones, whofe voice was not as yet arrived at its full tone. Moreover, Madam, they never hefitate in this country to place the fea-wolf in the rank of fifhes, tho' it is far from being dumb, is brought forth on fhore, on which it lives at leaft as much as in the water, is covered with hair, in a word, though nothing is wanting to it, which conftitutes an animal truly amphibious. But we are now in a new world, and it muft not be expected we fhould always fpeak the language of the old, and as cuftom, the authority of which is never difputed, has put it in poffeffion of all its own rights. Thus the war which is carried on againft the fea-wolf, though often on fhore,

and

and with muſkets, is called a fiſhery; and that carried on againſt the beaver, though in the water, and with nets, is called hunting.

The head of the ſea-wolf reſembles pretty much that of a dog; he has four very ſhort legs, eſpecially the hind legs; in every other circumſtance he is entirely a fiſh: he rather crawls than walks on his legs; thoſe before are armed with nails, the hind being ſhaped like fins; his ſkin is hard, and is covered with a ſhort hair of various colours. There are ſome entirely white, as they are all when firſt brought forth; ſome grow black, and others red, as they grow older, and others again of both colours together.

The fiſhermen diſtinguiſh ſeveral forts of ſeawolves; the largeſt weigh two thouſand weight, and it is pretended have ſharper ſnouts than the reſt. There are ſome of them which flounce only in water; our ſailors call them *braſſeurs*, as they call another ſort *nau*, of which I neither know the origin nor meaning. Another ſort are called *Groſſes têtes*, *Thick-heads*. Some of their young are very alert, and dextrous in breaking the nets ſpread for them; theſe are of a greyiſh colour, are very gameſome, full of mettle, and as handſome as an animal of this figure can be; the Indians accuſtom them to follow them like little dogs, and eat them neverthelefs.

M. Denis mentions two forts of ſea-wolves, which he found on the coaſts of Acadia; one of them, ſays he, are ſo very large, that their young ones are bigger than our largeſt hogs. He adds, that a little while after they are brought forth, the parents lead them to the water, and from time to time

conduct

conduct them back on shore to suckle them; that
this fishery is carried on in the month of February,
when the young ones, which they are not desirous
of catching, scarce ever go to the water; thus on
the first alarm the old ones take to flight, making
a prodigious noise to advertise their young, that they
ought to follow them, which summons they never
fail to obey, provided the fishermen do not quickly
stop them by a knock on the snout with a stick,
which is sufficient to kill them. The number of
these animals upon that coast must needs be prodigious; if it is true, what the same author assures
us, that eight hundred of these young ones have
been taken in one day.

The second fort mentioned by M. Denys are
very small, one of them yielding only a quantity
of oil sufficient to fill its own bladder. These last
never go to any distance from the sea-shore, and
have always one of their number upon duty by
way of sentry. At the first signal he gives, they
all plunge into the sea; some time after they approach the land, and raise themselves on their hind
legs, to see whether there is any danger; but in
spite of all their precautions great numbers of them
are surprized on shore, it being scarce possible to
catch them any other way.

It is by all agreed, that the flesh of the sea-wolf
is good eating, but it turns much better to account
to make oil of it, which is no very difficult operation. They melt the blubber fat of it over the
fire which dissolves into an oil. Oftentimes they
content themselves with erecting what they call *char-
niers*, a name given to large squares of boards or
plank, on which is spread the flesh of a number of
sea-wolves; here it melts of itself, and the oil runs
through

through a hole contrived for the purpofe. This oil when frefh is good for the ufe of the kitchen, but that of the young ones foon grows rank; and that of the others if kept for any confiderable time, becomes too dry. In this cafe it is made ufe of to burn, or in currying of leather. It keeps long clear, has no fmell, fediment, or impurity whatfoever at the bottom of the cafk.

In the infancy of the colony great numbers of the hides of fea-wolves were made ufe of for muffs. This fafhion has long been laid afide, fo that the general ufe they are now put to, is the covering of trunks and chefts. When tanned, they have almoft the fame grain with Morocco leather; they are not quite fo fine, but are lefs liable to crack, and keep longer quite frefh, and look as if new. Very good fhoes and boots have been made of them, which let in no water. They alfo cover feats with them, and the wood wears out before the leather; they tan thefe hides here with the bark of the oak, and in the dye ftuff with which they ufe black, is mixed a powder made from a certain ftone found on the banks of rivers. This is called thunderftone, or marcafite of the mines.

The fea-wolves couple and bring forth their young on rocks, and fometimes on the ice; their common litter is two, which they often fuckle in the water, but oftener on fhore; when they would teach them to fwim they carry them, fay they, on their backs, then throw them off in the water, afterwards taking them up again, and continue this fort of inftruction till the young ones are able to fwim alone. If this is true, it is an odd fort of fifh, and which nature feems not to have inftructed in what moft fort of land animals do the moment

they

they are brought forth. The sea-wolf has very
acute senses, which are his sole means of defence;
he is, however, often surprized in spite of all his
vigilance, as I have already taken notice; but the
most common way of catching them is the following.

It is the custom of this animal to enter the creeks
with the tide; when the fishermen have found out
such creeks to which great numbers of sea-wolves
resort, they enclose them with stakes and nets, leaving only a small opening for the sea-wolves to enter; as soon as it is high-water they shut this opening, so that when the tide goes out the fishes remain
a dry, and are easily dispatched. They also follow
them in canoes to the places to which many of
them resort, and fire upon them when they raise
their heads above water to breathe. If they happen to be no more than wounded they are easily taken; but if killed outright, they immediately sink
to the bottom, like the beavers; but they have
large dogs bred to this exercise, which fetch them
from the bottom in seven or eight fathom water.
Lastly, I have been told, that a sailor having one
day surprifed a vast herd of them ashore, drove
them before him to his lodgings with a switch, as
he would have done a flock of sheep, and that he
with his comrades killed to the number of nine
hundred of them. *Sit fides penes autorem.*

Our fishermen now take very few sea-cows, on
the coasts of the gulf of St. Lawrence; and I do
not certainly know whether any of them have ever
been catched any where else. The English formerly
set up a fishery of this sort on the island *de Sable*,
but without any degree of success. The figure of
this animal is not very different from that of the
sea-

ea-wolf, but it is larger. What is peculiar to it is two teeth of the thickness and length of a man's arm, bending somewhat upwards, which one might easily mistake for horns, and from which these animals probably had the name of sea-cows. The sailors have a simpler name for them, which is, the beast with the great tooth. This tooth is a very fine ivory, as well as all the rest in the jaws of this fish, and which are four fingers long.

There are two sorts of porpoises in the river St. Lawrence; those found in salt-water, that is, from a little below the Isle of Orleans, are exactly the same with those found in the ocean. Those in fresh water are perfectly white, and of the size of a cow; the first sort commonly go in herds; I have not observed this circumstance in the other sort, though I have seen many of them playing in the port of Quebec. They never go higher than this city; but there are many of them on the coasts of Acadia, as well as of the first sort, so that the difference of colour cannot proceed from the different qualities of fresh and salt-water.

The white porpoise yields a hogshead of oil, which is of much the same quality with that drawn from the sea-wolf. I have never found any person that had tasted the flesh of this animal, but as for those called dorcelles, a name given the grey porpoise, their flesh is said to be no bad eating; they make puddings and sausages of their guts; the pluck is excellent fricasied, and the head preferable to that of a sheep, though inferior to a calf's.

The skins of both are tanned and dressed like Morocco leather; at first it is as tender as lard or fat, and is an inch thick; they shave it down thin-

ner

ner for a confiderable while, till it becomes a tranf-
parent fkin; and let it be made ever fo thin, even
fo as to be fit for making into waiftecoats and
breeches, it is always exceffive ftrong and mufket-
proof. There are of them eighteen feet long and
nine broad; it is affirmed that there is nothing ex-
ceeds it for covering coaches.

There have been two porpoife fiſheries lately ſet
up below Quebec, one in the bay of St. Paul, and
the other feven or eight leagues lower down, oppofite to a habitation called *Camourafca*, from certain
rocks, rifing to a confiderable height above water.
The expence is no great affair, and the profits would
be confiderable, were the porpoifes animals haunt-
ing particular parts; but whether from inftinct or
caprice, they always find means to break all the
meafures of the fiſhermen, and to take a different
rout from that where they are expected. Befides
thefe fiſheries, which only enrich particular perfons,
occafion a general outcry among the people, which
is owing to their having caufed a confiderable diminution in the fiſhery for eèls, an article of great
benefit to the poor. For the porpoifes finding themfelves difturbed below Quebec, have retired elfewhere, and the eels no longer finding thofe large
fiſhes in their way, fwim down the river without
any hindrance; from whence it is, that between
Quebec and the Three Rivers, where prodigious
quantities of them were caught formerly, there are
now none caught at all.

The way of fiſhing for the porpoife is little different from that I laft mentioned with refpect to the
fea-wolf: when the tide is out, they plant pretty
near each other in the mud or fand ftakes to which
they tie nets in the form of a pouch the opening
of

of which is tolerably large ; but that in fuch manner, that when the fifh has once paffed through it,
he cannot find his way out again ; there are green
branches placed at top of the ftakes.   When the
flood comes, thefe fifhes which give chace to the
herrings, which always make towards the fhore,
and are allured by the verdure which they are extremely fond of, and intangled in the nets, where
they are kept prifoners.   In proportion as the tide
ebbs, you have the pleafure of feeing their confufion and fruitlefs ftruggles to efcape.   In a word,
they remain a dry, and fometimes heaped upon one
another in fuch numbers, that with one ftroke of a
ftick you may knock down two or three of them.
It is affirmed, that amongft the white fort fome
have been found to weigh three thoufand weight.

No body is ignorant of the manner of carrying
on the whale-fifhery, for which reafon I fhall take
no notice of it ; it is here faid, that the Bafques or
people of Bayonne in France, have left it over, only
that they might give themfelves up entirely to the
fur-trade, which requires neither fo large an expence, nor fo much fatigue, and whereof the profits were then more confiderable as well as fooner
returned.   But they wanted many conveniencies for
carrying it on, which are to be had now, there being fo many fettlements a great way towards the
gulf.   There has fome years fince been an attempt
to re-eftablifh it, but without fuccefs ; the undertakers either wanted the neceffary funds for making
the advances, or elfe wanted to reimburfe the fums
they had laid out too foon, or wanted conftancy.   It
appears, however, that this commerce might become highly ufeful to the colony, and that it might
be carried on with much inferior expence and danger than on the coaft of Greenland.   What fhould

hin-

hinder it even from being fixed and carried on from ſhore, as M. Denys propoſed to carry on the cod-fiſhery in Acadia. This is, Madam, what I have to ſay with regard to the fiſheries of Canada: I will inform you of ſome others, after I ſhall have taken notice of their manner of living in this country.

I have the honour to be, &c.

LETTER

L E T T E R IX.

Of fort Chambly, *with the fiſhes, birds, and
ſeveral animals peculiar to* Canada. *Of trees
common to it with* France, *and of ſuch as are
peculiar to this country.*

Chambly, April 11, 1721.

Madam,

ONE of the principal ſecurities and bulwarks
of Montreal againſt the Iroquois and New-
York, is the fort of Chambly, from which I now
have the honour to write you. I came here to pay
a viſit to the commandant, who is M. de *Sabrevois,*
one of the beſt families of Beauce, and my friend,
fellow-paſſenger, and a good officer. I am going in
two words to give you the ſituation and deſcription
of this important place.

In the firſt years of our ſettling in this country,
the Iroquois, that they might make incurſions even
as far as the center of our plantations, came down
a river which empties itſelf into the St. Lawrence,
a little above St. Peter, and which had for this reaſon given it the name of *the River of the Iroquois.*
It has been ſince called *Richelieu River,* on account

P 4　　　　　　　　　　　　　　　of

of a fort of this name, that had been built at its mouth. This fort having been demolifhed, M. de Sorel, captain in the regiment of Carignan Salieres, caufed build another, to which his name was given ; this name has been fince extended to the river, which ftill retains it, though the fort has long ceafed to exift. After failing up this river about feventeen leagues, always ftretching towards the fouth, and a little towards to the fouth-weft, you come to a *rapide*, and oppofite to it, a little lake formed by the fame river. On the banks of this *rapide*, and oppofite to the lake, the fort is placed. This was at firft built of wood by M. de Chambly, captain in the above-mentioned regiment, and at the time when M. de Sorel built the other. But it has fince been built of ftone, and flanked with four baftions, and has always a ftrong garrifon. The lands round it are excellent, they begin to make plantations, and many are of opinion that in time a city will be built here.

From Chambly to lake Champlain there are only eight leagues ; the river Sorel croffes this lake, and there is not perhaps a canton in all New France, which it would be more proper to people. The climate here is milder than in any part of the colony, and the inhabitants will have for neighbours, the Iroquois, who are, at bottom, a good fort of people enough, who will, probably, never think of coming to a rupture with us, after they fhall fee us in fuch a condition as not to fear them, and who, in my opinion would like us much better for neighbours than the people of New-York. There are many other reafons to induce us to make this fettlement ; but were I to mention all, I fhould leave myfelf nothing to tell you when I have the honour to fee you. I am going to make ufe of the leifure

I

I have here to continue my account of such things as are peculiar to this country. I left off at the article of the benefit which the gulph and river of St. Lawrence are capable of furnishing with respect to the commerce of New France. It remains to treat of the resources the inhabitants may find for the support of life in these parts.

In all parts where the water of the river is salt, that is from cape *Tourmente* to the gulf, may be caught such fishes as are found in the ocean ; such as the salmon, tunny, shad fish, smelt, sea-eels, mackerel, trout, lamprey, sole, herring, anchovy, pilchard, turbot, and many others, unknown in Europe. They are all caught with nets of different forms. In the gulph are caught thrashers, three sorts of *Rayes* ; the common, that called *Bouclee*, and which is by some preferred to ours in France ; and the sort termed *le Posteau*, not esteemed ; lencornets, a kind of cuttle-fish ; *Gobergues*, or St. Peter-fish ; plaise, requiems, sea-dogs, another sort of requiem not so mischievous when alive, and better beyond comparison when dead. Oisters are extremely plenty in winter, on all the coasts of Acadia, and their way of fishing them is very singular. They make a hole in the ice, through which they put two poles tied together, so as to play like pincers, and rarely draw them up without an oister.

I said the lencornet was a sind of cuttle-fish, its figure is, however, very different from the common sort of them. It is quite round, or rather oval ; it has above the tail, a sort of border, which serves it instead of a target, and its head is surrounded with prickles half a foot long, which he uses to catch other fishes ; there are two sorts of them which differ only in size ; some are as large as

a

a hogfhead, and others but a foot long; they catch only thefe laft, and that with a torch; they are very fond of light, they hold it out to them from the fhore at high-water, and they come to it, and fo are left a-ground. The lencornet roafted, boiled, or fricafied, is excellent eating; but it makes the fauce quite black.

The gobergue refembles a fmall cod. It has the fame tafte, and is dried like it. It has two black fpots on each fide the head, and the failors tell you that this is the fifh in which St. Peter found money to pay the Roman emperor's tribute for our Lord and himfelf, and that thefe two fpots are the two places by which he held it; this is the reafon it has got the name of St. Peter's fifh. The fea-plaife has firmer flefh and is of a better relifh than the frefh water fort; this is taken as well as the lobfter or fea-crab, with long poles armed with a pointed iron, ending in a fork or hook which hinders the fifh from getting loofe. Laftly, in feveral places, efpecially in Acadia, the pools are full of falmon trouts a foot long, and of turtles two foot diameter, the flefh of which is excellent, and the upper fhell, ftriped with white, red, and blue.

Amongft the fifhes which lake Champlain, and the rivers falling into it, abound, M. Champlain remarks one fingular enough, called *Chaourafou*; probably from the name given it by the Indians. This is a fpecies of the armed fifh, which is found in feveral other places; this is in figure pretty much like a pike, only it is covered with fcales which are proof againft a dagger; its colour is a filver grey, and from under its throat proceeds a bone which is flat, indented, hollow, and pierced or open at the end, from which it is probable the animal
breathes

breathes through this. The fkin which covers this bone is tender, and its length is in proportion to that of the fifh, of which it is one third part. Its breadth is two fingers in thofe of the fmalleft fize. The Indians affured M. Champlain they had found fome of thofe fifhes from eight to ten feet broad ; but the largeft of thofe he faw were not above five, and were as thick as a man's thigh.

We may well imagine this to be a real pirate amongft the inhabitants of the waters ; but no body could ever dream that he is full as dangerous an enemy to the citizens of the air ; this is, however, one of his trades, in which he acts like an able huntf-man ; the way he does it is as follows. He con-ceals himfelf amongft the canes or reeds, in fuch manner, that nothing is to be feen, befides his weapon, which he holds raifed perpendicularly above the furface of the water. The fowl which come to take reft imagining this weapon to be only a wither-ed reed, make no fcruple of perching upon it. They are no fooner alighted than the fifh opens his throat, and fo fuddenly makes at his prey, that it rarely efcapes him. The teeth which are placed on the fides of the bone, which he ufes fo dexteroufly, are pretty long and very fharp. The Indians pre-tend they are a fovereign remedy againft the tooth-ach, and that by pricking the part moft affected with one of thefe teeth the pain vanifhes that in-ftant.

Thefe people have a wonderful addrefs in dart-ing fifhes under water, efpecially in rapid currents. They alfo fifh with the bofom net, and prepare themfelves for it by a ceremony fingular enough. Before they ufe this net they marry it to two girls
who

who are virgins, and during the marriage-feaſt, place it between the two brides; they afterwards exhort it to catch plenty of fiſh, and believe they do a great deal to obtain this favour, by making large preſents to the ſham fathers-in-law.

The ſturgeon of this country is both a freſh and ſalt-water fiſh; for it is caught on the coaſts of Canada, and in the great lakes croſs which the river St Lawrence runs. Many believe this to be the true dolphin of the antients; if this is true, it was but fit the king of fiſhes ſhould reign both in the rivers and ocean. Be this as it will, we ſee here ſturgeons of from eight to ten, and twelve feet long, and of a proportionable thickneſs. This animal has on its head a ſort of crown about an inch high, and is covered with ſcales half a foot diameter, almoſt oval, and with ſmall figures on them, pretty much like the lily in the arms of France. The following is the way the Indians fiſh for them in the lakes. Two men place themſelves in the two extremities of a canoe; the next the ſtern ſteers, the other ſtanding up holding a dart to which is tied a long cord, the other extremity whereof is faſtened to one of the croſs timbers of the canoe. The moment he ſees the ſturgeon within reach of him, he lances his dart at him, and endeavours, as much as poſſible, to hit in the place that is without ſcales. If the fiſh happens to be wounded, he flies and draws the canoe after him with extreme velocity; but after he has ſwam the diſtance of an hundred and fifty paces or thereabouts, he dies, and then, they draw up the line and take him. There is a ſmall ſort of ſturgeon, the fleſh of which is exceeding tender, and prodigious delicate.

The

The river St. Lawrence breeds feveral fifhes, altogether unknown in France. Thofe moft efteemed are the *Achigau* and the *Gilthead*. The other rivers of Canada, and efpecially thofe of Acadia, are equally well provided with this river, perhaps, the moft plentifully ftocked with fifh in the whole world, and in which there is the greateft variety of different and thofe the beft forts.

There are fome feafons in which the fifhes in this river are alone capable of fuftaining the whole colony. But I am utterly at a lofs, what degree of credit ought to be given to what I have read in a manufcript relation of an ancient miffionary, who afferts, his having feen a Homme marin, or mermaid in the river Sorel, three leagues below Chambly ; this relation is wrote with abundance of judgment ; but in order to ftate the matter of fact, and to prove that he has not been deceived by a falfe and hafty appearance, the author ought to have added to his account a defcription of this monfter. People have often at firft look apprehended they faw the appearance of fomething, which vanifhes on the careful fcrutiny of a fage eye. Befides, had this fifh fo refembling a human creature come from the fea, he muft have made a long voyage before he got up as high as near Chambly, and it muft have been extraordinary enough he was never feen till he arrived at this fortrefs.

The forefts of Canada are far from being as well peopled with birds, as our lakes and rivers are with fifhes. There are fome, however, which are not without their merit, and which are even peculiar to the Americans. We find here eagles of two forts ; the largeft have the head and neck almoft quite white ; they give chace to the hares and rabbits, take
them

them in their talons, and carry them to their nests
and airies. The reft are entirely grey, and only
make war on birds. They are all excellent fifhers.
The falcon, the gofs-hawk, and taffel, are abfolutely the fame with thofe of Europe; but we have
here a fecond fort of them, which live folely by
fifhing.

Our partridges are of three forts; the grey, red,
and black partridge. The laft are the leaft efteemed; they favour too much of the grape, juniper,
and fir-tree. They have the head and eyes of a
pheafant, and their flefh is brown; they have all
long tails, which they fpread like a fan, or like the
tail of a turkey-cock. Thefe tails are exceeding
beautiful; fome of them are a mixture of grey,
red, and brown; others are that of a light and dark
brown. I faid the black partridge was not efteemed; fome there are, however, who prefer them
even to the red fort; they are all bigger than ours
in France, but fo ftupidly foolifh as to fuffer themfelves to be fhot, and even to let you come near
them, almoft without ftirring.

Befides fnipes which are excellent in this country,
and fmall water-game, which is every where in great
plenty, you meet with fome woodcocks about
fpring, but thofe in no great numbers. In the
country of the Illinois, and all over the fouthern
parts of New France, they are more common. M.
Denys afferts, that the raven of Canada is as good
eating as a pullet. This may be true on the coafts
of Acadia; but I don't find people of this opinion
in thefe parts; they are larger than in France, fomething blacker, and have a different cry from ours.
The ofpray, on the contrary is fmaller, and their
cry not fo difagreeable. The owl of Canada has no
diffe-

difference from that of France, but a fmall ring of white round the neck, and a particular kind of cry. Its flefh is good eating, and many prefer it to that of a pullet. In winter, its provifions are field mice, the legs of which he breaks, feeds carefully, and fattens till he wants them. The bat here is larger than that of France. The blackbird and fwallow are in this country birds of paffage, as in Europe ; the former are not a deep black, but inclining to red. We have three forts of larks the fmalleft of which are like fparrows. This laft is little different from ours ; he has quite the fame inclinations, but his mien is very indifferent.

There are in this country vaft multitudes of wild-ducks, of which I have heard reckoned to the number of two and twenty different fpecies. The moft beautiful and the moft delicate eating are thofe called *Canaras Branchus*, or bough wild ducks, from their perching on the boughs of trees. Their plumage is extreamly variegated, and very brilliant. Swans, turkey-cocks, water-hens, cranes, teale, geefe, buftards, and other large water-fowl, fwarm every where, except near our habitations, which they never approach. We have cranes of two colours ; fome quite white, and others of a light grey. They all make excellent foop. Our woodpecker is an animal of extreme beauty ; there are fome of all manner of colours, and others quite black, or of a dark brown all over the body, except the head and neck, which are of a beautiful red.

The thrufh of Canada is much the fame with that of France as to fhape, but has only one half his mufick ; the wren has robbed him of the other half. The goldfinch has the head lefs beautiful than that of France, and its plumage is a mixture of
black

black and yellow. As I have never feen any of
them in a cage, I can fay nothing of his fong.
All our woods are full of a bird of the fize of a
linnet, which is quite yellow, and has a delightful
pipe; his fong, however, is but fhort, and without
variety. This has no name to diftinguifh it, but
that of its colour. A fort of ortolan, the plumage
of which is of an afh-colour on the back, and white
under the belly, and which is called the *white-bird*,
is, of all the guefts in our forefts the beft fongfter.
This yields not to the nightingale of France, but
the male only is overheard to fing; the female
which is of a deeper colour, utters not a fingle
note even in a cage; this fmall animal is of a very
beautiful mien, and well deferves the name of ortolan for its flavour. I know not whither he bends
his courfe in the winter; but he is always the firft
to return, and to proclaim the approach of the
fpring. The fnow is fcarce melted in fome parts,
when they flock thither in great numbers, and then
you may take as many of them as you pleafe.

You muft travel a hundred leagues to the fouthward of this place before you meet with any of the
birds called cardinals. There are fome in Paris
which have been brought thither from Louifiana,
and I think they might thrive in France, could
they breed like the canary bird; the fweetnefs of
their fong, the brilliancy of their plumage, which
is of a fhining fcarlet incarnate; the little tuft on
their heads, and which is no bad refemblance of
the crowns the painters give to Indian and American kings, feem to promife them the empire of the
airy tribe; they have, however, a rival in this
country, who would even have the unanimous voice
of every one, were his pipe as grateful to the ear as
his outward appearance is to the fight; this is
what

what is called in this country *l'Oiſeau Mouche*, or the Fly-bird.

This name has two derivations; the firſt is that of the ſmallneſs of the animal; for with all its plumage, its volume is no larger than that of an ordinary May-bug. The ſecond is a loud ſort of humming noiſe, which he makes with his wings, and which is not unlike that of a large fly; its legs which are about an inch long are like two needles; his bill is of the ſame thickneſs, and from it he ſends forth a ſmall ſting, with which he pierces the flowers, in order to extract the ſap, which is his nouriſhment. The female has nothing ſtriking in her appearance, is of a tolerable agreeable white under the belly, and of a bright grey all over the reſt of the body; but the male is a perfect jewel, he has on the crown of his head a ſmall tuft of the moſt beautiful black, the breaſt red, the belly white, the back, wings, and tail of a green, like that of the leaves of the roſe-buſh; ſpecks of gold, ſcattered all over the plumage, add a prodigious *eclat* to it, and an imperceptible down produces on it the moſt delightful ſhadings that can poſſibly be ſeen.

Some travellers have confounded this bird with the *Coliby*; and in fact, this bird ſeems to be a ſpecies of it. But the coliby of the iſlands is ſomething bigger, has not ſo much livelineſs of colour in his plumage, and his bill is a little bent downwards. I might, however, be miſtaken with regard to the brightneſs and luſtre of his plumage, as I never ſaw any of them alive : ſome affirm he has a melodious pipe; if this is true, he has a great advantage over the oiſeau mouche, which no one

Q
has

has as yet ever heard to fing; but I myfelf have heard a female one whiftle notes exceeding fhrill and difagreeable. This bird has an extremely ftrong and an amazingly rapid flight; you behold him on fome flower, and in a moment he will dart upwards into the air almoft perpendicularly; it is an enemy to the raven, and a dangerous one too. I have heard a man worthy of credit affirm, that he has feen one boldly quit a flower he was fucking, lance himfelf upwards into the air like lightning, get under the wing of a raven that lay motionlefs on his extended wings at a vaft height, pierce it with his his fting, and make him tumble down dead, either of his fall or the wound he had received.

The oifeau mouche felects fuch flowers as are of the ftrongeft fcent, and fucks them, always hopping about at the fame time; he, however, alights now and then to reft himfelf when we have an opportunity of beholding him at our leifure. Some of them have been kept for fome time, by feeding them with fugar-water and flowers; I formerly kept one of them for twenty-four hours; he fuffered himfelf to be taken and handled, and counterfeited himfelf dead; the moment I let him go, he flew away, and continued fluttering about my window. I made a prefent of him to a friend, who found him dead the next morning, and that very night there was a little froft. Thus thefe diminutive animals are extremely watchful to prevent the firft advent of cold weather.

There is great reafon to think, that they retire to Carolina, where we are affured they are never feen but in winter; they make their nefts in Canada, where they fufpend them on the branch of fome

tree

tree, and turn them towards such an expofure, that they are fheltered from all the injuries of the air and weather. Nothing can be neater than thefe nefts. The foundation confifts of tiny bits of wood interwoven bafket-wife, and the infide is lined with I don't know what fort of down, which feems to be filk; their eggs are of the fize of a pea, with yellow fpots on a black ground. Their common litter is faid to be three and fometimes five.

Amongft the reptiles of this country, I know of none as yet but the rattle fnake, that merits the leaft attention. There are fome of them as thick as a man's leg, and fometimes thicker, and long in proportion; but there are others, and thofe I believe the greater number, which are neither longer nor thicker than our largeft fnakes of France; their figure is abundantly odd; on a neck, which is flat and very broad, they have but a fmall head. Their colour is lively without being dazzling, and a pale yellow, with very beautiful fhades, is the colour which predominates.

But the moft remarkable part of this animal is its tail; this is fcaly like a coat of mail, fomewhat flattifh, and it grows, fay they, every year a row of fcales; thus its age may be known by its tail, as that of a horfe is by his teeth; when he ftirs he makes the fame noife with his tail as the grafhopper does when he leaps or flies; for your Grace, no doubt knows, that the pretended mufick of the grafhopper is no more than the noife of his wings. Moreover, the refemblance I fpeak of is fo perfect, that I have been deceived with it myfelf. It is from this noife, this fort of ferpent has obtained the name it bears.

Q 2

Its

Its bite is mortal, if the remedy be not applied immediately, but Providence has provided againſt this misfortune. In all places where this dangerous reptile is found, there grows an herb, called the rattle-ſnake plant, *Herbe a ſerpent a ſonettes,* the root of which is a never-failing antidote againſt the venom of this animal. You have only to bray or chew it, and to apply it in the nature of a plaiſter upon the wound. This plant is beautiful and eaſily known. Its ſtem is round, and ſomewhat thicker than a gooſe quill, riſes to the height of three or our feet, and terminates in a yellow flower of the igure and ſize of a ſingle daiſy ; this flower has a very ſweet ſcent, the leaves of the plant are oval, narrow, ſuſtained, five and five, in form of a turkey cock's foot, by a pedicle, or foot-ſtalk an inch long.

The rattle-ſnake rarely attacks any paſſenger who gives him no provocation. I had one juſt at my foot, which was certainly more afraid than I was, for I did not perceive him till he was flying. But ſhould you tread on him you are ſure to be bitten, and if you purſue him, if he has ever ſo little time to recover himſelf, he folds himſelf up in a circle with his head in the middle, and darts himſelf with great force againſt his enemy. The Indians, how-ever, give chace to him, and eſteem his fleſh ex-cellent. I have even heard Frenchmen, who had eaten of it, ſay, that it was no bad eating ; but they were travellers, a ſort of cattle who hold every thing excellent, being often expoſed to be extreme hungry. It is, however, for certain, abundantly innocent food.

I don't

I don't know, Madam, whither I ought to entertain you with an account of the forefts of Canada. We are here furrounded with the vafteft woods in the whole world; in all appearance, they are as ancient as the world itfelf, and were never planted by the hand of man. Nothing can prefent a nobler or more magnificent profpect to the eyes, the trees hide their tops in the clouds, and the variety of different fpecies of them is fo prodigious, that even amongft all thofe who have moft applied themfelves to the knowledge of them, there is not perhaps one who is not ignorant of at leaft one half of them. As to their quality, and the ufes to which they may be applied, their fentiments are fo different, both in the country in which we now are, as well as in that where your grace is, that I defpair of being ever able to give you the information I could defire on this head. At prefent, at leaft I ought to confine myfelf to fome obfervations on what I have myfelf feen, and on what I have heard people who have more experience fay, and who are greater adepts in this fcience.

What moft ftruck my eyes on my firft arrival in this country, was, the pines, fir-trees, and cedars, which are of a height and thicknefs perfectly aftonifhing. There are two forts of pines in this country, all of them yielding a refinous fubftance very fit for making pitch and tar. The white pines, at leaft fome of them, fhoot out at the upper extremity a kind of mufhroom, which the inhabitants call Guarigûe, and which the Indians ufe with fuccefs againft diforders in the breaft and in the dyfentery. The red pines are more gummy and heavier, but do not grow to fuch a thicknefs. The lands which produce both are not the moft proper

for

for bearing of corn ; they are generally a mixture of gravel, sand, and clay.

There are four sorts of fir-trees in Canada ; the first resembles ours ; the three others are the Epinette Blanche, and Epinette Rouge, or the White and Red Prickly firs, and that called *la Peruffe*. The second and fourth sorts rife to a vast height, and are excellent for masts, especially the white prickly sort, which are also extremely fit for carpenter's work. This grows generally in moist, and black lands, but which after being drained, are fit for bearing all sorts of grain. Its bark is smooth and shining, and there grows on it a kind of small blisters of the size of kidney-beans, which contain a kind of turpentine, which is sovereign in wounds, which it cures speedily, and even in fractures. We are assured that it cures fevers, and pains in the breast and stomach ; the way to use it is to put two drops of it in some broth. This is what is called in Paris *White Balsam*.

The epinette rouge has scarce any resemblance to the epinette blanche. Its wood is heavy, and may be of good use in ship-building, and in carpenter's work. The lands where it grows are a mixture of gravel and clay. The peruffe is gummy, but yields not a quantity sufficient to be made use of ; its wood remains long in the ground without rotting, which renders it extremely fit for paling or inclosures. The bark is excellent for tanners, and the Indians make a dye of it, resembling that of a turky-blue. Most of the lands where this tree grows are clayey ; I have, however, seen some very thick ones in sandy-grounds, though perhaps there was clay under the sand.

The

The cedar is of two forts, the white and the red ;
the former are the thickeft of the two ; of thefe are
made palings, and this too is the wood moft commonly
made ufe of for fhingles, on account of its light-
nefs. There diftills a fort of incenfe from it, but
it is without any fruit like thofe of Mount Liba-
nus. The red cedar is fhorter and thinner in proportion. The moft fenfible difference between
them, is, that all the odour of the former is in the
leaves, and that of the fecond in its wood ; but
the latter is the more agreeable flavour. The
cedar, at leaft the white fort grows only in good
ground.

There are all over Canada two forts of oaks,
diftinguifhed by the names of the white and red
oaks. The firft are often found in lands which are
low, fwampy, fertile, and proper for producing
corn and legumes. The red, the wood of which
is the leaft efteemed, grow in dry fandy lands, both
of them bear acorns. The maple is likewife very
common in Canada, is very large and is made into
good furniture ; this grows on high grounds, and
fuch as are fit for bearing fruit-trees, which they
call *Rhene.* Here is the female maple, the wood
of which is ftreaked and clouded very much, but is
paler than the male ; befides it has all its qualities
as well as its colour ; but it muft have a moift and
rich foil.

The cherry-tree, which is found promifcuoufly
amongft the maple and white wood-trees, is very
fit for making furniture ; it yields a much greater
quantity of juice than the maple, but this is bitter
and the fugar made of it never lofes this quality.
The Indians ufe its bark againft certain difeafes,

Q 4   which

which are incident to women. There are in Canada, three forts of afh-trees; the free, the mongrel, and the baftard. The firft grows among maples is fit for carpenter's work, and for ftaves for dry ware cafks. The fecond has the fame qualities, and like the baftard, will grow only in low and good lands.

They reckon alfo in this country three forts of walnut-trees, the hard, the foft, and a third fort which has a very thin bark. The hard fort bears a very fmall walnut, good to eat, but very coftive. The wood is only fit for fire-wood. The tender, bears a long fruit, as large as thofe in France, but the fhell is very hard. The kernels of them are excellent. The wood is not fo pretty as ours; but to make amends it is almoft incorruptible in water, or in the ground, and is difficult to confume in the fire. The third produces a nut of the fame fize with the firft, but in greater quantity, and which is bitter, and inclofed in a very tender hufk; they make excellent oil of it. This tree yields a fweeter fap than that of the maple, but in a fmall quantity. This grows only, as doth the foft walnut tree, in the beft lands.

The beech is here fo plentiful, that whole tracts are covered with them; I have feen them growing on fandy hills, and in exceeding fertile low lands. They bear great quantities of nuts, from which it would be an eafy matter to extract an oil. The bears make this their principal nourifhment, as do alfo the partridges. The wood of it is exceeding tender, and very fit for oars and for fhallops. But thofe of canoes are made of maple. The tree called white-wood, which grows amongft maples, and

the

the cherry-tree is exceeding plentiful. Thefe trees grow to a great thicknefs and very ftrait ; very good planks and boards may be made of them, and even ftaves for dry ware cafks. It is foft and eafily worked; the Indians peel off the bark of this tree to cover their cabins.

Elms are very plenty all over this country. There are white and red elms ; the wood of this tree is difficult to work but lafts longeft. The bark of the red elm is that of which the Iroquois make their canoes. Some of them which are made of one fingle piece, will contain twenty perfons ; fome of them are likewife hollow, and to thefe the bears and wild cats retire in the month of November, and remain till April. The poplar grows commonly on the banks of rivers and on the fea-fhore.

In the thickeft woods are found great numbers of prune or plumb-trees, loaden with a very four fruit. The vinage-tree is a very pithy fhrub, which produces a four cluftering fruit, of the colour of bullock's blood ; they caufe infufe it in water, and make a fort of vinegar of it. The *Pemime*, is another fhrub growing along rivulets, and in meadows ; it bears alfo a cluftering fruit yielding a red and very aftringent liquor. There are three forts of goofeberry trees in this country ; thefe are the fame with thofe of France. The *Bluet* grows here as in Europe in woods. This fruit is a fovereign and fpeedy cure for the dyfentery. The Indians dry them as we do cherries in France.

The *Atoca* is a ftone-fruit of the fize of a cherry. This plant which creeps along the ground in fwamps, pro-

produces its fruit in water; this fruit is sharp, and is made into a confection. The white-thorn is found along rivulets, and produces a quantity of fruit with a treble kernel; this is the food of several wild beasts. What they call here the cotton-tree, is a plant which sprouts like asparagus, to the heighth of about three feet, and at the end grow several tufts of flowers. In the morning before the dew has fallen off, they shake the flowers, and there falls from it, with the humidity, a kind of honey, which by boiling is reduced to a kind of sugar. The seed is formed in a sort of pod, which contains a kind of very fine cotton.

The *soleil* is another very common plant in the fields of the Indians, and which rises to the height of seven or eight feet. Its flower, which is very thick has much the same figure with that of the marigold, and the seed is disposed in the same manner; the Indians extract an oil from it by boiling, with which they anoint their hair. The legumes they cultivate most, are, Maize, or Turkey-corn, French-beans, gourds, and melons. They have a sort of gourds smaller than ours, and which taste much of sugar; they boil them whole in water, or roast them under the ashes, and so eat them without any other preparation.

The Indians were acquainted before our arrival in their country with the common and water melon. The former are as good as those in France, especially in this island, where they are in great plenty. The hop-plant and capilaire are likewise the natural produce of Canada; but the latter grows to a much greater height, and is infinitely better than in France. I now finish a letter, by
which

which you may eafily difcover a traveller, **rambling** over the forefts and plains of Canada, and who **is** diverted with every thing which prefents itfelf **to** his view. But what could you expect from one who travels through fuch a country as this is.

I am, &c.

LETTER

L E T T E R X.

Of the caufes of the exceffive cold in Canada. *Of the refources it affords for the fupport of life. The character of the* French Canadians.

Montreal, April 22d, 1721.

Madam,

IT is furprifing, that in France, where they fo often meet with perfons who have fpent great part of their lives in Canada, they fhould have fo imperfect a notion of the country. This undoubtedly proceeds from this, that the greateft number of thofe, to whom they apply for information, are acquainted only with its bad fide. The winter commonly begins before the veffels fet fail in order to return to France, and always in fuch a manner as to aftonifh every one except the natives of the place. The firft frofts in a few days fill the rivers with ice, and the earth is foon covered with fnow, which continues for fix months, and is always fix feet deep in places not expofed to the wind.

It is true there is no want of wood to guard againft the cold, which very foon becomes extreme, and encroaches greatly on the fpring : but it is, however, fomething extremely fhocking, not to be able to stir out of doors without being frozen, at least, without being wrapt up in furs like a bear. Moreover, what a spectacle is it to behold one continued tract of snow, which pains the sight, and hides from your view all the beauties of nature ? No more difference between the rivers and fields; no more variety, even the trees are covered with snowfrost, with large icicles depending from all their branches, under which you cannot pass with safety. What can a man think who sees the horses with beards of ice more than a foot long, and who can travel in a country, where, for the space of six months, the bears themselves dare not shew their faces to the weather ? Thus I have never passed a winter in this country without seeing some one or other carried to the hospital, and who was obliged to have his legs or arms cut off on account of their being benumbed and frozen. In a word, if the sky is clear, the wind which blows from the west is intolerably piercing. If it turns to the south or east, the weather becomes a little more moderate, but so thick a snow falls, that there is no seeing ten paces before you, even at noon-day. On the other hand, if a compleat thaw comes on, farewel to the yearly stock of capons, quarters of beef and mutton, poultry and fish, which they had laid up in granaries, depending on the continuance of the frost ; so that in spite of the excessive severity of the cold, people are reduced to the necessity of wishing for its continuance.

It is in vain to say that the winters are not now as severe as they were four and twenty years ago, and that in all probability they will become still milder in the sequel: the sufferings of those who have gone before us, and the happiness of such as may come after us, are no remedies against a present evil, under

der which we ourfelves labour. What comfort would it have been to a Creole of Martinico, who had arrived in France for the firft time during the hard froft in 1709, fhould I, who had juft then returned from Quebec, have told him that the cold he now felt was ftill inferior to that of Canada? I fhould however have told him truth, and could have fupported it by good evidences; but he might very well have anfwered me, that he found the cold in France not a whit the lefs piercing, by being informed it was ftill more fo in Canada.

But as foon as the month of May begins, we have reafon to change our language, the mildnefs of this latter part of the fpring being by fo much the more agreeable, as it fucceeds fo rigorous a feafon. The heat of the fummer, which in lefs than four months, fhews us both the feed and the crop *, the ferenity of autumn, during which there is a feries of fine weather, very feldom to be feen, in the greateft part of the provinces of France: all which, joined to the liberty which is enjoyed in this country, makes many find their ftay here as agreeable as in the kingdom where they were born, and it is certain that our Canadians would without hefitation give it the preference.

After all, thefe colds fo long and fo fevere, are attended with inconveniencies which can never thoroughly be remedied. I reckon in the firft place the difficulty of feeding the cattle, which during the

---

* The ground is tilled in Autumn, and the feed fown between the middle of April and the tenth of May. The crop is cut down between the 15th of Auguft and 20th of September. The lands which are not tilled till the Spring yield fmaller crops, becaufe the nitrous particles of the fnow are not fo well able to penetrate into them.

whole winter feafon can find nothing in the fields, and confequently the preferving them muft be extremely expenfive, while their flefh, after being kept fix months on dry food, muft have loft almoft all its relifh. Corn is alfo neceffary for the poultry, and great care muft be taken to keep them alive during fo long a time. If to avoid expence all thofe beafts are killed about the end of October, which are intended for confumption before the month of May, you may eafily judge how infipid this fort of victuals muft be; and from the manner in which they catch fifh through the ice, it appears this cannot be very plentiful, befides its being frozen from the very firft, fo that it is almoft impoffible to have it frefh in the feafon when it is moft wanted. Were it not for the cod-fifh and eels there would hardly be any fuch thing as keeping Lent; with refpect to butter and frefh eggs there can be no queftion, nor indeed is much more account to be made of garden-ftuff, which is kept as well as may be in the cellars, but lofes almoft all its virtue after it has been there for fome months.

Add to this, that excepting apples, which are of an excellent quality, and fmall fummer fruit which does not keep, the fruits natural to France have not as yet fucceeded in Canada. Thefe, Madam, are all the difadvantages occafioned by this exceffive cold feafon. We are, notwithftanding, as near the fun as in the moft fourthern provinces of France, and the farther you advance into the colony, you ftill approach the nearer to it. Whence then can arife this difference of temperatures under the fame parallels of latitude? This is a queftion, which in my opinion no one has as yet anfwered in a fatisfactory manner.

Moft

Moſt authors who have handled this matter are contented with ſaying that this long and ſevere cold is occaſioned by the ſnow lying ſo long on the ground, that it is not poſſible it can ever be thoroughly warmed, eſpecially in places under cover: But this anſwer removes the difficulty only one ſtep; for it may be aſked what produces this great quantity of ſnow in climates as warm as Languedoc and Provence, and in countries at a much greater diſtance from the mountains.

The Sieur Denys, whom I have already quoted oftner than once, affirms that the trees reſume their verdure before the ſun is ſufficiently elevated above the horizon to melt the ſnow or warm the earth; this may be true in Acadia, and over all the ſea coaſt, but it is certain that every where elſe the ſnow is melted in the thickeſt foreſts before there is a ſingle leaf upon the trees. This author ſeems to have no better authority for ſaying that the ſnow melts rather by the heat of the earth than that of the air, and that it always begins to melt from below: but will he perſuade any man that the earth when covered with frozen water, is warmer than the air, which immediately receives the rays of the ſun. Beſides, this is no anſwer to the queſtion about the cauſe of that deluge of ſnow which overwhelms this immenſe country ſituated in the middle of the temperate zone.

There is no queſtion but that generally ſpeaking the mountains, foreſts, and lakes contribute greatly to it, but it appears to me that we ought to ſeek out for other cauſes beſides. Father Joſeph Bretani, an Italian Jeſuit, who ſpent the beſt part of his life-time in Canada, has left behind him in his own language, an account of New France, wherein he en-

deavours

deavours to clear up this point of natural philoſophy. He will not allow that the cold, the cauſes of which we are enquiring into, ought to be attributed to any of thoſe juſt mentioned, but methinks he goes too far ; for no reply can be made to experience, which convinces us of the decreaſe of the cold, according as the country is cleared, tho' that may not happen in the proportion it ought, were the thickneſs of the woods its principal cauſe.

He himſelf confeſſes that it is no rare thing to ſee a froſty night ſucceed a very hot ſummer day ; but this way of reaſoning appears to me to furniſh an argument againſt himſelf; for how can this phœnomenon be explained otherwiſe than by ſaying that the ſun having opened the pores of the earth in the day time, the humidity which was ſtill contained in it, the nitrous particles which the ſnow had left behind it in quantities, and the heat which an air equally ſubtle with that in this country ſtill preſerves after ſun-ſet, all together form theſe gentle froſts in the ſame manner as we make ice upon the fire. Beſides, the humidity of the earth has evidently a large ſhore in the exceſſive colds of this climate ; but whence could this humidity proceed in a country, the ſoil of which has for the moſt a great mixture of ſand in it, if it was not from the number and extent of its lakes and rivers, the thickneſs of its foreſts, its mountains covered with ſnow, which as it melts overflows the plains, and the winds which carry the exhalations every where along with them.

But ſhould Father Bretani be miſtaken, as I believe he is, when he excludes all thoſe from being the cauſes of the exceſſive cold in Canada, yet what he ſubſtitutes in their room ſeems, in my opinion, to contribute greatly to it. There are, fays he, hu-mid foils in the warmeft climates, and very dry foils in the coldeft; but a certain mixture of wet and dry forms ice and fnow, the quantity of which deter-mines the degree and duration of cold. Now, who-ever has travelled ever fo little in Canada muft be fenfible that this mixture obtains there in a very re-markable manner. There is undoubtedly no coun-try in the world which abounds more with water, and there are few which have a greater mixture of ftones and fand. With all this it rains very feldom, and the air is extremely pure and wholefome, an e-vident proof of the natural drynefs of the foil. In effect, Father Bretani tells us, that during the fix-teen years he was employed as miffionary in the country of the Hurons, there were there at the fame time to the number of fixty French, feveral of whom were of a very delicate complexion, all of them had been very ill fed, and had befides endured hardfhips beyond what could be imagined, and yet that not one of that number had died.

It is true, this prodigious number of rivers and lakes, which take up as much fpace in new France as one half the continent of Europe, ought to fur-nifh the air with a continual fupply of frefh vapours, but befides that the greateft part of thefe waters are extremely clear, and upon a fandy bottom, their great and continual agitation by blunting the effi-cacy of the fun's rays, prevents vapours from being exhaled in great quantities, or foon caufes them to fall again in mifts. For the winds raife as frequent and violent tempefts upon thefe frefh-water feas as upon the ocean, which is likewife the true reafon why it rains fo feldom at fea.

The

The fecond caufe of the extreme cold of Canada, according to father Bretani, is the neighbourhood of the North Sea, covered with enormous iflands of ice for more than eight months of the year, there, Madam, you may call to mind what I told you in my fecond letter, of the cold we felt even in the dog-days, from the neighbourhood of one of thefe iflands of ice, or rather from the wind which blew upon us from that fide on which it lay, and which ceafed that moment it fell to the leeward of us. It is, befides, certain that it never fnows here but with a north-eaft wind, which blows from that quarter in which the northern ice lyes; and tho' the cold is not fo very piercing when the fnow falls, yet it cannot be doubted that it greatly contributes to render the weft and north-weft winds fo extremely fharp, which before they reach us blow over immenfe countries, and a great chain of mountains entirely covered with it.

Laftly, if we believe the Italian miffionary, the height of the land is not the leaft caufe of the fubtility of the air of this country, and confequently of the feverity of its cold. Father Bretani endeavours to prove this height of the land from the depth of the fea, which encreafes according to him in proportion as you approach Canada, and from the number and height of the falls fo frequent in the rivers. But in my opinion the depth of the fea abfolutely proves nothing, and the falls of St. Lawrence and fome other rivers in New France, no more than the cataracts of the Nile. Moreover, it is not obferved that, from Montreal where the falls commence to the fea, the river St. Lawrence is much more rapid than fome of our rivers in Europe. I am therefore of opinion that we muft confine our reafoning to the ices of the north; and that

even

even notwithftanding this, if Canada were as well cleared and as populous as France, the winters would become much fhorter and lefs fevere. They would not however be always fo mild as in France, on account of the ferenity and purenefs of the air ; for it is certain that in the winter feafon every thing elfe being equal, the froft is always fharper when the fky is clear, and the fun has rarified the air.

After winter is paft, fifhing and hunting fupply thofe who will take the trouble with provifions in abundance; befides the fifh and the game which I have already fpoken of, the river St. Lawrence and the forefts furnifh the inhabitants with two articles, which are a great refource to them. From Quebec as high as Trois Rivieres, a prodigious quantity of large eels are caught in the river, which eels come down from Lake Ontario, where they are bred in the marfhes on the north fide of the Lake, and meeting, as I have already obferved, with the white porpoifes which give them chace, the greateft part endeavour to return back, which is the reafon of their being taken in fuch numbers. This fifhery is carried on in the following manner.

Thro' that whole extent of ground, which is co-vered at high water, but left dry during the ebb, boxes are fet at convenient diftances, which are fup-ported by a pallifade of ofier hurdles, contrived in fuch a manner that no free paffage is left for the eels. Large cafting nets of the fame materials and ftructure are fixed by the narroweft end in thefe boxes, while the other extremity, which is very wide, is backed againft the hurdles, upon which green branches are placed at intervals. When all is covered by the tide, the eels which love to be near the banks, and are attracted by the verdure, gather

in

in great numbers along the pallifade, go in to the nets, which lead them into the prifons prepared for them, fo that all the boxes are often filled in the fpace of one tide.

Thefe eels are larger than ours, and yield a great deal of oil. I have already obferved that with whatever fauce they are dreffed, they ftill retain a difagreeable relifh, to which people cannot eafily accuftom themfelves. This perhaps is the fault of our cooks. All their bones terminate in a point fomewhat crooked, which I do not remember to have feen in thofe of France. The beft method of preparing this fifh, is to hang them up in a chimney, and fuffer them to fry flowly in their fkins, which come off of themfelves, and all the oil runs out. As great quantities of them are taken during the time this fifhery lafts, they are falted and barreled up like herrings.

The other article I mentioned, is a fort of woodpigeon, which ufed to come hither in the months of May and June, as was faid, in fuch numbers as to darken the air, but the cafe is different at prefent. Neverthelefs, a very great number ftill come to reft themfelves upon the trees, even in the neighbourhood of the towns. They are commonly called turtles, and differ from the wood and other pigeons in Europe, fufficiently to conftitute a fourth fpecies. They are fmaller than our largeft pigeons, and have the fame eyes and changing fhadows upon their necks. Their plumage is a dark brown, excepting their wings, in which there are fome feathers of a very fine blue.

Thefe birds may be faid to feek only an opportunity of being killed, for if there is a naked branch
upon

upon a tree, on that they chufe to perch, and fit in
fuch a manner, that the moft inexperienced gunner
can hardly fail of bringing down at leaft half a dozen at a fingle fhot.   Means have likewife been
found of catching many of them alive; they are fed
till the firft fetting in of the frofts, then killed, and
thrown into the ftore-room, where they are preferved all the winter.

Thus it appears, Madam, that every one here is
poffeffed of the neceffaries of life; but there is little
paid to the King; the inhabitant is not acquainted
with taxes; bread is cheap; fifh and flefh are not
dear; but wine, ftuffs, and all French commodities
are very expenfive.   Gentlemen, and thofe officers
who have nothing but their pay, and are befides
encumbered with families, have the greateft reafon
to complaim.   The women have a great deal of fpirit and good nature, are extremely agreeable, and
excellent breeders; and thefe good qualities are for
the moft part all the fortune they bring their hufbands; but God has bleffed the marriages in this
country in the fame manner he formerly bleffed
thofe of the Patriarchs.   In order to fupport fuch
numerous families, they ought likewife to lead the
lives of Patriarchs, but the time for this is paft.
There are a greater number of nobleffe in New
France than in all the other colonies put together.

The king maintains here eight and twenty companies of marines, and three etats majors.   Many
families have been ennobled here, and there ftill remain feveral officers of the regiment of Corignan-
Salieres, who have peopled this country with gentlemen who are not in extraordinary good circumftances, and would be ftill lefs fo, were not commerce

allowed

allowed them, and the right of hunting and fishing, which is common to every one.

After all, it is a little their own fault if they are ever exposed to want; the land is good almost every where, and agriculture does not in the least derogate from their quality. How many gentlemen throughout all our provinces would envy the lot of the simple inhabitants of Canada, did they but know it? And can those who languish here in a shameful indigence, be excused for refusing to embrace a profession, which the corruption of manners and the most salutary maxims has alone degraded from its ancient dignity? There is not in the world a more wholesome climate than this; no particular distemper is epidemical here, the fields and woods are full of simples of a wonderful efficacy, and the trees distill balms of an excellent quality. These advantages ought at least to engage those whose birth providence has cast in this country to remain in it; but inconstancy, aversion to a regular and assiduous labour, and a spirit of independence, have ever carried a great many young people out of it, and prevented the colony from being peopled.

These, Madam, are the defects with which the French Canadians are, with the greatest justice, reproached. The same may likewise be said of the Indians. One would imagine that the air they breathe in this immense continent contributes to it; but the example and frequent intercourse with its natural inhabitants are more than sufficient to constitute this character. Our Creoles are likewise accused of great avidity in amassing, and indeed they do things with this view, which could hardly be believed if they were not seen. The journeys they undertake; the fatigues they undergo; the dangers to which

which they expofe themfelves, and the efforts they make, furpafs all imagination. There are however few lefs interefted, who diffipate with greater facility what has coft them fo much pains to acquire, or who teftify lefs regret at having loft it. Thus there is fome room to imagine that they commonly undertake fuch painful and dangerous journeys out of a tafte they have contracted for them. They love to breathe a free air, they are early accuftomed to a wandering life ; it has charms for them, which make them forget paft dangers and fatigues, and they place their glory in encountering them often. They have a great deal of wit, efpecially the fair fex, in whom it is brilliant and eafy ; they are, befides, conftant and refolute, fertile in refources, courageous, and capable of managing the greateft affairs. You, Madam, are acquainted with more than one of this character, and have often declared your furprife at it to me. I can affure you fuch are frequent in this country, and are to be found in all ranks and conditions of life.

I know not whether I ought to reckon amongft the defects of our Canadians the good opinion they entertain of themfelves. It is at leaft certain that it infpires them with a confidence, which leads them to undertake and execute what would appear impoffible to many others. It muft however be confeffed they have excellent qualities. There is not a province in the kingdom where the people have a finer complexion, a more advantageous ftature, or a body better proportioned. The ftrength of their conftitution is not always anfwerable, and if the Canadians live to any age, they foon look old and decrepid. This is not entirely their own fault; it is likewife that of their parents, who are not fufficiently watchful over their children to prevent their ruining

their

their health at a time of life, when if it fuffers it is feldom or never recovered. Their agility and addrefs are unequalled ; the moft expert Indians themfelves are not better markfmen, or manage their canoes in the moft dangerous *rapids* with greater fkill.

Many are of opinion that they are unfit for the fciences, which require any great degree of application, and a continued ftudy. I am not able to fay whether this prejudice is well founded, for as yet we have feen no Canadian who has endeavoured to remove it, which is perhaps owing to the diffipation in which they are brought up. But nobody can deny them an excellent genius for mechanics ; they have hardly any occafion for the affiftance of a mafter in oider to excel in this fcience ; and fome are every day to be met with who have fucceeded in all trades, without ever having ferved an apprenticefhip.

Some people tax them with ingratitude, neverthelefs they feem to me to have a pretty good difpofition ; but their natural inconftaney often prevents their attending to the duties required by gratitude. It is alledged they make bad fervants, which is owing to their great haughtinefs of fpirit, and to their loving liberty too much to fubjeft themfelves willingly to fervitude. They are however good mafters, which is the reverfe of what is faid of thofe from whom the greateft part of them are defcended. They would have been perfeft in charafter, if to their own virtues they had added thofe of their anceftors. Their inconftancy in friendfhip has fometimes been complained of ; but this complaint can hardly be general, and in thofe who have given occafion for it, it proceeds from their not being accuftomed to conftraint, even in their own affairs. If
they

they are not eafily difciplin'd, this likewife proceeds from the fame principle, or from their having a difcipline peculiar to themfelves, which they believe is better adapted for carrying on war againft the Indians, in which they are not entirely to blame. Moreover, they appear to me to be unable to govern a certain impetuofity, which renders them fitter for fudden furprifes or hafty expeditions, than the regular and continued operations of a campaign. It has likewife been obferved, that amongft a great number of brave men who diftinguifhed themfelves in the laft wars, there were very few found capable of bearing a fuperior. This is perhaps owing to their not having fufficiently learned to obey. It is however true, that when they are well conducted, there is nothing which they will not accomplifh, whether by fea or land; but in order to this they muft entertain a great opinion of their commander. The late M. d' Iberville, who had all the good qualities of his countrymen without any of their defects, could have led them to the end of the world.

There is one thing with refpect to which they are not eafily to be excufed, and that is the little natural affection moft of them fhew to their parents, who for their part difplay a tendernefs for them, which is not extremely well managed. The Indians fall into the fame defect, and it produces amongft them the fame confequences. But what above all things ought to make the Canadians be held in much efteem, is the great fund they have of piety and religion, and that nothing is wanting to their education upon this article. It is likewife true, that when they are out of their own country they hardly retain any of their defects. As with all this they are extremely brave and active, they might be of great fervice in war, in the marine and in the arts;

and

and I am opinion that it would redound greatly to the advantage of the ftate, were they to be much more numerous than they are at prefent. Men conftitute the principal riches of the Sovereign, and Canada, fhould it be of no other ufe to France, would ftill be, were it well peopled, one of the moft important of all our colonies.

I am, &c.

LETTER

L E T T E R XI.

Of the Iroquoife *village of the Fall of St.*
Lewis. *Of the different nations inhabiting*
Canada.

Fall of St. Lewis, May 1, 1721.

Madam,

I Came hither to fpend a part of the Eafter holi-
days ; this is a time of devotion, and in this
village every thing infpires one with fentiments of
piety. All the exercifes of religion are carried on
in a very edifying manner, and we ftill feel the impreffion which the fervor of the firft inhabitants has
left behind it ; for it is certain, that this for a long
time was the only place in Canada, where you could
perceive the great examples of thofe heroick virtues
with which God has been ufed to enrich his churches
when in their infancy ; and the manner in which it
has been erected is fomething very extraordinary.

The miffionaries after having for a long time wa-
tered the Iroquo'fe cantons with the fweat of their
brows, and fome of them even with their blood,
were at laft fenfible that it was impracticable to efta-
blifh the chriftian religion amongft them upon a folid
foundation ; but they ftill had hopes of reducing a

I   con-

confiderable number of thefe Indians under the yoke
of the faith.   They perceived that God had an elect
few among thefe barbarians as in every nation ; but
they were perfuaded, that *to make their calling and
election fure*, they muft feparate from their brethren ;
and therefore came to a refolution to fettle all thofe
who were difpofed to embrace Chriftianity in a colony by themfelves.   They made known their defign
to the governor-general and intendant, who carrying their views ftill farther, highly approved it, being fenfible that this fettlement would be greatly
advantageous to New France, as it has indeed been,
as well as another fimilar to it, which has fince been
fet on foot in the ifland of Montreal, under the name
of *la Montagne*, of which the fuperiors of the feminary of St. Sulpicius have always had the direction.

To return to this which has ferved as a model
for the other, one of the Iroquois miffionaries communicated his defign to fome *Aquiers* ; they relifhed
his propofal, and this fettlement was formed chiefly
out of that canton, which had at all times been
the moft averfe to the minifters of the gofpel, and
had even treated them the moft cruelly.   Thus to
the great aftonifhment of the French and Indians,
thofe formidable enemies to God and our nation
were touched with that victorious grace, which takes
delight in triumphing over the hardeft and moft re-
bellious hearts, abandoning every thing that was
deareft to them, that they might have no impedi-
ment in ferving the Lord with all liberty.   A facri-
fice ftill more glorious for Indians, than for any
other nation, becaufe there are none fo much attached as they are to their families and their native
country.

Their

Their numbers encreafed greatly in a fhort time, and this progrefs was, in a great meafure, owing to the zeal of the firft converts who compofed this chofen flock. In the very height of a war, and even with the hazard of their lives they have travelled over all the cantons, in order to make profelites, and when they have fallen into the hands of their enemies, who were often their neareft relations, reckoned themfelves happy when dying in the midft of the moft frightful torments, as having expofed themfelves to them, folely for the glory of God and the falvation of their brethren. Such were the fentiments even of the murtherers of the minifters of Jefus Chrift, and perhaps this oracle of St. Paul, Ep. Rom. c. 20. *Ubi autem abundavit delictum, fuperabundavit Gratia*, was never fo literally accomplifhed as now. It was moft commonly left to their choice, either to renounce Jefus Chrift and return to their canton, or to fuffer the moft cruel death, and there was not an example of one who accepted life upon that condition. Some have even perifhed worn out with miferies in the prifons of New-York, when they could have had their liberty on changing their belief, or engaging not to live among the French, which they imagined they could not do without running the rifque of lofing their faith.

Thofe converts, who on fuch occafions difplayed fo much fidelity and greatnefs of foul, muft undoubtedly have been prepared for it by the pureft virtue ; we cannot in reality call in queftion certain facts, which have been notorious over the whole colony, and which render thofe very credible for which we have only the evidence of the Indians themfelves and their paftors. M. de St. Valier, who is head of this church to this day, wrote as follows in the
year

year 1688. " The lives of all the Chriftians of this miffion are very extraordinary, and the whole village would be taken for a monaftery. As they have quitted the allurements of their native country, entirely to make fure of their falvation, they are all led to the practice of the moft perfect refignation, and they preferve amongft them fuch excellent rules for their fanctification that nothing can be added to them."

This village was at firft placed in the meadow *de la Madeleire*, about a league lower than the Fall of St. Lewis on the fouth-fide. But the foil being found improper for the culture of maïz, it was tranfported to a place oppofite to the Fall itfelf, from whence it has taken the name it ftill bears, though it has been carried from thence a few years ago a league higher up. I have already obferved, that its fituation is charming, that the church, and the houfe of the miffionaries, are two of the fineft edifices in this country, which makes me imagine, that they have taken fuch good meafures as not to be obliged to make a new tranfmigration.

On my arrival here, I had laid my account with departing immediately after the feftivals ; but nothing is more fubject to difappointments of all kinds than this manner of travelling. I am, therefore, ftill uncertain as to the day of my departure ; and as in fuch voyages as mine, advantage is to be taken of every occurrence, I fhall now make the beft ufe I can of this prefent delay. I have fpent my time in the company of fome old miffionaries, who have lived a long time among the Indians, and I fhall now, Madam, give you an account of what I have heard from them concerning the different nations inhabiting this immenfe continent.

The

The firſt land of America which is diſcovered on a voyage from France to Canada is Newfoundland, one of the largeſt iſlands we are acquainted with. It has never yet been fully determined, whether its inhabitants are natives of the country; and its bar-tenneſs, were it really as great as it is ſuppoſed to be, would be no ſufficient proof that they are not ; for hunting and fiſhing afford ſufficient ſubſiſtence for Indians. What is certain is, that none but Eſkimaux have ever been ſeen upon it, who are not originally of this iſland. Their real native country is the land of *Laborador*, or *Labrador*, it is there, at leaſt, they paſs the greateſt part of the year ; for, in my opinion, it would be profaning the grateful appellation of a native country, to apply it to wandering barbarians who have no affection for any country, and who being ſcarce able to people two or three villages, yet occupy an immenſe extent of land. In effect, beſides the coaſts of Newfoundland, which the Eſkimaux wander over in the ſummer-time, there are none but that people to be ſeen throughout all that vaſt continent lying betwixt the river St. Lawrence, Canada, and the North-ſea. Some of them have been even found at a great diſtance from hence up the river Bourbon, which runs from the weſtward, and falls into Hudſon's-Bay.

The origin of their name is not certain, but it is probably derived from the Abenaquiſe word *Eſquimantris*, which ſignifies an eater of raw fleſh. The Eſquimaux are in fact the only ſavages we know of who eat raw fleſh, though they are likewiſe in uſe to broil or dry it in the ſum. It is likewiſe certain, that there is no nation known in America, which anſwers better to the firſt idea Europeans are apt to conceive of ſavages. They are almoſt the only nation amongſt whom the men have beards, which grow up to their eyes, and are fo thick, that it is with difficulty the features of their faces are to be diftinguifhed. They have likewife fomething very frightful in their air and mien, fmall fiery eyes, large and very ugly teeth, hair commonly black, fometimes fair, always very much in diforder, and their whole external appearance extremely brutifh. Their manners and character do not bely the deformity of their phifiognomy; they are fierce, favage, fufpicious, turbulent, and have a conftant propenfity to do mifchief to ftrangers, who ought to be perpetually on their guard againft them. As to the qualities of their mind we have had fo little intercourfe with this nation that we do not as yet know their real temper; but they have always had a fufficient bent towards mifchief.

They have been frequently known to go in the night-time, and cut the cables of fhips at anchor, in order to make them drive on fhore, and then plunder the wrecks; they are not afraid to attack them even in open day on difcovering their crews to be weak. It has never been poffible to tame them, and it is not fafe to hold any difcourfe with them but at the end of a long pole. They not only refufe to come near the Europeans, but they will not fo much as eat any thing they prefent to them; and in all things take fo many precautions on their fide, which mark an extreme diftruft, that they muft mutually infpire the fame with refpect to every thing which comes from them. They are of an advantageous ftature, and are tolerably well made. Their fkin is as white as ours, which proceeds undoubtedly from their never going naked even in the warmeft weather.

Their

Their beards, their fair hair, the whiteneſs of
their ſkin, and the little reſemblance and intercourſe
they have with their neareſt neighbours leave no
room to doubt of their having a different original
from the reſt of the Americans; but the opinion of
their being deſcended from the Baſques ſeems to
me to have little foundation, if it is true, as I am
informed it is, that the languages of the two nations have no affinity with one another. This alliance at any rate can be of no honour to any nation ; for if there is not on the ſurface of the earth a
region leſs fit to be inhabited than Newfoundland
and Labrador, ſo there is not, perhaps, a people
which deſerves better to be confined to it than the
Eſkimaux. For my part, I am of opinion, that
they are originally from Greenland.

These ſavages are covered in ſuch a manner that
only a part of their faces and the ends of their
hands are to be ſeen. Over a ſort of a ſhirt made
of bladders, or the inteſtines of fiſh cut into fillets,
and neatly enough ſewed together, they throw a
kind of a ſurtout made of bear-ſkin, or of the
ſkin of ſome other wild beaſt, nay, ſometimes of
the ſkins of birds, whilſt their head is covered with
a cowl of the ſame ſtuff, with the ſhirt fixed to it ;
on the top of which is a tuft of hair, which hangs
down and ſhades their forehead. The ſhirt falls
no lower than their loins, the ſurtout hangs down
behind to their thighs, and terminates before in a
point ſomewhat lower than their girdle ; but in the
women it deſcends on both ſides as far as the mid-
leg, where it is fixed by a girdle, at which hang
little bones. The men wear breeches made of
ſkins, with the hairy ſide inwards, and faced on the
outſide with ermine, and ſuch like furs. They
likewiſe wear on their feet pumps of ſkins, the

hairy

hairy fide of which is alfo inwards; and above
them furred boots of the fame, and over thefe a fecond pair of pumps, then another pair of boots
over that. It is affirmed they are fometimes fhod
in this manner three or four times over, which,
however, does not prevent thefe Indians from being
extremely active. Their arrows, the only weapons
they ufe, are pointed with the teeth of the fea-cow,
to which they likewife add iron when they can get
it. In the fummer they live in the open air, night
and day, but in the winter under ground, in a fort
of caverns, where they lie pell-mell one above another.

We are but little acquainted with the other nations living beyond Hudfon's-bay, and in its neighbourhood. In the fouthern parts of this bay, the
trade is carried on with the Mataffins, the Monfo-
nis, the Chriftinaux, and Affiniboils; thefe laft
muft come from a great diftance as they inhabit the
borders of a lake to the north or north-weft of the
Sioux, and likewife fpeak a dialect of their language. The three others fpeak the Algonquin
tongue. The Chriftinaux or Killiftinons, come from
the northward of Lake Superior. The Indians in
the neighbourhood of the river Bourbon *, and the
river St. Therefa, have no affinity in their language
either with the one or the other. Perhaps, they
may be better underftood amongft the Efkimaux,
who have been feen, as is faid, a great way above
the mouth of this river. It has been obferved that

---

* It is faid that a hundred leagues from the mouth of this
river, it is unnavigable for fifty more, but that a paffage is found
by means of rivers and lakes which fall into it, and that afterwards it runs through the middle of a very fine country, which
continues as far as the Lake of the Affiniboils, from whence it
takes its rife.

they

they are extremely superstitious, and use some kind of sacrifices. Those who have had the greatest intercourse with them, assure us, that in common with the Indians of Canada, they have a notion of a good and of an evil genius, that the Sun is their great divinity, and that when they deliberate upon any affair of importance, they make him an offering of smoke which is done in the following manner. At break of day they assemble in the cabbin of one of their chiefs, who, after having lighted his pipe, presents it three times to the rising sun, and then turning it with both his hands from the east to the west, he supplicates this luminary to be propitious to his people. This being done, all those who compose the assembly, smoke in the same pipe. All these Indians, though of four or five different nations are known in the French accounts under the general name of the *Savanois*, because the country they inhabit is low, marshy, and ill-wooded, and in Canada, all those wet lands, which are good for nothing are called Savannahs.

Coasting along the north-shore of the Bay, you meet with two rivers, the first of which is called *Danish-River*, and the second the river of the *Sea-Wolf*; on the banks of both these rivers there are Indians, who, I know not why, have got the name, or rather nickname of *Plats côtez de Chiens*, or Flat-sided Dogs, and are often at war with the Savanois; but neither of them treat their prisoners with that barbarity which is usual among the Canadians, being contented with keeping them in slavery. Want sometimes reduces the Savanois to strange extremities; and whether it be idleness on their part, or that their lands are absolutely good for nothing, they find themselves entirely destitute of provisions when their hunting and fishing prove

unsuc-

unfuccefsful, and then they are faid to make no difficulty of eating one another. The moft daftardly
are the firft facrifices ; it is further pretended, that
when a man arrives at fuch an age that he can only
be a burthen and expence to his family, he himfelf
paffes a cord round his own neck, the extremities
of which he prefents to the child who is deareft to
him, who ftrangles him as expeditioufly as he can,
believing that in fo doing, he performs a good action, not only by putting an end to the fufferings
of his father, but likewife by advancing his happi-
nefs ; for thefe Indians imagine, that a man who
dies old is born again in the other world at the age
of a child at the breaft ; and that, on the contrary,
thofe who finifh their courfe foon, become old when
they arrive at the country of fouls.

The young women among thefe people never
marry but with the advice of their parents, and the
fon-in law is obliged to ftay with his father-in-law,
and be fubfervient to him in every thing, till he has
children himfelf. The young men leave their father's houfes very early. Thefe Indians burn their
dead bodies, and wrap the afhes in the bark of a
tree, which they lay into the ground. Afterwards
they erect upon the grave a fort of monument with
pofts, to which they fix tobacco, in order that the
deceafed may have materials for fmoaking in the
other world If he was a hunter, his bow and arrows are fufpended there likewife. The mothers
lament their children for twenty days, and prefents
are made to the fathers, who make an acknowledg-
ment for them by a feaft. War is held in lefs efti-
mation amongft them than hunting ; but before
any perfon can be efteemed a good hunter, he muft
faft for three days running, without tafting any
thing whatever, and all that time he muft have his

face

face painted with black. The feaſt being ended, the candidate offers up a ſacrifice to the great ſpirit, conſiſting of a morſel of each of the animals he has been uſed to hunt, being commonly the tongue and muzzle, which, except on ſuch occaſions, are always the portion of the hunter himſelf. His parents and relations would rather die of hunger than touch it, and he is allowed to regale his friends and ſtrangers only in this manner.

It is further aſſerted, that theſe Indians are perfectly diſintereſted, that they poſſeſs a fidelity proof againſt all temptation, that they cannot endure a lie, and hold deceit in abhorrence. This, Madam, is what I have been able to learn with reſpect to theſe northern people, with whom we have never maintained any regular commerce, and have only ſeen them in a tranſient manner. We ſhall now proceed to thoſe with whom we are better acquainted, who may be divided into three claſſes diſtinguiſhed by their languages and their peculiar geniuſes.

In this vaſt extent of country, properly called New-France, and bounded on the north by Hudſon's-Bay, which was diſmembered from it by the treaty of Utrecht, on the eaſt by the ſea, by the Engliſh colonies on the ſouth, by Louiſiana on the ſouth-eaſt, and by the Spaniſh poſſeſſions on the weſt; I ſay, in this vaſt extent of country there are but three mother-tongues, from which all the reſt are derived; theſe are, the Sioux, Algonquin, and Huron languages; we are but little acquainted with the people who ſpeak the firſt, and nobody knows how far they extend. We have hitherto had no trade with any but the Sioux and Aſſiniboils, and

even

even this trade has not been very regularly carried on.

Our missionaries have endeavoured to make a settlement amongst the first, and I knew one who regretted very much his not being able to succeed, or rather his not staying longer amongst them, as they seemed to be extremely docile. There is, perhaps, no people to the north-west of the Mississippi, of of whom we can receive better and more authentic information than this, by reason that they can carry on a trade with all the other nations on this immense continent. They dwell commonly in meadows under large tents made of skins, which are very well wrought, and live on wild oats, which grow in great plenty in their meadows and rivers, and by hunting, especially the buffalo which are covered with wool, and are found by thousands in their meadows. They have no fixed abode, but travel in great companies like the Tartars, never stopping in any place longer than they are detained by the chace.

Our geographers divide this people into the *wandering Sioux*, and the *Sioux of the Meadows*, into the *Sioux of the East*, and the *Sioux of the West*. This division does not seem to me to be well founded. All the Sioux live in the same manner, whence it happens, that a village which the year before was on the eastern bank of the Mississippi, shall be this year on the western bank, and that those who have lived for some time on the banks of the river St. Peter, shall, perhaps, be at present in some meadow a great distance from it. The name Sioux, which we have given to these Indians, is entirely of our own invention, or rather the two last syllables of of the word *Nadouessioux*, a name by which several nations distinguish them. Others call them *Na-*
douessis.

doueffis. This nation is the moſt populous we know in Canada. They were ſufficiently pacific, and but little addicted to war, before the Hurons and Outawais when they fled from the fury of the Iroquois, took refuge in their country. They laughed at them for their ſimplicity, and made them warlike at their own expence. The Sioux have a plurality of wives, and ſeverely puniſh ſuch as are wanting in conjugal fidelity. They cut off the tip of their noſes, and make a circle in the ſkin on the top of their heads, and afterwards tear it off. I have ſeen ſome perſons, who were perſuaded theſe people ſpoke with the Chineſe accent; it would be no difficult matter to determine this fact, or if their language has any affinity with that of China.

Thoſe perſons who have had intercourſe with the Affiniboils, tell us, that they are tall, well-made, robuſt, active, and inured to cold, and all manner of fatigue; that they are pricked over all the body, and marked with the figures of ſerpents and other animals; and that they are in uſe to undertake very long journeys. There is nothing in all this which diſtinguiſhes them from the other nations of this continent which we are acquainted with; but what particularly characterizes them, is, their being extremely phlegmatick, at leaſt they appear ſo in reſpect of the Chriſtinaux who trade with them, and who are indeed of an extraordinary vivacity, continually dancing and ſinging, and ſpeaking with precipitation and a volubility of tongue, which is not obſerved in any other Indian nation.

The true country of the Affiniboils, is in the neighbourhood of a lake which bears their name, with which we are but little acquainted. A Frenchman, whom I ſaw at Montreal, aſſured me he had

been

been there, but had feen it only in a tranfient manner, as one fees the fea in a harbour. It is the
common opinion, that this lake is fix hundred
leagues in circumference; that there is no paffage
to it but through roads almoft impracticable; that
all its banks are delightful; that the climate is very
temperate, though it lies to the north-weft of Lake
Superior, where it is extremely cold, and that it
contains fo great a number of iflands, that it is called in that country, the *Lake of Iflands*; fome Indians call it *Michinipi*, which fignifies the *Great Water*; and it feems in effect to be the refervoir or
fource of the greateft rivers, and all the great lakes
of North-America; for on feveral accounts, all the
following rivers are faid to have their rife from it;
the river Bourbon, which runs into Hudfon's-Bay;
the river St. Laurence, which carries its waters to
the ocean; the Miffiffippi, which falls into the
gulph of Mexico; the Miffouri, which mixes with
this laft, and till their junction is in nothing inferior to
it; and a fifth, which runs as they fay, weftward,
and confequently difcharges its waters into the South-
Sea. It is a great pity that this lake was not known
to thofe learned men who have fought for the ter-
reftrial paradife all over the world; it might have
been placed here with at leaft as great propriety as
in Scandinavia. I do not, however, warrant all
thefe facts, which are fupported only by the accounts
of travellers, and much lefs what the Indians have
related, that in the neighbourhood of the Lake of
the Affiniboils, there are men refembling the Europeans, who are fettled in a country where gold and
filver are fo common, that they are employed in
the meaneft ufes. Father Marquette, who difcovered the Miffiffippi in 1673, fays in his relation,
that the Indians not only talked to him of the river
which runs from this lake weftward, but likewife
added

added, that they had feen large fhips at its mouth.
It appears befides, that the Affiniboils are the fame
people who in the old maps are marked under the
name of *Poualaks*, and of whom fome accounts
fay, that their country is contiguous to that of the
Chriftinaux or Killiftinons.

The Algonquin and Huron languages fhare betwixt them almoft all the Indian nations of Canada,
with whom we have any commerce. A perfon well
acquainted with both might travel over above fifteen hundred leagues of a country without an interpreter, and make himfelf underftood by above
a hundred different nations, who have each of them
their peculiar language. The Algonquin particularly has a prodigious extent. It begins at Acadia and the gulph of St. Laurence, and makes a
circuit of twelve hundred leagues, turning from
the fouth eaft by the north to the fouth-weft. It is
even faid, that the Makingans or Wolves, and the
greateft part of the Indians of New-England and
Virginia fpeak dialects of this language.

The *Abenaquis*, or *Conibas* bordering upon New-
England, have, for their neareft neighbours the
Etechemins, or *Malécites* in the country about the
river Pentagoët, and further to the eaft are the *Mic-
maks* or *Souriquois*, whofe country is properly Accadia, all along the coaft of the gulph of St. Laurence as far as Gafpey, whence a certain author has
called them *Gafpefians*, as well as the neighbouring iflands. Going up the river St. Laurence, you
do not meet with any Indian nations at prefent till
you come to Saguenay. Yet when Canada was difcovered and fome years afterwards, feveral Indian
nations were found in that territory, which fpread
themfelves over the ifland of Anticofti, towards the

moun-

mountains of Notre Dame, and along the northern side of the river. Thofe moft frequently mentioned in ancient accounts are the *Berfiamites*, the *Papinachois*, and the *Montagnez*, who were likewife called, efpecially the latter, the *inferior Algonquins*, on account of their dwelling on the lower part of the river with refpect to Quebec; but the greateft part of the reft are reduced to a few families which you meet with, fometimes in one place fometimes in another.

There were fome nations which ufed to come down to the colony from the northern parts, fometimes by the Saguenay, but oftener by *Trois Rivieres*, of whom we have heard no mention made for fome time paft. Such were amongft others the *Attikamegues*, who came from a great diftance, and were furrounded by feveral other nations who extended themfelves to the country about Lake *St. John*, and as far as the lakes of the *Miftafirus* and *Nemifcan*. Thefe are almoft all put to the fword by the Iroquois, or deftroyed by diftempers, a confequence of the mifery the fear of thefe barbarians has reduced them to; which is much to be regretted, as they were a people without vice, of a mild temper, and might have been eafily gained over to Jefus Chrift, and to the intereft of the French nation. Between Quebec and Montreal, and towards Trois Rivieres we ftill find a few Algonquins who trade with the French, but do not form a village. In the time of the firft difcoveries this nation poffeffed all the northern fide of the river, from Quebec, where M. Champlain found them fettled and made an alliance with them, as far as the lake of St. Peter.

From

From the ifland of Montreal, always taking a
north courfe, you find a few villages of the *Nipif-
fings*, the *Temifcamings*, the *Têtes de Boule*, or *Roundheads*, the *Amikouês*, and *Outaways*. The firft,
who were the true Algonquins, and have alone
preferved the Algonquin language in its purity, have
given their name to a fmall lake lying between Lake
Huron, and the river of the Outaways. The Temifcamings poffefs the banks of another fmall lake,
which likewife bears their name, and feems to be
the true fource of the river of the Outaways. The
Roundheads are at no great diftance, who have their
name from the roundnefs of their heads ; they think
there is a great beauty in this figure, and it is very
probable the mothers give it to their children,
while in their cradles. The Amikouês, otherwife
called the *nation of the Beaver*, are reduced almoft
to nothing ; the few remaining of them are found
in the ifland *Manitoualin* in the northern part of
Lake Huron. The Outaways who were formerly
very numerous inhabited the banks of that great river which bears their name, and of which they
pretended to be the lords. I know not but of three
villages of them, very indifferently peopled, of
which I fhall fpeak in the fequel.

Between Lake Huron and Lake Superior, even
in the ftreight itfelf, by which the fecond difcharges its waters into the firft, there is a fall called
by us *Sault St. Marie*, or the Fall of St. Mary.
The country round about it was formerly peopled
by Indians, who it is faid came from the fouthern
banks of Lake Superior, and were called *Saulteurs*,
that is to fay, *Inhabitants of the Fall*. This name
was probably given them to fave the labour of pro-
nouncing that which they gave themfelves, which
could not poffibly be done without taking breath

two

two or three times *. There is no nation, at leaft
that I know of, fettled on the banks of Lake Superior; but in the pofts which we poffefs there a
trade is carried on with the Chriftinaux, who come
from the north-eaft, and fpeak the Algonquin language, and with the Affiniboils, who come from
the north-weft.

Lake *Michigan*, which is almoft parallel to Lake
Huron, into which it difcharges itfelf, and is feparated from it by a peninfula, about a hundred leagues
in length, growing continually narrower towards
the north, has but few inhabitants on its banks; I
do not even know if ever any nation was fixed there,
and it is without foundation, that it has been called
in fome maps the lake of the Illinois. Going up the
River St. Jofeph, the waters of which it receives, you
find two villages of different nations, who have come
from fome other place not long fince. On the
weft fide of this lake is a large bay, extending eight
and twenty leagues to the fouth, and called the *Baye
des Puans*, or fimply the *Bay*. Its entrance is very
large, and interfperfed with iflands, fome of which
are from fifteen to twenty leagues in circumference.
They were formerly inhabited by the *Poutewatamies*,
whofe name they bear, excepting fome few on the
right hand, where there are ftill fome Indians called
Noquets. The Poutewatamies poffefs at prefent one
of the fmalleft of thefe iflands, and have befides
two other villages, one at the river St. Jofeph, and
the other at the Narrows. At the bottom of this
bay are the *Sakis* and *Otchagras*, which laft are likewife called *Puans* or Stinkards, for what reafon I
know not; but before you arrive amongft them you
leave upon your right hand, another fmall nation

* PANOIRIGOUEIOUHAK.

called

called *Malhomines*, or *Folles Avoires*; that is, wild Oat Indians.

A small river very much incommoded with falls, discharges itself into the bottom of this bay, and is known under the name of the *Riviere des Renards*, or, river of the Foxes, on account of its neighbourhood to the *Outagamies*, commonly called the *Renards* or Foxes. All this country is extremely beautiful, and that which stretches to the southward as far as the river of the Illinois is still more so; it is, however, inhabited by two small nations only, who are the *Kicapous*, and the *Muscoutins*. Some of our geographers have been pleased to give the latter the title of the *Nation of Fire*, and their country that of the *Land of Fire*. An equivocal expression has given rise to this denomination.

Fifty years ago, the Miamis were settled on the southern extremity of Lake Michigan, in a place called Chicagou, from the name of a small river, which runs into the lake, the source of which is not far distant from that of the river of the Illinois; they are at present divided into three villages, one of which stands on the river St. Joseph; the second on another river which bears their name, and runs into Lake Erié, and the third upon the river Ouabache, which empties its waters into the Mississippi; these last are better known by the appellation of *Ouyatanons*. There can be no doubt, that this nation and the Illinois were not long ago the same people, considering the great affinity which is observed between their languages; but I shall be able to speak of this with greater certainty when I shall be on the spot. I shall only observe farther, that the greatest part of the Algonquin nations, if we except those who are farther advanced to the

south-

southward, busy themselves very little in cultivating the ground, but live almost entirely by fishing and hunting, and are likewise very little disposed to a sedentary life. A plurality of wives is in use amongst some of them; yet, so far from encreasing, they diminish every day. There is not one nation in which there are reckoned above six thousand souls, and in some there are not above two thousand.

The Huron language is not so extensive as the Algonquin, which is undoubtedly owing to the nations who speak it, having always been of a less wandering disposition than the Algonquins. I say, the Huron language, to conform myself to the opinion most commonly received, for some still maintain, that the Iroquoise is the mother-tongue; be this as it will, all the Indians to the southward of the river St. Laurence, from the river Sorel to the extremity of Lake Erié, and even bordering upon Virginia, belong to this language, and whoever is acquainted with the Huron understands them all. Its dialects are multiplied extremely, and there are almost as many as there are villages. The five cantons which compose the Iroquois republick, have each their own, and all that was heretofore indifferently called Huron was not the same language. I have not been able to learn to what language the *Cherokees* belong, a pretty numerous nation, inhabiting those vast meadows between Lake Erié and the Missisippi.

But it ought to be observed, that as the greatest part of the Indians of Canada have had at all times an intercourse with one another, sometimes as allies, sometimes as enemies, though the three mother-tongues of which I have spoken have no sort of affinity or analogy with one another, these people, have

have, notwithſtanding found means to do buſineſs together without having occaſion for an interpreter; whether through long cuſtom they have acquired a facility of making themſelves underſtood by ſigns; or, whether they have formed a ſort of a common jargon which they have learned by practice. I am juſt now informed I muſt embark, I ſhall conclude this article the firſt leiſure I have.

I have the honour to be, &c.

L E T T E R XII.

Voyage to Catarocoui. *Defcription of the country, and of the* Rapides *or falls in the river*
St. Lawrence. *Defcription and fituation of
the Fort. Character and genius of the languages and nations of* Canada. *Origin of the
war between the* Iroquois *and* Algonkins.

Catarocoui, May 14, 1721.

Madam,

I Set out from the Fall of St. Lewis on the 1ft of
May, after clofing my laft epiftle, and lay at
the weftern extremity of the ifland of Montreal,
where I did not however arrive till midnight.   On
the morrow I employed the whole morning in vifiting this country, which is exceeding fine   In the
afternoon I croffed Lake St. Lewis, to go to the
place called *les Cafcades*, where I found fuch of my
people, as had gone directly thither, employed in
fewing their canoe, which they had let fall, as they
were carrying it on their fhoulders, and which was
thus fplit from one end to the other.   This, Madam, is the pleafure, and at the fame time the inconvenience of travelling in fuch fmall vehicles, the

T 2   leaft

leaſt thing in the world breaks them, but then the remedy is both ready and eaſy : all you have to do, is to provide yourſelf with a ſufficient quantity of bark, gum, and roots ; beſides, there are few places where you may not meet with gum and roots ſufficient for ſtitching your canoe.

What they call *les Caſcades*, is a *rapide* or fall, ſituated exactly at the upper end of the iſland Perrot, which ſeparates lake St. Lewis from the lake *des deux Montagnes*. To ſhun this, you keep a little to the right, and make your canoes go empty over a part of the river called *le Trou :* you afterwards bring them on ſhore, and then make over a carrying place of half a quarter of a leaguè ; that is to ſay, you carry your canoe and all your baggage on your ſhoulders. This is to ſhun a ſecond *rapide* called *le Bouiſſon* or the buſh, being a fine ſheet of water, falling from a flat rock of about a foot and a half high. One might be delivered from this trouble by hollowing a little the bed of a ſmall river, which diſcharges itſelf into another above the *Caſcades*. The expence would be no great matter.

Above the *Bouiſſon*, the river is a large quarter of a league broad, and the lands on both ſides are excellent and well wooded. They begin to clear thoſe lying on the northern bank, and it would be very eaſy to make a highway from the point oppoſite to the iſland of Montreal, as far as the height or creek called *La Galette*. By this means one might ſhun a paſſage of forty leagues, and a navigation rendered almoſt impracticable with *Rapides*, and always exceding tedious. A fort would even be better placed at *La Galette*, where it would alſo be of more ſervice than at Catarocoui, becauſe not a ſingle canoe can paſs it without being ſeen ; whereas at Catarocoui, they

they may flip thro' between the iflands without being perceived. Morever, the lands about *La Galette* are excellent, and for this reafon there muft always be plenty of provifions, which would fave a
confiderable expence. Befides, a veffel might fail
from hence to Niagara in two days with a favourable wind. One of the objects in view, in building the fort of Cataracoui, was the commerce with
the Iroquois; but thofe Indians would as readily
come to *La Galette* as to Catarocoui. They would
indeed have a little farther to travel, but they would
fhun a paffage of eight or ten leagues crofs lake Ontario: laftly, the fort at Galette would cover the
whole country lying between the river of the Outawais and the river St. Lawrence; for this country
cannot be attacked on the fide towards the river, by
reafon of the *Rapides*, and nothing is more eafy than
to defend the banks of the great river. I owe thefe
obfervations to a commiffary of the marine, who
was fent by the king in 1706 to vifit all the remote
parts of Canada.

The fame day, the 3d of May, I advanced three
leagues, and arrived at the place called *Aux Œdres*.
This is the third fall or *rapide*, and has taken its
name from the great number of cedars which were
formerly in this place: but they have fince been
moftly cut down. On the 4th I could get no farther than to the fourth rapid, called *le Côteau de Lac*,
tho' no more than two leagues and a half from the
preceeding, becaufe one of my canoes happened to
fplit near it. Your Grace will not be furprifed at
the frequency of thefe fhipwrecks, after you have
been informed of the conftruction of thefe diminitive
gondolas. I think I have already told you there are
two forts of them; the one of the bark of elm,
wider, and of very coarfe workmanfhip, but commonly

monly the largeſt. I know no nation but the Iroquois, which have any of this ſort. The others are
of the bark of the birch tree, of a breadth leſs proportioned to their length, and much better and
neater built. It is theſe latter I am going to de-
ſcribe to you, as all the French, and almoſt all the
Indians uſe no other.

They extend the pieces of bark, which are very
thick on flat and extremely thin timbers of Cedar-
wood. All theſe timbers from head to ſtern are
kept in form by little croſs bars, which form the different ſeats in the canoe. Two girders of the ſame
materials, to which theſe bars are faſtened or ſewed,
bind the whole fabric. Between the timbers and
the bark are inſerted ſmall pieces of cedar, ſtill more
ſlender than the timbers, and which for all that contribute to ſtrengthen the canoe, the two extremities
of which riſe gently, and terminate in two ſharp
points bending inwards. Theſe two extremities are
perfectly alike ; ſo that in order to go backward,
the canoe-men have only to change offices. He
who happens to be behind ſteers with his oar, ſtill
rowing at the ſame time ; and the chief employment of he who is forwards, is to take care that the
canoe touch nothing that may break it. They all
ſit low down, or on their knees, and their oars are
a ſort of paddles from five to ſix feet long, commonly of maple. But when they are to ſtem any
ſtrong current, they are obliged to make uſe of a
pole, and to ſtand upright, and this is called *picquer
le fond*, or piercing the bottom. They muſt be
well experienced to be able to preſerve their balance
in this work, for nothing can be lighter, and conſequently eaſier to overſet, than theſe vehicles, the
largeſt of which, with their whole loading, do not
draw above half a foot water.

The

The bark of which they are built, as well as the timbers, are fewed with the roots of fir-trees, which are more pliant, and lefs apt to dry than the ofier. All the feams are gummed within fide and without, but they muft be examined every day, to fee whether the gum has fcaled off. The largeft canoes carry twelve men, two and two, and four thoufand weight, or two tons. Of all the Indians, the moft expert builders are the Outawais, and in general the Algonquin nations excel the Huron Indians in this trade. There are few French who can make a canoe even fo much as tolerably well, but in conducting them, they are at leaft full as fure to truft to as the natives. as they exercife themfelves at it from their infancy. All thefe canoes, the fmalleft not excepted, carry fail, and with a favourable wind, make twenty leagues a-day. Without fails you muft have able canoe-men, to make twelve in ftill water.

From Coteau de Lac, to lake St. Francis, you have only a large half league. This lake which I croffed on the 5th, is feven leagues long, and at moft three in breadth where broadeft. The lands on both fides of it are low, but feem indifferent good. The rout from Montreal thither lies fomewhat fouth-weft, and lake St. Francis lies weftfouth weft and eaft-fouth eaft. I encamped immediately above it, and in the night was awakened with piercing cries, as of people making lamentations. I was frightened at firft, but they foon made me eafy, by telling me that it was a kind of cormorants called *Huarts* from their howling. They alfo told me thefe howlings were a fign of wind the next day, and it actually was fo.

On

On the fixth I paffed what they call *les Chefnaux du Lac.*, This they call the channels, formed by a multitude of iflands, which occupy almoft all the river in this place. I never faw a more charming country, and the foil appears excellent. The reft of the day we did nothing but clear the *rapides* : the moft confiderable called *le Moulinet*, terrified me only to look at it, and we had much ado to extricate ourfelves from it. I made however this day, almoft feven leagues, and encamped at the foot of the fall called *le long Sault :* this is a *rapide* half a league in length, where canoes cannot fail up, but half loaded. We paffed it on the 7th in the morning. We afterwards went on till three in the afternoon under fail, when the rain obliged us to encamp, and detained us all next day. There even fell on the 8th a little fnow, and on the night it froze as in France in the month of January. We were however under the fame parallel with Languedoc. On the ninth we paffed *le Rapide plat*, or flat fall, about feven leagues from the *Sault*, and five from *le Galots*, which is the laft of the *Rapides.* La Galette is a league and a half farther, where we arrived on the 10th. I could never have wearied of admiring the country between this creek and the Gallots. It is impoffible to fee nobler forefts. I remarked efpecially oaks of an amazing height.

Five or fix leagues from la Galette, is an ifland called Tonihata, the foil of which appears tolerably fertile, and which is about half a league long. An Iroquois, called the Quaker, for what reafon I know not, a man of excellent good fenfe, and much devoted to the French, had obtained the right to it from the Compte de Frontenac. and he fhews his patent to every body that defires to fee it. He has however fold his lordfhip for four *pots* of brandy ;

but

but he has reserved the usufruit for his own life, and has got together, on it eighteen or twenty families of his own nation. I arrived in his island on the 12th, and paid him a visit. I found him at work in his garden; this is not usual with the Indians; but this person affects to follow all the French manners. He received me very well, and would have regaled me, but the fine weather invited me to pursue my voyage. I took my leave of him, and went to pass the night two leagues from hence in a very pleasant spot. I had still thirteen leagues to sail before I could reach Catarocoui; the weather was fine, and the night very clear; this prevailed with us to embark at three in the morning. We passed thro' the middle of an archipelago called the thousand islands, and I am fully persuaded there are above five hundred of them. After you have got from among them, you have only a league and an half to sail to reach Catarocoui. The river here is opener, and is full half a league over. You leave afterwards on your right three large creeks of a good depth, and on the third the fort stands.

This fort has four bastions built of stone, which occupy a quarter of a league in circuit. Its situation is truly exceeding pleasant. The banks of the river present on all side landskips of great variety, which is also the case at the entry of lake Ontario, at no more than a short league's distance: it is adorned with a number of islands of different extent, all of them well wooded, and without any thing to confine the prospect on that side. This lake bore for some time the name of St. Lewis, it afterwards obtained that of Frontenac, as did also the fort of Catarocoui, of which Count Frontenac was the founder. The lake however insensibly recovered its ancient

cient appellation, which is Huron in Iroquois, and
the fort that of the place where it ſtands.

The ſoil from la Galette hither is barren enough;
but this is only on the out ſkirts; beyond that it is
excellent. There is oppoſite to the fort a very pleaſant iſland in the middle of the river. They formerly put ſome hogs in it, which multiplied greatly,
and whoſe name it bears. There are two other ſmall
iſlands below this, and half a league diſtant from each
other; one is called l'Iſle aux Cedres, and the other
l'Iſle aux Cerfs. The creek of Catarouoi is double,
that is, there is a point very near the middle which
advances a great way into the water, and under
which there is excellent anchoring ground for the
largeſt veſſels. Monſ. de la Salle, ſo celebrated for
his diſcoveries and misfortunes, who was once lord
of Catarocoui, and governor of the fort, had two
or three veſſels here which were ſunk, and are ſtill
to be ſeen. Behind the fort is a morafs, which ſwarms
with game. This is at once a diverſion, and an advantage to the garriſon. There was formerly a very
large commerce carried on at this place, eſpecially
with the Iroquois, and it was to hinder them from
carrying their furs to the Engliſh, and to hold themſelves in reſpect, the fort was built. But this commerce laſted not long, and the fort has not been
able to prevent thoſe Barbarians from doing us a-
bundance of miſchief. They have ſtill a few families without the fort, as well as ſome of the *Miſſiſa-
guez*, an Algonquin nation, who have ſtill a town
on the weſtern ſhore of lake Ontario, another at
Niagara, and a third at *le Detroit*, or the Narrows.

I found here, Madam, an occaſion of ſending my
letters to Quebec; I am going to lay hold of ſome
hours

hours leifure to fill this with what I have ftill to inform you of, with refpect to the different languages
of Canada. Thofe who have ftudied them to the
bottom, pretend that the three of which I formerly
made mention, have all the marks of primitive languages : and it is certain that they have not any
common origin. Their pronounciation would be
alone fufficient to prove this. The Sioux Indian hif-
fes rather than fpeaks. The Huron knows none of
the labial letters, fpeaks thro' the throat, and afpi-
rates almoft all the fyllables ; the Algonquin pronounces with a fofter tone, and fpeaks more naturally.
I have not been able to learn any thing particular,
with refpect to the firft of thefe three tongues ; but our
ancient miffionaries have laboured much on the two
others, and on their principal dialects : the following is what I have heard faid by the moft able of
them.

The Huron language has a copioufnefs, an energy, and a noblenefs, which are fcarce to be found
united in any of the fineft we know, and thofe whofe
native tongue it is, tho' but a handful of people,
ftill retain a certain elevation of foul, which agrees
much better with the majefty of their difcourfe,
than with the wretched eftate to which they are reduced. Some have imagined they found fome refemblance with the Hebrew in it ; others, and a
much greater, pretend that it has the fame origin
with that of the Greeks ; but nothing can be more
frivolous than the proofs they alledge in fupport of
it. We are in a fpecial manner to beware of re-
lying on the vocabulary of the Friar *Gabriel Sagbard*
a Recollect, which has been cited in favour of this
opinion : ftill lefs on that of James Cartier, and of
the Baron de la Hontan. Thefe three authors took
at random a few words, fome from the Huron, and
others

others from the Algonquin tongues, which they very
ill remembered, and which often fignified fomething
very different from what they imagined. How many
errors have been occafioned by fuch miftakes in travellers!

The Algonquin language has not the fame force
with the Huron, but much more fweetnefs and ele-
gance. Both have a richnefs of expreffion, a variety of turns and phrafes, a propriety of diction, and
a regularity, which are perfectly aftonifhing. But
what is ftill more wonderful is, that amongft Barbarians, who never ftudied the graces of elocution,
and who never knew the ufe of letters or writing, they
never introduce a bad word, an improper term, or
a faulty conftruction, and that the very children retain the fame purity in their lighteft and moft familiar difcourfe.

Befides, their manner of animating whatever they
fay leaves no room to doubt their comprehending all
the force of their expreffions, and all the beauty and
delicacy of their language. The dialects which are
derived from both, have retained neither the fame
force nor the fame graces. The Tfonnonthouans
for inftance, one of the five Iroquoife cantons, pafs
amongft the Indians for being the moft ruftick in
their fpeech of any Indians.

In the Huron language every word is inflected
or conjugated ; there is a certain art which I cannot
well explain to you, by which they diftinguifh
verbs from nouns, pronouns, adverbs, &c. Simple
verbs have a twofold conjugation ; one abfolute,
and the other relative or reciprocal. The third perfons have two genders, which are all known in
their tongues: to wit, the noble and ignoble. As
for

for number and tenfe, they have the fame difference
as the Greeks. For inſtance, to relate the account
of a voyage, you uſe a different expreſſion, if it is by
land, from that you would make uſe of had it been
by water. Active verbs are multiplied as often as
there are different objects of their action. Thus the
verb which fignifies to eat, has as many different
variations as there are different forts of eatables.
The action is differently expreſſed of an animated or
inanimate thing : thus, to fay you fee a man or you
fee a ſtone, you muſt make uſe of two different
verbs. To make uſe of any thing which belongs
to him who uſes it, or to the perſon to whom
he addreſſes himſelf, there are ſo many different
verbs.

There is fomething of all this in the Algonquin
language, but the manner of it is different, and I
am by no means in a condition to inform you of it.
However, Madam, if it ſhould follow from the
little I have been telling you that the richnefs and
variety of theſe languages render them expreſly difficult to be learned, the poverty and barrennefs into
which they have fince fallen cauſe an equal confufion. For as theſe people, when we firſt begun to
have any intercourſe with them, were ignorant of
every thing which was not in uſe among themſelves,
or which fell not under the cognizance of their fenfes, they wanted terms to expreſs them, or elſe had
let them fall into deſuetude and obſcurity. Thus
having no regular form of worſhip, and forming
confuſed ideas of the deity and of every thing relating
to religion, and never reflecting on any thing but the
objects of their fenfes, or matters which concerned
themfelves or their own affairs, which were fufficiently confined, and being never accuſtomed to diſcourfe
of virtues, paſſions, and many other matters which

are

are the common fubjects of converfation with us, as they neither cultivated the arts, except fuch as were neceffary to them, and which were reduced to a very fmall number ; nor any fcience, minding only fuch things as were within the reach of their capacity, and having no knowledge or defire of fuperfluities, nor any manner of luxury or refinement; when we had occafion to fpeak of all thefe topicks to them, there was found a prodigious void in their language, and it became neceffary, in order to be underftood by them, to make ufe of troublefome and perplexing circumlocutions to both them and us. So that after learning their language, we were under a neceffity to teach them a new one partly compofed of their own terms, and partly of ours, in order to facilitate the pronounciation of it. As to letters or characters they had none, and they fupplied this want by a fort of hieroglyphicks. Nothing confounded them more than to fee us exprefs ourfelves in writing with the fame eafe as by word of mouth.

If any one fhould afk me how I came to know that the Sioux, Huron and Algonkin languages are mother tongues rather than fome others, which we look upon as dialects of thefe, I anfwer that it is impoffible to be miftaken in this point, and I afk no other Proof of it than the words of Monf. l'Abbè Dubos, which I have already cited : but laftly, as we cannot judge in this cafe but by comparifon, if by fuch reflections we are able to determine that all the languages of Canada are derived from thefe three already mentioned, I will acknowledge they do not amount to an abfolute proof of their being primitive, and as old as the firft inftitution or invention of languages. I add, that all thefe nations have
fome

fomewhat of the Afiatic genius in their difcourfe, which gives a figurative turn and expreffion to things, and which is what has probably made fome conclude that they are of Afiatic extraction, which is moreover probable enough in other refpects.

Not only the nations of the Huron language have always occupied themfelves more than the other Indians in hufbandry and cultivation of their lands; they have alfo been lefs difperfed, which has produced two effects; for firft, they are better fettled, lodged and fortified, but have alfo always been under a better fort of police, and a more diftinct and regular form of government. The quality of chief, at leaft among the true Hurons who are Tionnontatez, is always hereditary. In the fecond place, till the wars of the Iroquois, of which we have been witneffes, their country was the moft populous, tho' polygamy never was in ufe in it. They have alfo the character of being the moft induftrious, moft laborious, moft expert in the management of their affairs, and moft prudent in their conduct, which can be attributed to nothing but to that fpirit of fociety which they have better retained than the others. This is in a fpecial manner remarked of the Hurons, who forming at prefent but one nation or people, and being reduced to two middling villages very remote from each other, are, notwithftanding the foul of all their councils in all matters regarding the community. 'Tis true that notwithftanding this difference, which is not to be difcovered at firft glance, there is a ftrong refemblance in the genius, manners, and cuftoms of all the Indians of Canada; but this is owing to the mutual commerce they have carried on with each other for many ages.

This

This is the proper place to take notice of the government of these Indians, as well as of their customs
and religion : but I can as yet discover nothing but
a chaos and confusion, which it is impossible for me
to unravel. You would certainly blame me should
I, like certain travellers, fill up my journal with
every thing I had heard, without giving myself any
trouble to ascertain the truth, and should retail to
you all the extravagant stories, charged to the account of our Indians, or which have probably been
drawn from their traditions. These traditions are
moreover so very uncertain, and almost always contradict themselves so grosly, that it is almost impossible
to pick out any thing certain or coherent. In fact,
how should a people such as they have been found
really to be, how should such persons transmit a
faithful account of what has passed amongst them
so many ages, since without any means of easing or
assisting their memory ? And can it be conceived
that men who think so little of the future, should
have so much concern about the past, as to preserve
faithful registers of it ? Thus, after all the re-
searches that could possibly be made, we are yet in
the dark and to seek, as to the situation of Canada,
when we first discovered it towards the middle of the
sixteenth century.

The sole point of their history which has come
down clothed with any degree of probability, is
the origin of the war, which Monsf. Champlain
found kindled between the Iroquois on one side,
and the Hurons and Algonquins on the other, and
in which he engaged much too far for our real interests. I have ever been unable to discover the epo-
cha of it, but I do not believe it of very old stand-
ing. I will not put an end to this letter with this
account : but I warn you before hand, that I don't
pretend

pretend to vouch for this historical piece, tho' I have
it from pretty good hands.

The Algonquins, as I have already observed, occupied all that tract of country lying between Quebec, and possibly from Tadoussac to the Lake Ni-
pissing, running along the north shore of the river
St. Lawrence, and tracing upwards the great river,
which discharges itself into the former above the
island of Montreal. This would incline us to judge
that this people was then pretty numerous, and it is
certain it has long made a very great figure in this
part of America, where the Hurons only were able
to dispute the superiority with them over all the rest.
With respect to skill in hunting, they had no equal,
and stood also foremost in the lists of fame for pro-
wess in war. The few remaining of them at this
day, have not degenerated from the ancient renown
of their fathers, nor have their misfortunes in the
least tarnished their reputation.

The Iroquois had concluded a kind of treaty of
alliance with them, which was equally and greatly
advantageous to either party, but which too, in the
estimation of Indians, (with whom a great hunts-
man and great warrior are in equal veneration) gave
the Algonquins a real superiority over the Iroquois.
The latter almost wholly taken up with the cultivating their fields, had stipulated to pay a certain
proportion of their harvests to the Algonkins, who
were on their part obliged to share with them the
fruits of their huntings, and to defend them against
all invaders. These two nations lived in harmony
for a considerable while, but an unreasonable piece
of pride in the one, and a certain, sudden, and un-
expected disgust on the other, broke all bounds of

concord, and embroiled thofe two nations in an ir-
reconcileable quarrel.

As the winter feafon is that of their great hunting, and as the earth being covered with fnow, furnifhes no employment to the hufbandman, the Indians of both confederate nations joined 'camps and
wintered abroad in the forefts. But the Iroquois generally left the hunting to the Algonquins, and contented themfelves with fleaing the beafts, curing their
flefh, and dreffing the fkins. This is now every
where the bufinefs of the women : poffibly this was
not then the cafe : be this as it will, the Iroquois
were perfectly fatisfied. Now and then however
fome particular perfons among them had a fancy to
make an effay at hunting, the Algonquins making
no oppofition to this practice. In this they acted
like bad politicians. It happened one winter that a
company of the two nations halted in a place where
they made fure of a fuccefsful hunting; and fix
young Algonquins, accompanied with as many Iroquoife of the fame age, were fent out to begin the
work.

They faw at firft a few elks, and immediately
prepared to give them chace. But the Algonquins
would not fuffer the Iroquois to accompany them, and
gave them to underftand that they would have employment enough in fleaing the beafts they fhould
catch. As ill luck would have it for thefe bragga-
docio's, three days paffed without their being able
to kill a fingle elk, tho' they ftarted a great number.
This fmall fuccefs mortified them, and probably
highly pleafed the Iroquois, who earneftly defired
to be allowed to go fome other way, where they
flattered themfelves they would prove more fortu-
nate. Their propofal was agreed to by the Algonquins,

quins, juſt as David's brethren did formerly, when
that young ſhepherd aſked leave to go and fight the
giant Goliah.   They told them it was vain to pretend to be abler huntſmen than the Algonquins; that
their office was to turn the glebe, and that it became them to leave the honourable profeſſion of
hunting to their betters, to whom that exerciſe was
more ſuitable.

The Iroquois affronted at this anſwer made no
reply, but on the night following, they ſet out pri-
vately to hunt.   The Algonquins, when they a-
woke, were ſurpriſed to find the Iroquois gone, but
their ſurpriſe was ſoon changed into the moſt violent
hatred.   For the ſame evening they had the morti-
fication to ſee the Iroquois returning loaded with
the fleſh of elks.   There are no mortals more ſuſ-
ceptible of an affront, or who carry their reſentment
farther than the Indians.   The effects of this were
ſudden, for the Iroquois had ſcarce cloſed their eyes,
when they were all butcher'd.   Such a murder could
not be long concealed, and tho' their bodies were
buried ſecretly, it was very ſoon known to their nation.   They at firſt made their complaints with
great moderation, but they inſiſted on having juſtice
done on the murderers.   They were too much deſ-
piſed to obtain their requeſt, nor were they thought
worthy of receiving the ſmalleſt ſatisfaction.

The Iroquois being thus drove to deſpair, came
to a determined reſolution to revenge the contempt
ſhewn them, and piqued themſelves more on puniſh-
ing this, than even the murder itſelf.   They bound
themſelves by oath to periſh to a man, or to have
their revenge ; but as they did not believe themſelves in a condition to try their fortune againſt the
Algonquins, the terror of whoſe name alone kept

all

all the other nations in awe, they went to a distance from them, to try their strength against some other less dreadful enemy, whom they provoked on purpose, and after they thought themselves sufficiently inured to warfare, they poured all at once upon the Algonquins, and commenced that war of which we saw only the conclusion, and which set all Canada on fire. This has been continued by the Iroquois with unparallel'd fury, and with a fierceness so much the more dreadful, as it was deliberate, and as it had nothing of that headstrong rage, which hurries men into bad measures, and which is soon over. Besides, Indians never think they have enough of revenge, till they have entirely exterminated their enemies; which is likewise more true of the Iroquois than of the other nations. They commonly say of them, that they advance like foxes, attack like lions, and fly like birds. Thus they are almost always sure of their blow, and their conduct has succeeded so well with them, that, had it not been for the French, there would not have been left so much as the memory of any of those nations which dared to oppose themselves to this deluge.

Those who suffered most were the Hurons, who engaged in this war as allies, auxiliaries, or neighbours to the Algonquins, or because they lay in the way of both. We have seen with astonishment one of the most populous and warlike nations on this continent, and the most esteemed of them all either for wisdom or good sense, almost wholly disappear in a few years. We may even say that there is not any nation in all this part of America who have not paid very dearly, for the Iroquois being obliged to take up arms, and I know none in all Canada except the Abenaquis, whom they have not molested in their own countries. For after they were once entered,

entered, and proved their fuccefs in war, and had tafted of the fweets of conqueft, they could no longer remain quiet, like lions, whofe thirft after blood is only encreafed by tafting of it. One would hardly imagine to what an immenfe diftance they have gone to feek out their enemies, and to give them battle. Notwithftanding, by dint of making continual war, as they were not without feveral checks at different times, they have found themfelves extremely diminifhed ; and were it not for the flaves they have made on all hands, moft of whom they have adopted, their fituation would be equally miferable with that of the nations they have fubdued.

What happened in this refpect to the Iroquois, may with ftill more reafon be faid of the other Indians in this country, and we are not to wonder if, as I have already remarked, thefe nations diminifh daily in a very fenfible manner. For tho' their wars appear lefs ruinous than ours at firft fight, they are however much more fo in proportion. The moft numerous of thefe nations perhaps never contained above fixty thoufand fouls, and there fometimes happen battles, in which cafe there is much blood fpilt. A furprife, or *coup de main*, fometimes deftroys a whole town ; oftentimes the fear of an irruption of an enemy makes a whole canton be deferted, when the fugitives to fhun the fword of the enemy, or their torturing punifhments, expofe themfelves to die of hunger and mifery in the woods, or on mountains, having feldom leifure or confideration enough to carry the neceffary provifions to fuch places. This happened in the laft age to a great number of Hurons and Algonquins, whofe fate it has been impoffible to learn.

I am, &c.

LETTER.

L E T T E R XIII.

Description of the country to the river of the Onnontagués. Of the flux and reflux in the great lakes of Canada. Manner in which the Indians sing the war-song. Of their God of War. Manner of declaring war. Of the collars of Wampum or Porcelain, and the Calumet, with their customs relating to peace and war.

Anse de la Famine, May 16th, 1721.

Madam,

HERE I am detained by a contrary wind, which has the appearance of lasting some time, and keeping me above a day in one of the worst places in the world. I shall endeavour to divert my chagrin by writing to you. Whole armies of those pigeons we call turtles are continually passing here, and if one of them would take charge of my letters, perhaps, you might hear of me before I leave this place; but the Indians have not as yet thought of training up these birds to this piece of dexterity, as it is said the Arabians and several other nations did formerly.

I

I embarked on the 14th, precisely at the same hour, on which I arrived the evening before at Catarocoui. I had only six leagues to make, in order to gain the island *aux Chevreuils*, or of Roebucks, where there is a good harbour capable of receiving large barks; but my Canadians having forgot to examine their canoe, and the sun having melted the gum in several places, it admitted the water on all sides, and I was obliged to stop two hours in order to repair it in one of the islands at the entrance of Lake Ontario; we continued our course afterwards till past ten at night, but not being able to gain the island *aux Chevreuils*, we were obliged to pass the remainder of the night at the corner of the forest.

Here I observed for the first time vines in the woods. There were almost as many as there were trees, and they always climbed quite to their top. This was the first time I had made this observation having never stopt before but in open fields; but I am told this continues all the way to Mexico. These vines are very thick at bottom, and bear great plenty of grapes, which, however, are no larger than pease, but this cannot be otherwise, seeing they are neither pruned nor cultivated. When ripe they afford excellent feeding for the bears, who climb to the tops of the highest trees in quest of them. After all, they have only the leavings of the birds, which would soon rob whole forests of their vintage.

Next day I set out early in the morning, and at eleven o'clock stopt at the island *aux Gallots*, three leagues beyond the island *aux Chevres*, in 43 deg. 33 min. lat. I reimbarked a little after mid-day, and made a traverse of a league and a half, in order

der to gain the *Point of the Traverse*; for had I coasted along the main-land in order to get at that place, from that where I spent the night, I should have had a course to make of above forty leagues, which way, however, must be taken when the lake is not very calm; for if it be ever so little agitated, the waves are as heavy as those at open sea. It is not even possible to range along the coast when the wind is any thing large.

From the point of the Isle *aux Gallots*, you see to the westward the river of *Chauguen*, formerly the river of *Onnontagué*, at the distance of fourteen leagues. As the lake was calm, as there was no appearance of bad weather, and as we had a small breeze at east, just sufficient to fill our sails, I took a resolution to steer directly for that river, in order to save a circuit of fifteen or twenty leagues. My guides who had more experience than I, imagined this enterprize hazardous, but yielded out of complaisance to my opinion. The beauty of the country which lay on the left hand, did not tempt me, any more than the salmon and great quantities of other excellent fish, which are taken in the six fine rivers, which lie at the distance of two or three leagues from one another*. We therefore bore away, and till four o'clock had no reason to repent it; but then the wind rose all on a sudden, and we should have been very well pleased to have been close in with the land. We made towards the nearest, from which we still were three leagues, and had great difficulty to gain it. At last about seven

---

* The river of Assumption is a league from the point of the Traverse, that of Sables three leagues farther; that of la Planche two leagues beyond the former, that of La Grande Famine two leagues more, that of La Petite Famine one league, and that of La grosse Ecorce another league.

in

in the evening we landed at *Anfe de la Famine*, or the Creek of Famine, fo called, becaufe M. de la Barre, governor-general of New-France, had very near loft his whole army there by hunger, and other diftempers, when he was going upon an expedition againft the Iroquois.

It was high time we fhould arrive, the wind was ftrong, and the waves ran fo high that no one durft have croffed the Seine oppofite to the Louvre, in fuch a fituation as we were then in. This place is indeed very proper for deftroying an army which fhould depend on hunting and fifhing for fubfiftence, befides that the air feems to be extremely unwholfome. Nothing, however, can exceed the beauty of the foreft, which covers all the banks of this lake. The white and red oaks raife their heads as high as the clouds, and there is another tree of a very large kind, the wood of which is hard but brittle, and bears a great refemblance to that of the plane-tree; its leaves have five points, are of a middle fize, of a very beautiful green in the infide, but whitifh without. It has got the name of the cotton-tree, becaufe it bears a fhell nearly of the thicknefs of an Indian Chefnut-tree, containing a fort of cotton which, however feems to be good for nothing.

As I was walking on the banks of the lake I obferved that it fenfibly lofes ground on this fide, the land being here much lower and more fandy for the fpace of half a league, than it is beyond it. I likewife obferved that in this lake, and I am told that the fame thing happens in all the reft; there is a fort of flux and reflux almoft inftantaneous, the rocks near the banks being covered with water, and uncovered again feveral times in the fpace of

a

a quarter of an hour, even fhould the furface of the lake be very calm, with fcarce a breath of wind. After reflecting for fome time on this appearance, I imagined it was owing to the fprings at the bottom of the lakes, and to the fhock of their currents with thofe of the rivers, which fall into them from all fides, and thus produce thofe intermitting motions.

But would you believe it, Madam, that at this feaion of the year, and in the 43d deg. of latitude, there is not as yet fo much as a fingle leaf upon the trees, though we have fometimes as hot weather as with you in the month of July. This is undoubtedly owing to the earth's having been covered with fnow for feveral months, and not being as yet fufficiently warm to open the pores of the roots, and to caufe the fap to afcend. The *Grande* and *Petite Famine* fcarce deferve the name of rivers ; they are only brooks, efpecially the latter, but are pretty well ftocked with fifh. There are eagles here of a prodigious fize, my people have juft now thrown down a neft, in which there was a cart-load of wood and two eaglets, not as yet feathered, but as big as the largeft Indian pullets. They have eat them, and declare they were very good. I return to Catarocoui, where, the night I paffed there, I was witnefs to a pretty curious fcene.

About ten or eleven o'clock at night, juft as I was going to retire, I heard a cry, which I was told was the war-cry, and foon after faw a troop of the Miffifaquez enter the fort finging all the way. It feems, for fome years paft, thefe Indians have been engaged in a war which the Iroquois carried on againft the Cherokees, a numerous nation inhabiting a fine country to the fouthward of Lake Erié ;
and

and fince that time their young men have had a
ftrange itching to be in action. Three or four of
thefe bravoes equipped as if they had been going to
a mafquerade, with their faces painted in fuch a
manner as to infpire horror, and followed by almoft
all the Indians in the neighbourhood of the fort,
after having gone through all the cabbins finging
their war fongs to the found of the chichikoué,
which is a fort of calabafh filled with little flint
ftones, came to perform the fame ceremony through
all the apartments in the fort, in order to do honour to the commandant and the reft of the officers.

I own to you, Madam, that this ceremony has
fomething in it which infpires one with horror when
feen for the firft time, and I had not been as yet fo
fully fenfible as I then was, that I was among barbarians. Their fongs are at all times melancholy
and doleful ; but here they were to the laft degree
frightful, occafioned perhaps entirely by the dark-
nefs of the night, and the apparatus of this feftival,
for fuch it is amongft the Indians. This invitation
was made to the Iroquois, who finding the war
with the Cherokees begin to turn burthenfome, or
not being in the humour, required time for deliberation, after which every one returned home.

It fhould feem, Madam, that in thefe fongs they
invoke the god of war, whom the Hurons call
Arefkoui, and the Iroquois *Agrefkoué* ; I know not
what name he bears in the Algonquin languages.
But it is not a little furprifing, that the Greek word
Aϱης, which is Mars, and the god of war in all thofe
countries which have followed the theology of Ho-
mer, fhould be the root whence feveral terms in
the Huron and Iroquoife languages feem to be derived,

rived, which have a relation to war. *Aregouen* signifies to make war, and is conjugated in this manner: *Garego*, I make war; *Sarego*, thou makeſt war; *Arego*, he makes war. Moreover, Areſkoui is not only the Mars of theſe people, but likewiſe the ſovereign of the gods, or as they expreſs it, the Great Spirit, the Creator and Maſter of the Univerſe, the Genius who governs all things; but it is chiefly in warlike expeditions that they invoke him; as if the attribute, which does him greateſt honour, was, that of being the God of armies. His name is their war-cry before battle, and in the heat of the engagement: in their marches likewiſe they repeat it often, as if to encourage one another, and to implore his aſſiſtance.

To take up the hatchet, is to declare war; every private perſon has a right to do it, and nothing can be ſaid againſt him; unleſs it be among the Hurons and Iroquois, where the matrons command and prohibit a war as ſeems good unto them; we ſhall ſee in its proper place how far their authority extends in theſe matters. But if a matron wants to engage any one who does not depend on her, to levy a a party for war, whether it be to appeaſe the manes of her huſband, ſon, or near relation, or whether it be to procure priſoners, in order to replace thoſe in her cabbin, of whom death or captivity has deprived her; ſhe muſt make him a preſent of a collar of Wampum, and ſuch an invitation is ſeldom found ineffectual.

When the buſineſs is to declare war in form between two or three nations, the manner of expreſſing it is *to hang the kettle over the fire*; which has its origin without doubt from the barbarous cuſtom of eating their priſoners, and thoſe who have been
killed

I

killed after boiling them. They likewise say simply, that they are going to *eat such a nation*, which signifies that they are going to make war against them in the moſt deſtructive and outrageous manner, and indeed they ſeldom do otherwiſe. When they intend to engage an ally in the quarrel, they ſend him a porcelain or wampum, which is a large ſhell, in order to invite him to drink the blood, or as the terms made uſe of ſignify, the broth of the fleſh of their enemies. After-all, this practice may have been very antient, without our being able to infer from thence, that theſe people have always been Anthropophagi, or Man-eaters. It was, perhaps, at firſt, only an allegorical manner of ſpeaking, with examples of which the ſcripture often furniſhes us. David, in all appearance, had not to do with enemies who were accuſtomed to eat human fleſh, when he ſays: *Dum appropriant ſuper me nocentes ut edunt carnes meas.* Pſalms xxvi. 2. Afterwards ſome nations becoming ſavage and barbarous, may have ſubſtituted the reality in the room of the figure.

I took notice that the porcelain in theſe countries are ſhells ; theſe are found on the coaſts of New-England and Virginia ; they are channelled, drawn out lengthwiſe, a little pointed, without ears and pretty thick. The fiſh contained in theſe ſhells are not good to eat ; but the inſide is of ſo beautiful a varniſh with ſuch lively colours, that it is impoſſible to imitate it by art. When the Indians went altogether naked, they made the ſame uſe of them which our firſt parents did of the leaves of the fig-tree, when they diſcovered their nakedneſs and were aſhamed at it. They likewiſe hung them at their necks, as being the moſt precious things they had, and to this day their greateſt riches and fineſt

fineſt ornaments conſiſt of them. In a word, they entertain the ſame notion of them that we do of gold, ſilver, and precious ſtones; in which they are ſo much the more reaſonable, as in a manner they have only to ſtoop to procure riches as real as ours, for all that depends upon opinion. James Cartier in his memoirs makes mention of a ſhell of an uncommon ſhape, which he found, as he ſays, in the iſland of Montreal; he calls it *Eſurgni*, and affirms it had the virtue of ſtopping a bleeding at the noſe. Perhaps, it is the ſame we are now ſpeaking of; but they are no longer to be found in the iſland of Montreal, and I never heard of any but the ſhells of Virginia which had the property Cartier ſpeaks of.

There are two ſorts of theſe ſhells, or to ſpeak more properly two colours, one white and the other violet. The firſt is moſt common, and perhaps, on that account leſs eſteemed. The ſecond ſeems to have a finer grain when it is wrought; the deeper its colour is, the more it is valued. Small cylindrical grains are made of both, which are bored through and ſtrung upon a thread, and of theſe *the branches and collars* of Porcelain or *Wampum* are made. The branches are no more than four or five threads, or ſmall ſtraps of leather, about a foot in length, on which the grains or beads of Wampum are ſtrung. The collars are in the manner of fillets or diadems formed of theſe branches, ſewed together with thread, making four, five, ſix or ſeven rows of beads, and of a proportionable length; all which depends on the importance of the affair in agitation, and dignity of the perſon to whom the collar is preſented.

By

By a mixture of beads of different colours, they form such figures and characters as they have a mind, which often serve to distinguish the affairs in question. Sometimes the beads are plaited, at least it is certain that they frequently send red collars when a war is in agitation. These collars are carefully preserved, and not only compose part of the publick treasures, but are likewise their regifters or annals, and ought to be studied by those who have the charge of the archives, which are deposited in the cabbin of the chief. When there are two chiefs in a village of equal authority, they keep the treasures and archives by turns for one night, but this night, at least at present, is a whole year. Collars are never used but in affairs of consequence; for those of less importance they make use of branches, or strings of porcelain, skins, blankets, maïz, either in grain or flour, and such like things; for all these make a part of the publick treasure. When they invite a village or a nation to enter into an alliance, sometimes they send them a pair of colours tinged with blood; but this practice is modern, and there is good reason to believe, they have taken the hint from the white colours of the French, and the red of the English. It is even said, that we ourselves first introduced it amongst them, and that they have thought of tinging theirs with blood, when the question was to declare war.

The calumet is no less sacred among the Indians than the collar of Wampum; it has even, if we may believe them a divine original, for they maintain, it was a present made them by the Sun. It is more in use among the southern and western nations, than among the eastern and northern, and is more frequently employed for peace than for war. *Calumet* is a Norman word, being a corruption of *Chaliorveau,*

liorveau, and the calumet of the Indians is properly
the ftalk of the pipe, but under that name is underftood the whole pipe as well as the ftalk. The
ftalk is very long in calumets of ceremony, and the
pipe has the fhape of our old hammers for arms ;
it is commonly made of a fort of reddifh marble,
very eafy to work, and found in the country of the
Aiouez, beyond the Miffiffippi. The ftalk is of a
light wood, painted with different colours, and a-
dorned with the heads, tails, and feathers of the
moft beautiful birds, which in all probability is only
intended for ornament.

The cuftom is to fmoke in the calumet when it
is accepted, and perhaps, there is no example of an
engagement entered into in this manner being vio-
lated. The Indians at leaft are perfuaded, that the
great fpirit never fuffers an infraction of this kind
to efcape with impunity. If in the midft of a battle, an enemy prefents a calumet, it may be refufed ; but if it is accepted, their arms on both fides
muft immediately be laid down. There are calumets for all different forts of treaties. When an
exchange is agreed upon in trade they prefent a calumet, in order to cement the bargain, which renders it in fome meafure facred. When a war is in
agitation, not only the ftalk, but even the feathers
with which it is adorned are red ; fometimes they
are red only on one fide, and it is pretended, that
from the manner in which the feathers are difpofed,
they know at firft fight to what nation it is to be
prefented.

It cannot be doubted, but that the Indians, by
caufing thofe to fmoke in the calumet, with whom
they feek to enter into a treaty of alliance or commerce, intend to take the fun for a witnefs, and in

some measure for a guarantee of their mutual engagements ; for they never fail to blow the smoke towards that luminary ; but that from this practice, and from the ordinary use of the calumet, we ought to infer as some have done, that this pipe might originally be the Caduceus of Mercury, appears to me by so much the less probable, as the Caduceus had no manner of relation to the Sun, and as nothing is to be found in the traditions of the Indians, by which we can imagine they had ever the least acquaintance with the Grecian Mythology. It would, in my opinion, be much more natural to suppose, that these people, informed by experience that the smoke of their tobacco dissipated the vapours of the brain, made their heads clearer, raised their spirits, and put them into a better condition for managing affairs, have for that reason introduced it into their councils, where, indeed, they have the pipe continually in their mouths, and that after having maturely deliberated and taken their resolutions, they imagined they could not find a more proper symbol for affixing a seal to what had been agreed upon, nor a pledge more capable of securing its execution, than the instrument which had had so much share in their deliberations. Perhaps, Madam, you may think it more simple, still to say, that these people imagined nothing could be a more natural sign of a strict union, than smoking out of the same pipe, especially, if the smoke be offered to a Divinity, who sets the seal of religion upon it. To smoke then out of the same pipe, in sign of alliance, is the same thing as to drink out of the same cup, as has been at all times the practice among several nations. Such customs as these are too natural an offspring of the human mind, for us to seek for mysteries in them.

The

The fize and ornaments of the calumets, which are prefented to persons of diftinction, on occafions of importance, are not fo particular that we need fearch far for their motives. When men begin to have ever fo little commerce together, or to entertain mutual refpect for one another, they are foon accuftomed to have certain regards for one another, chiefly on occafions when publick affairs are in agitation, or when they want to engage the good-will of thofe with whom they have bufinefs to tranfact, and hence proceeds the care they take to give a greater magnificence to the prefents they make one another. But it is to the *Panis*, a nation fettled on the banks of the Miffouri, who extend themfelves a good way towards New Mexico, that it is pretended the Sun gave the calumet. But thefe Indians have probably done like a great many other people, endeavoured to ennoble by the marvellous, a cuftom of which they were the authors; and all that can be concluded from this tradition, is, that the Panis paid the Sun a more ancient and diftinguifhed worfhip than the other nations of that part of the continent of America, and that they were the firft who thought of making the calumet a fymbol of alliance. In the laft place, if the calumet had been in its inftitution the caduceus of Mercury, it would have only been employed in affairs relating to peace or commerce, whereas it is certain, that it is ufed in treaties that have war for their object.

Thefe hints, Madam, I thought neceffary, in order to give you a perfect knowledge of what relates to the wars of the Indians, about which I fhall entertain you in my next letters till I have exhaufted the fubject; at leaft, if they are digreffions, they are not altogether foreign to my defign. Befides,

a

a traveller endeavours to difpofe in the leaft difagreeable manner he can every thing that he learns
upon his rout.

I am, &c.

LETTER

L E T T E R XIV.

Defcription of the country from the Anfe de la Famine *to the* Riviere des Sables. *Motives of the Indians for going to war. Departure of the warriors for the campain, with what precedes their fetting out. Their manner of taking leave of their relations and countrymen. Their arms offenfive and defenfive. Their care in taking along with them their tutelary gods. Particularities of the country as far as Niagara.*

Riviere des Sables, May 19, 1721.

Madam,

I Am now once more ftopped by a contrary wind, which arofe the moment we were likelieft to make moft fpeed. It even furprifed us fo abruptly, that we would have been in great danger had we not fortunately met with this fmall river to take fanctuary in. You muft acknowledge there are a multitude of inconveniencies and difappointments to cope with in fuch a voyage as this. It is a very fad thing to fail a hundred, and fometimes two hundred leagues without meeting with a fingle houfe,

or

or feeing one human creature; to be engaged in a voyage of two or three hundred leagues to fhun a paffage of twenty, made with many difficulties, and with the hazard of lofing one's life by the caprice of the winds; to be ftopped, as it fometimes happens, for whole weeks, on fome point or barren fhore, or if it fhould happen to rain, to be obliged to take up one's lodging under fome canoe, or in a tent: if the wind proves ftrong we muft feek for fhelter in fome wood, where we are expofed to be crufhed to death by the fall of fome tree. Thefe inconveniencies might be fhunned in part by the building veffels for failing on the lakes; but in order to have this advantage, the trade muft be better able to afford it.

We are now on the borders of the Iroquois cantons, which is an exceeding delightful country. We embarked early yefterday in the fineft weather imaginable. There was not a fingle breath of wind, and the lake was as fmooth as glafs. About nine or ten o'clock we paffed by the mouth of the river of Onnantague, which feemed to me to be about 120 feet in breadth. The lands near it are fomewhat low, but exceeding well wooded. Almoft all the rivers which water the Iroquois cantons difcharge themfelves into this, the fource of which is a fine lake called *Gannentatha*, on the banks of which are faltpits. Towards half an hour paft eleven we made fail by favour of a fmall breeze at north-eaft, and in a few hours pufhed on as far as the Bay *des Goyogouins*, which is ten leagues from the Riviere of Onnontague. The whole coaft in this tract is diverfified with fwamps and high lands fomewhat fandy, covered with the fineft trees, efpecially oaks, which feem as if planted by the hand of men.

A ftrong

A ſtrong gale of wind from the land, which o·
vertook us oppoſite to the Bay des Goyogouins,
obliged us to take ſanctuary in it. This is one of
the fineſt ſpots I have ever ſeen. A peninſula well
wooded advances from the middle, and forms a
kind of theatre. On the left as you enter, you perceive in a bight a ſmall iſland which conceals the
mouth of a river, by which the Goyogouins deſcend
to the lake. The wind did not continue long, we
therefore ſet out again, and made three or four
leagues farther. This morning we embarked before
ſun-riſe, and have actually made five or ſix leagues.
I know not how long the north-weſt wind may de-
tain us here. Whilſt I wait till a favourable gale
ariſes, I will reſume my relation of the wars of the
Indians, where I left it off.

Theſe Barbarians rarely refuſe to engage in a war,
when invited by their allies. They commonly do
not even want any invitation to take up arms; the
ſmalleſt motive, even a very nothing, is with them
cauſe ſufficient. But above all, vengeance is their
darling paſſion ; they have always ſome old or new
grudge to ſatisfy ; for no length of time ever cloſes
thoſe ſort of wounds, let them be ever ſo ſlight.
Thus one can never be ſure that the peace is fully
eſtabliſhed between two nations who have been long
enemies : on the other hand, the deſire of replacing
the dead by priſoners to appeaſe their manes ; the
caprice of a private perſon, a dream which every
one explains at random, with other reaſons and pre-
texts equally frivolous, will often occaſion a party
to go to war, who thought of nothing leſs the day
before.

'Tis true, theſe ſmall expeditions, without con·
ſent of the council, are generally without any great

con-

confequence, and as they demand no great preparations, there is little attention paid to them ; but ge-
gerally fpeaking, they are not much difpleafed to
fee the youth exercifed, and keep themfelves in
breath, and they muft have very cogent reafons to
oppofe fuch a refolution ; befides, they rarely employ authority to this end, every one being mafter
of his own actions : But they try to intimidate fome
by falfe reports which they take care to fpread a-
broad ; others they follicit underhand ; they engage
the chief to break off the party by prefents, which
is no difficult matter ; for a dream, true or falfe, no
matter which, is all that is requifite to accomplifh
it. Amongft fome nations their laft refource is to
addrefs themfelves to the nations, which is generally efficacious, but they never have recourfe to this
method, but when the affair is of much confequence.

A war in which the whole nation is concerned,
is not fo eafily put an end to : they weigh with much
deliberation the advantages and difadvantages of it,
and whilft they are confulting, they take great care
to remove every thing that may give the enemy the
leaft fufpicion of their intention of breaking with
him. The war being once refolved upon, they confider firft the providing the neceffary provifions, and
the equipage of the warriors, which require no long
time. Their dances, fongs, feafts, and certain fu-
perftitious ceremonies which vary greatly in different nations, require a much greater length of
time.

He who is to command never thinks of levying
foldiers, till he has obferved a faft of feveral days,
during which he is bedawb'd with black, holds no
manner of difcourfe with any one, invokes day and
night his tutelar genius, and above all he is very
careful

careful to obferve what dreams he has. Their firm perfuafion, according to the prefumptuous genius of thofe Barbarians, that he is marching forth to certain victory, never fails to infpire him with fuch dreams as he defires. The faft being ended, he affembles his friends, and holding a collar of porcelain in his hand, addreffes them in words like thefe: My brethren, the Great Spirit is the author of what I fpeak, and has infpired me with the thought of what I am going to put in execution. The blood of fuch an one is not yet wiped away, his corpfe is not yet covered, and I am going to perform this duty to him. He fets forth in like manner the other motives which move him to take up arms. " I am therefore refolved to march to fuch a place " to take fcalps, or to make prifoners;" Or, " I will " eat fuch a nation. Should I perifh in this glo- " rious enterprize, or fhould any of my compa- " nions in it lofe his life, this collar will ferve to re- " ceive us, that we may not be for ever hid in the " duft, or in the mire." That is, perhaps, it will be the recompence of him who buries the dead.

As he pronounces thefe laft words, he lays the collar on the ground, and he who takes it up, by fo doing declares himfelf his lieutenant; he then thanks him for his zeal to revenge his brother, or to maintain the honour of the nation. Then they fet water on to warm, wafh the chief from his dawbing, drefs, anoint with oil or fat, or paint his hair. They paint his face with different colours, and clothe him in his fineft robe. Thus adorned, he fings with a hollow voice the fong of death; his foldiers, that is to fay, all thofe who have offered themfelves to accompany him (for no one is ever compelled) thunder out one after another their war fong; for every one has one peculiar to himfelf, which no other per-

fon

fon is allowed to ufe; and there are even fome which are coveted by certain families.

After this previous meafure, which paffes in fome remote place, and often in a ftove, the chief communicates his project to the council, who fit upon it, without ever admitting him who is the author of it, to be prefent. As foon as his project is approved of he makes a feaft; at which the chief, and fometimes the only, difh is a dog. Some pretend that this animal is offered to the god of war, before he is put in to the kettle, and poffibly this may be the practice amongft fome nations. I am glad, Madam, to have this opportunity of advertifing you once for all, that I don't pretend to fay that what I relate on this fubject, is abfolutely univerfal amongft all the nations. But it feems certain, that on the occafion I here fpeak of they make many invocations to their genii, good and evil, and above all to the god of war.

All this takes up feveral days, or rather the fame thing is repeated for feveral days running: but tho' every one feems wholly employed in thefe feftivals, each family takes its meafures for obtaining a fhare of the prifoners, either to replace their loffes, or to revenge their dead. In this view they make prefents to the chief, who on his fide gives both his promife and pledges befides. In default of prifoners they demand fcalps, which are more eafily obtained. In fome places, as amongft the Iroquois, as foon as a military expedition is refolved on they fet on the war kettle, and advertife their allies to fend or bring fomething to it, to fhew their approbation of the enterprize, and their readinefs to take part in it.

All

All thofe who enlift themfelves, give alfo to the chief, as a token 'of their engagement, a bit of wood with their mark upon it, and he who after that fhould draw back, would never be fafe while he lived; at leaft he would be difhonoured for ever. The party once formed, the war chief prepares a a new feaft, to which the whole village is invited, and before any thing is tafted, he, or an orator for him, and in his name, accofts them in fuch words as thefe : " My brethren, I know I am not worthy " to be called a man, tho' you all know that I " have more than once looked an enemy in the " face. We have been flaughtered ; the bones of " fuch and fuch perfons are yet unburied, they cry " out againft us, and we muft fatisfy their requeft. " They were once men as well as we; how there- " fore could we fo foon forget them, and fit fo long " in this lethargy on our matreffes ? In a word, the " genius who is the guardian of my honour and " the author of my renown, infpires me with " the refolution to revenge them. Youth, take " courage, anoint your hair, paint your vifages, " fill your quivers, caufe the forefts refound with " the voice of your military fongs, let us eafe and " comfort the deceafed, and fhew them that we " have avenged them."

After this difcourfe, and the applaufes with which it never fails to be attended, the chief proceeds into the midft of the affembly, his hatchet in his hand, and fings his fong ; all his foldiers make refponfes in the fame manner, and fwear to fecond him or to die in the attempt. All this is accompanied with gef- tures highly expreffive of their refolution never to give ground to an enemy ; but it is to be remarked that not a fyllable efcapes any foldier, which figni- fies the leaft dependance. The whole confifts in

a promise to act with perfect unanimity and in concert. Befides, the engagement they lay themfelves
under, requires great acknowledgements on the part
of the chief. For inftance, as often as any one in
the public dances ftrikes the poft with his hatchet,
and recals to memory his moft fignal exploits, as is
always the cuftom, the chief under whofe conduct
he performed them, is obliged to make him a prefent ; at leaft this is ufual among fome nations.

Thefe fongs are followed with dances ; fometimes
this is no more than a fierce fort of march, but in
cadence ; at others it is done by very lively geftures,
expreffive of the operations of a campaign, and always in cadence. Laftly, the whole ceremony concludes with a feaft. The war chief is no more than
a fpectator of it, with his pipe in his mouth ; it is
even common enough in every confiderable feaft,
for him who does the honours of it, to touch nothing at all himfelf. The following days, and till
the departure of the warriors, many things pafs,
the recital of which is not worth notice, and which
are befides neither effential nor generally practifed :
but I cannot forget a cuftom fingular enough, and
with which the Iroquois in particular never difpenfe :
it feems to have been devifed to difcover fuch perfons as are endued with natural good fenfe, and what
is called mother-wit, and are capable of govern-
ing themfelves as well as others ; for thefe Indians
whom we imagine barbarous people, believe it impoffible for any one to poffefs true courage without
being abfolute mafter of his paffions, or if he cannot endure the moft cruel reverfes that can poffibly happen. The affair is this.

The moft ancient of the military company treat
the young people, at leaft fuch as have never feen

an

an enemy, with all the fcorn and infults they are
capable of devifing. They throw hot embers on
their heads; they throw the moft cruel reproaches in
their teeth; they in fhort load them with all manner
of injuries, and carry this treatment to the greateft
excefs. All this muft be endured with the utmoft
infenfibility; to give at fuch occafions the leaft fign
of impatience, would be fufficient to caufe them be
declared for ever incapable of bearing arms : But
when this is done by perfons of the fame age, as it
often happens, the aggreffor muft take care to do
nothing wantonly, or out of private pique, or otherwife he would be obliged, when the fport is ended,
to attone for the affront by a prefent. I fay, when
the fport is ended, for whilft it lafts they are obliged to bear every thing without being angry, tho'
this fort of paftime often goes fo far as the throwing big burning brands at each others heads, and
giving heavy blows with cudgels.

As the hope of having their wounds cured, fhould
they happen to receive any, is no fmall encourage-
ment for the braveft to expofe themfelves boldly to
danger, they afterwards prepare the drugs for this
purpofe, and this is the office of their jugglers. I
will fome other time tell you what fort of perfons
thefe are. The whole town being affembled, one
of thefe quacks declares he is going to communicate to the roots and plants, of which he takes care
to provide good ftore, the virtue of healing all forts
of wounds, and even of reftoring the dead to life. He
falls immediately a finging; the other quacks make refponfes to him, and it is believed that during the concert, which would not appear to your ear very me
lodious, and which is accompanied with many gri-
maces on the part of the actors, the medicinal quality is communicated to the plants. The chief juggler

gler then makes trial of them; he begins with bleeding his own lips, he applies his remedy; the blood which the impoftor fucks in very dextroufly ceafes to flow, and the whole auditory cries out, *A miracle, a miracle*. After this, he takes a dead animal, and leaves the fpectators as much time to confider as they chufe, when by means of a canule or pipe inferted under the tail, he caufes it to move by blowing his herbs into its throat when the exclamations of admiration are redoubled. Laftly, the whole company of jugglers makes the tour of the cabbins, finging the praifes and virtues of their remedies. Thefe tricks at bottom deceive no one, but ferve to amufe the multitude, and cuftom muft be obeyed.

The following is another ufage peculiar to the Miamis, and perhaps to fome other nations in the neighbourhood of Louifiana. I have extracted it from the memoirs of a Frenchman who was eye-witnefs of it. After a folemn feaft they placed, fays he, on a kind of altar, fome figures of pagods, made of bears fkins, the heads of which were painted green. All the Indians paffed before this altar, making their genuflexions, or bending their knees, and the quacks led the band, holding in their hand a fack, in which were inclofed all thefe things which were wont to be ufed in their invocation or worfhip. He was the clevereft fellow who made the moft extravagant contortions, and in proportion as any one diftinguifhed himfelf this way, he was applauded with great fhouts. After they had thus paid their firft homage to the idols, they all danced in a very confufed manner, to the found of the drum and chichicoué; and during this the jugglers pretended to bewitch or charm feveral Indians, who
feemed

seemed to be expiring under the power of their in-
cantations: afterwards, by applying a certain powder to their lips, they restored them to life.

When this farce had lasted some time, he who
presided at the feast, having two men and two women near him, run over all the cabbins, to intimate
that the sacrifices were going to begin. On meeting any one in his way, he rested both hands on
his head, and the other embraced his knees. The
victims were to be dogs, and the cries of these animals, which were howling, and of the Indians who
howled as if to answer them, with all their might
were heard on all sides. When the viands were
ready, they were offered to the pagods, they were
afterwards eaten, and the bones were burnt. Mean
time the juggler continued to restore the dead to
life, and the whole concluded with distributing to
these quacks a portion of whatever was most to their
fancy in the whole town.

From the time of their coming to the resolution
of making war, to the departure of the warriors,
the nights are spent in singing, and the days in
making the necessary preparations. They depute
warriors to sing the war song amongst their neighbours and allies, whom they often take care to dif-
pose to their desires before hand, and by secret negociations. If their rout is by water, they build or
repair their canoes; if it happen to be in the winter
season, they provide themselves in sledges and snow
shoes. These snow shoes, which are absolutely necessary for walking in the snow, are about three
feet long, and from fifteen to sixteen inches in their
extreme width. They are of an oval shape, except
that the hind part terminates in a point; there are
small bits of wood placed cross wise five or six inches
from

from either end, which ferve to ftrengthen them,
and that on the fore part is as it were the ftring of a
bow, under an opening in which the foot is inferted, and made faft with thongs. The tiffue or covering of the fnow fhoe is made of ftraps of leather
two fingers broad, and the border is of a light
wood hardened in the fire. To walk well on
thefe fhoes, you muft turn your knees inwards,
keeping your legs at a good diftance from each o-
ther. It is very difficult to accuftom one's felf to
them; but when once you attain it, you walk eafily and without fatiguing yourfelf any more than
if you had nothing on your feet. It is impoffible
to make ufe of thefe fnow fhoes with common fhoes.
One muft wear thofe of the Indians, which are a
kind of facks made of dried hides, folded over the
extremity of the foot, and tied with cords.

Their fledges, which ferve to tranfport the baggage, and in cafe of neceffity the fick and wounded, are two fmall and very thin boards half a foot
broad each, and fix or feven long. The fore part
is fomewhat raifed, and the fides bordered with
fmall bands, to which the thongs for binding whatever is laid upon the carriage, is faftened. Let thefe
carriages be ever fo much loaded, an Indian draws
it without difficulty, by means of a long thong or
ftrap, which is pafs'd round his breaft, and is called a collar. They ufe them likewife for carrying
burdens, and mothers for carrying their children
with their cradles; but in this cafe the thong or
collar is placed upon their forehead, and not on
their breafts.

Every thing being ready, and the day of their
departure come, they take their leave with great
demonftrations of real affection. Every one is defirous

firous of having fomething the warriors have been in ufe to wear or carry about them, and gives them in return pledges of their friendfhip, and affurances of an everlafting remembrance of them. They fcarce ever enter any of their cabins without carrying away their robe, in order to give them a better, or at leaft one full as good in its ftead. Laftly, they all repair to the chief. They find him armed as on the firft day of his addreffing himfelf to them, and as he has appeared in publick ever fince. They again have their faces painted, every one after his own fancy or caprice, and all of them generally fo as to ftrike terror. The chief makes them a fhort harangue: afterwards he comes out of his cabin finging the death fong. They all follow him in file, or one after another, obferving a profound filence; and the fame thing is repeated every morning when they begin their march. Here the women lead the van with their provifions; and when the warriors have joined them, they deliver to them all their baggage, and remain almoft naked; at leaft as much fo as the feafon will allow.

Formerly the arms of the Indians were the bow and arrow, and a kind of javelin, both pointed with a kind of bone worked in different manners; and laftly, the hatchet or break-head. This was formerly a fhort club of a very hard wood, the head of which was partly round, and partly fharp edged. Moft had no defenfive weapon; but when they attacked any entrenchment, they covered their whole body with fmall light boards. Some have a fort of cuirafs, or breaft plate, of fmall pliable rings very neatly worked. They had even formerly a kind of mail for the arms and thighs made of the fame materials. But as this kind of armour was found not to be proof againft fire arms, they have renounced

Y them

them, without putting any thing in their place
The weftern Indians always ufe bucklers of buffaloes hide, which are very light, and proof againft
mufket-fhot. It is pretty furprifing, the other Indian
nations never ufe them.

When they ufe our fwords, which is very rare,
they handle them like our half pike : but when they
can have fire arms, powder and fhot, they abandon
their bows, and are excellent markfmen. We
have no caufe to repent having given them thefe
arms, tho' we were not the firft to do it. The Iroquois had got them of the Dutch, who were then in
poffeffion of New-York ; which laid us under the
neceffity of giving them to our allies. They have a
kind of ftandards or colours to know one another
by, and to enable them to rally ; thefe are fmall
pieces of bark cut into a round form, which they
fix to the head of a pole, and on which is drawn
the mark of their nation or village. If the party is
numerous, each family or tribe has its peculiar enfign with its diftinguifhing mark. Their arms are
alfo adorned with different figures, and fometimes
with the mark of the chief.

But that which they are as careful not to forget,
as even their arms, and which they guard with ftill
more care, is their manitous. I fhall treat more
particularly of them elfewhere ; it fuffices here to
fay, that they are fo many fymbols, under which
every one reprefents his tutelar genius. They in-
clofe them all in a bag made of rufhes, and painted
with different colours ; and often to do honour to
the chief, they place this bag in the prow of his canoe. if there are too many manitous to be contained in one bag, they diftribute them amongft feveral bags, which are entrufted to the care of the
lieutenant

lieutenant and of the elders of each family. To thefe they join the prefents which have been made them in order to obtain prifoners, together with the tongues of all the animals killed during the campaign, and which are to be facrificed to the genii at their return.

In their marches by land, the chief carries his own bag called his matrafs, but may difcharge this burden on any one at pleafure, and need not fear being refufed, this being looked upon as an honour done the perfon to whom it is given : this is alfo a fort of right of furvivorfhip to the command in cafe the chief and his lieutenant fhould happen to die in the campaign. But whilft I write you, behold me arrived in the river Niagara, where I fhall meet with agreeable company, and remain fome days. I fet out from Riviere des Sables, the 21ft before fun rife, but the wind proving always contrary, we were obliged at ten o'clock to enter the bay of the Tfonnonthouans. At half way between this bay and Riviere des Sables, there is a fmall river which I would not have failed to vifit, had I been fooner informed of what it has that is fingular, which I learnt juft after my arrival here.

This river is called Cafconchiagon, and is very narrow, and fhallow at its difcharge into the lake. A little higher it is 240 feet in breadth, and it is affirmed that there is water to float the largeft fhips. Two leagues from its mouth you are ftopped by a fall, which feems to be about fixty feet high, and 240 feet broad ; a mufket fhot above this, you find a fecond of the fame breadth, but not fo high by a third : and half a league higher ftill a third, which is full a hundred feet high, and 360 feet broad. You meet after this with feveral rapids,

and

and after failing fifty leagues higher, you difcover
a fourth fall, nothing inferior to the third. The
courfe of this river is an hundred leagues, and after
you have failed up fixty leagues on it, you have no
more than ten to make over land, turning towards
the right, to arrive at the Ohio, otherwife, *la Belle
Riviere*. The place where you arrive at is called
Ganos, where, an officer worthy of credit, and from
whom I have received all I have been relating to
you, affures me he faw a fountain, the water of
which refembles oil, and has the tafte of iron. He
added, that a little farther there is another exactly of
the fame kind, and that the Indians make ufe of
its water to mitigate all kinds of pains.

The bay of the Tfonnonthouans is a delightful
place : here is a fine river which meanders between
two beautiful meadows fkirted with hills, between
which you difcover vallies which ftretch a great
way, the whole forming the nobleft profpect in the
whole world, and is furrounded with a magnificent
foreft of the talleft and largeft timber trees : but the
foil feemed to me a little light and fandy. We fet
out again at half an hour paft one, and continued
our voyage till ten at night. Our defign was to
take up our night's lodgings within a fmall river
called Buffaloe's river ; but we found the entry fhut
up with fand banks, which often happens to fmall
rivers which difcharge themfelves into thefe lakes,
by reafon of their carrying a great quantity of fand
along with them : for when the wind blows directly
towards their mouths, the fand is ftopped by the
waves, and gradually forms a dike, fo high and
ftrong that the current of the rivers cannot force a
paffage thro' it, except at fuch times as they are
fwoln by the melting of the fnow.

I was

I was obliged to pafs the reft of the night in my
canoe, where I was expofed to a very hard froft.
Thus the trees were fcarce obferved to bud, but
were all in the fame ftate as in the middle of winter.
We fet out thence at half an hour paft three in the
morning of the 22d, being afcenfion day, and went
to fay mafs at nine o'clock, at what is called *le
Grand Marais*. This is much fuch another place
as that of the Tfonnonthouans, but the lands feem
better. Towards two o'clock in the afternoon, we
entered the river of *Niagara* formed by the great
fall, whereof I fhall fpeak prefently, or rather it is
the river St. Lawrence, which proceeds from lake
Eriè, and paffes thro' lake Ontario after fourteen
leagues of Narrows. It is called the river Niagara
from the fall being a courfe of fix leagues. After
failing three leagues, you find on the left fome cabins of the Iroquois, Tfonnonthouans, and of the
Miffifagues as at Catarocoui. The Sieur de Joncaire, lieutenant of our troops, has alfo a cabbin at
this place, to which they have before hand given the
name of Fort * : for it is pretended that in time this
will be changed into a great fortrefs.

I found here feveral officers, who were to return
in a few days to Quebec. For this reafon I am
obliged to clofe my letter, which I fhall fend by that
way. As for my own part, I forefee I fhall have
time fufficient to write you another after they are
gone, and the place itfelf will in a great meafure
furnifh me materials enough to fill it, together with

* A fort has been fince built in the mouth of the river of
Niagara on the fame fide, and exactly at the place where Monf.
de Denonville had built one, which fubfifted not long. There
even begins to be formed here a French town.

what

what I fhall be able to learn of the officer I have
mentioned.

I have the honour to be, &c.

Niagara, May 23, 1721.

LETTER

L E T T E R   XV.

Tranſactions between the Tſonnonthouans *(à tribe of the* Iroquois) *and the* Engliſh, *on occaſion of building a* French *fort at* Niagara. *Deſcription of the country. Fire-dance ; ſtory on this occaſion. Deſcription of the Fall of* Niagara.

From the Fall of Niagara, May 14, 1721.

Madam,

I Have already had the honour to acquaint you, that we have a ſcheme for a ſettlement in this place ; but in order to know the reaſon of this project, it will be proper to obſerve, that as the Engliſh pretend, by virtue of the treaty of Utrecht, to the ſovereignty of all the Iroquoiſe country, and by conſequence, to be bounded on that ſide, by Lake Ontario only ; now it is evident, that, in caſe we allow of their pretenſions, they would then have it abſolutely in their power to eſtabliſh themſelves firmly in the heart of the French colonies, or at leaſt, entirely to ruin their commerce. In order, therefore, to prevent this evil, it has been judged proper, without, however, violating the treaty, to

make

make a fettlement in fome place, which, might fecure to us the free communication between the lakes,
and where the Englifh fhould not have it in their
power to oppofe us. A commiffion has therefore
been given to M. de Joncaire, who having in his
youth been prifoner amongft the Tfonnonthouans,
fo infinuated himfelf into the good graces of thofe
Indians, that they adopted him, fo that even in the
hotteft of their wars with us, and notwithftanding
his remarkable fervices to his country, he has always enjoyed the privileges of that adoption.

On receiving the orders I have been now mentioning to you, he repaired to them, affembled their
chiefs, and after having affured them, that his greateft pleafure in this world would be to live amongft
his brethren ; he added, that he would much oftener
vifit them, had he a cabin amongft them, to which
he might retire when he had a mind to be private.
They told him, that they had always looked upon
him as one of their own children, that he had only
to make choice of a place to his liking in any part
of the country. He afked no more, but went immediately and made choice of a fpot on the banks
of the river, which terminates the canton of Tfonnonthouan, where he built his cabbin. The news
of this foon reached New-York, where it excited fo much the more the jealoufy of the Englifh,
as that nation had never been able to obtain the favour granted to the Sieur de Joncaire, in any Iroquoife canton.

They made loud remonftrances, which being fe-
conded with prefents, the other four cantons at once
efpoufed their interefts. They were, however, never the nearer their point, as the cantons are not
only independant of each other, but alfo very jealous

lous of this independance. It was therefore neceffary to gain that of Tfonnonthouan, and the Englifh omitted nothing to accomplifh it ; but they were
foon fenfible they fhould never be able to get Joncaire difmiffed from Niagara. At laft they contented themfelves with demanding, that, at leaft, they
might be permitted to have a cabin in the fame
place ; but this was likewife refufed them. " Our
country is in peace, faid the Tfonnonthouans, the
French and you will never be able to live together,
without raifing difturbances. Moreover, added
they, it is of no confequence that Joncaire fhould
remain here ; he is a child of the nation, he enjoys
his right which we are not at liberty to take from
him."

Now, Madam, we muft acknowledge, that nothing but zeal for the publick good could poffibly
induce an officer to remain in fuch a country as this,
than which a wilder and more frightful is not to be
feen. On the one fide you fee juft under your feet,
and as it were at the bottom of an abyfs, a great
river, but which in this place is liker a torrent by
its rapidity, by the whirlpools formed by a thoufand
rocks, through which it with difficulty finds a paffage, and by the foam with which it is always covered ; on the other the view is confined by three
mountains placed one over the other, and whereof
the laft hides itfelf in the clouds. This would have
been a very proper fcene for the poets to make the
Titans attempt to fcale the heavens. In a word,
on whatever fide you turn your eyes, you difcover
nothing which does not infpire a fecret horror.

You have, however, but a very fhort way to go,
to behold a very different profpect. Behind thofe
uncultivated and uninhabitable mountains, you enjoy

joy the fight of a rich country, magnificent forefts, beautiful and fruitful hills ; you breathe the pureft air, under the mildeft and moft temperate climate imaginable, fituated between two lakes the leaft of which * is two hundred and fifty leagues in circuit.

It is my opinion that had we the precaution to make fure of a place of this confequence, by a good fortrefs, and by a tolerable colony, all the forces of the Iroquoife and Englifh conjoined, would not have been able, at this time to drive us out of it, and that we ourfelves would have been in a condition to give law to the former, and to hinder moft part of the Indians from carrying their furs to the fecond, as they daily do with impunity. The company I found here with M. de Joncaire, was compofed of the baron de Longueil, king's lieutenant in Montreal †, the marquis de Cavagnal, fon of the marquis de Vaudreuil, the prefent governor of New-France ; M. de Senneville, captain, and the Sieur de la Chauvignerie, enfign, and interpreter of the Iroquoife language. Thefe gentlemen are about negotiating an agreement of differences with the canton of Onontagué, and were ordered to vifit the fettlement of the Sieur de Joncaire, with which they were extremely well fatisfied. The Tfonnonthouans renewed to them the promife they had formerly made them, to maintain it. This was done in a council, in which Joncaire, as they told me, fpoke with all the good fenfe of a Frenchman, whereof he enjoys a large fhare, and with the fublimeft eloquence of an Iroquoife.

* Lake Ontario. Lake Erie is three hundred leagues round.
† He died governor of this city,

On the eve of their departure, that is, on the 29th, a Miſſiſuague regaled us with a feſtival, which has ſomething in it ſingular enough. It was quite dark when it began, and on entering the cabin of this Indian, we found a fire lighted, near which ſat a man beating on a kind of drum; another was conſtantly ſhaking his *Chichicoué*, and ſinging at the ſame time. This laſted two hours, and tired us very much as they were always repeating the ſame thing over again, or rather uttering half articulated ſounds, and that without the leaſt variation. We entreated our hoſt not to carry this prelude any further, who with a good deal of difficulty ſhewed us this mark of complaiſance.

Next, five or ſix women made their appearance, drawing up in a line, in very cloſe order, their arms hanging down, and dancing and ſinging at the ſame time, that is to ſay, they moved ſome paces forwards, and then as many backwards, without breaking the rank. When they had continued this exerciſe about a quarter of an hour, the fire, which was all that gave light in the cabbin, was put out, and then nothing was to be perceived but an Indian dancing with a lighted coal in his mouth. The concert of the drum and chichicoué ſtill continued, the women repeated their dances and ſinging from time to time; the Indian danced all the while, but as he could only be diſtinguiſhed by the light of the coal in his mouth he appeared like a goblin, and was horrible to ſee. This medley of dancing, and ſinging, and inſtruments, and that fire which never went out, had a very wild and whimſical appearance, and diverted us for half an hour; after which we went out of the cabin, though the entertainment laſted till morning. This Madam is all I ſaw of the fire-dance, and I have not been able to learn what

passed

paſſed the remainder of the night. The muſick, which I heard for ſome time after, was a great deal more ſupportable at a diſtance than when near it. The contraſt of male and female voices at a certain diſtance had a pleaſant effect enough ; and if the Indian women were taught muſick, I am confident they would make very agreeable ſingers.

I was very deſirous to know how a man was able to hold a lighted coal in his mouth ſo long, without being burnt, and without its going out ; but all I have been able to learn of this point is, that the Indians are acquainted with a plant which renders the part that has been rubbed with it inſenſible to fire, but whereof they would never communicate the diſcovery to the Europeans. We know that the onion and garlick will produce the ſame effect, though for a very ſhort while *. Beſides, how could this coal remain ſo long lighted ? be this as it will, I remember to have read in the letters of one of our ancient miſſionaries of Canada, a thing that has ſome relation to this, and which he learned from another miſſionary who was an eye witneſs. This perſon ſhewed him one day a ſtone, which one of their juglers or quacks had thrown into the fire in his preſence, leaving it there till it became red hot ; after which falling into a ſort of enthuſiaſtick frenzy, he took it between his teeth, and carrying it always in that manner, went to viſit a patient, the miſſionary following him ; as he caſt the ſtone upon the ground, the father on taking it up, perceived the marks of the Indian's teeth in it, but yet could not obſerve the leaſt ſign of burning in his mouth. He does not mention what the quack

---

* It is pretended that the leaves of the anemoné of Canada, in other reſpects very cauſtick, have this virtue.

did

did afterwards for the relief of the patient; but here is another incident of the fame kind, and proceeding from the fame fource, and of which your Grace will judge as you think proper.

A Huron woman, after having had a vifion, true or falfe, was feized with a giddinefs, and an almoft univerfal contraction of the nerves. As this woman from the beginning of the diforder, never flept without having many troublefome dreams, fhe began to fufpect fomething preternatural in it, and took it into her head, fhe fhould be cured by means of a feaft whereof fhe herfelf regulated all the ceremonies, according to what fhe faid, fhe remembered to have feen formerly practifed. Firft, fhe would have them carry her to the village where fhe was born, the elders whom fhe caufed to be advertized of her defign exhorting all the people to accompany her. In a moment's time her cabin was crowded with people, who came to offer her their fervice. She accepted them, inftructed them in what they were to do, and immediately the ftouteft of them placed her in a kind of litter, and carried her by turns, finging with all their might.

When they were come near the village, they affembled a great council to which the miffionaries were invited by way of compliment, who did all in their power, but ineffectually, to diffuade them from a thing, in which they juftly fufpected equal folly and fuperftition. They calmly heard all they had to fay on this fubject, but when they had done fpeaking, one of the chiefs of the council, undertook to refute their arguments, but with no better. fuccefs. Then leaving the miffionaries where he found them, he exhorted all the affiftants to acquit themfelves exactly of what fhould be prefcribed them,

them, and to maintain the ancient cuftoms. Whilſt
he was ſtill ſpeaking, two deputies from the patient entered the aſſembly, and requeſted on her
behalf, to have ſent her two young boys and two
young girls, attired in robes and belts of Wampum, with certain preſents, which ſhe mentioned,
adding, that ſhe would make known her further in-
tentions to theſe four perſons.

This was immediately put in execution, a ſhort
while afterwards, the four young perſons returned,
empty handed, and almoſt naked, the patient having ſtript them of all they had, even to their very
robes. In this condition they entered the council
which was ſtill aſſembled, and ſet forth the demands
of this woman, conſiſting of two and twenty articles, amongſt which one was a blue covering, to
be furniſhed by the miſſionaries, and all of them to
be delivered within an hour. They tried all their
rhetorick to obtain the covering, but this being pe-
remptorily refuſed, they were obliged to go without it. As ſoon as the ſick perſon received the other
preſents, ſhe entered the village, being carried, as
I have already ſaid, all the way. Towards evening, a publick crier, by her order, made procla-
mation, to have fires lighted in every cabbin, ſhe
being to viſit them all, which accordingly ſhe did
as ſoon as the ſun was ſet, being ſupported by two
men, and followed by the whole village. She
paſſed through the middle of all the fires, her feet
and legs naked, without receiving any harm, whilſt
her two ſupporters, though they did their utmoſt
endeavours to keep clear of being ſcorched ſuffered
greatly, as they were obl'ged to conduct her in this
manner acroſs upwards of three hundred fires : as
for her part, her conſtant complaint was of the
cold ;

cold ; at the end of this courfe, fhe declared fhe
felt herfelf better.

On the morrow, at funrife, they began, and by
her order too, a kind of Bacchanalian feftival, which
lafted three days. On the firft, all the people run
through the cabins, breaking and overturning every
thing, and, in proportion as the noife and hubbub
encreafed, the patient declared that her pains diminifhed. The other two days were fpent in running
over all the fires through which fhe had paffed, pro-
pofing her defires in ænigmatical terms, which they
were obliged to divine, and to perform accordingly,
that inftant ; fome of thefe were obfcene even to a
horrible degree. The fourth day, the fick perfon
made, a fecond time, the tour of all the cabbins,
but in a very different manner from the firft. She
was placed in the midft of two troops of Indians,
marching one after another, with a fad and languifhing air, and obferving a profound filence. No
perfon was fuffered to be in her way, and thofe who
formed the vanguard of her efcort, cleared the road
of all they met. As foon as fhe entered any cabin
they made her fit down, and placed themfelves
round her ; fhe fighed, related with a moving accent, all her evils, and gave to underftand that her
being perfectly cured, depended on the accomplifh-
ment of fome wifh, which fhe kept to herfelf, and
which muft be divined. Every one did his beft
to interpret it, but this defire was very complex,
and confifted of a great number of particulars, fo
that in proportion as they hit upon one of them,
they were obliged to give her what fhe fought for,
fhe fcarce ever left any cabbin, till fhe had got all
it contained.

When

When she saw them at a loss to guess her meaning, she expressed herself somewhat more clearly, and when they had guessed all, she caused every thing to be restored. There was no longer any doubt of her being perfectly cured, and a festival was made on the occasion, which consisted in cries, or rather, hideous howlings, and all manner of extravagancies. Lastly, she paid her acknowledgments, and, the better to testify her gratitude, she visited all the cabbins a third time, but without any ceremony. The missionary, who was witness to this ridiculous scene, says, that the sick person was not entirely cured, but that she was, however, a great deal better, though the most healthy and robust person would have died under such an operation. The father was at great pains to cause her take notice, that her pretended genius or familiar, had promised her a perfect cure, but had failed of his promise. He was answered, that amongst such a number of things as were to be done, it was hardly possible something should not have been omitted. He expected they would have chiefly insisted on the refusal of the blue covering ; it is true they made no mention of it, only they said, that after this refusal, the genius had appeared to the patient, and assured her that this refusal should do her no prejudice, because, the French not being natives of the country, the genii had no power over them. I return to my voyage.

The officers having departed, I ascended those frightful mountains, in order to visit the famous Fall of Niagara, above which I was to take water ; this is a journey of three leagues, though formerly five ; because the way then lay by the other, that is, the west-side of the river, and also because the place for embarking lay full two leagues above the
Fall.

Fall. But there has since been found, on the left, at the distance of half a quarter of a league from this cataract, a creek, where the current is not perceivable, and consequently a place where one may take water without danger. My first care, after my arrival, was to visit the noblest cascade perhaps in the world; but I presently found the baron de la Hontan had committed such a mistake with respect to its height and figure, as to give grounds to believe he had never seen it. It is certain, that if you measure its height by that of the three mountains, you are obliged to climb to get at it, it does not come much short of what the map of M. Deslisle makes it; that is, six hundred feet, having certainly gone into this paradox, either, on the faith of the baron de la Hontan or father Hennepin; but after I arrived at the summit of the third mountain, I observed, that in the space of three leagues, which I had to walk before I came to this piece of water, though you are sometimes obliged to ascend, you must yet descend still more, a circumstance to which travellers seem not to have sufficiently attended. As it is impossible to approach it but on one side only, and consequently to see it, excepting in profil, or sideways; it is no easy matter to measure its height with instruments. It, has, however, been attempted by means of a pole tied to a long line, and after many repeated trials, it has been found only one hundred and fifteen, or one hundred and twenty feet high. But it is impossible to be sure that the pole has not been stopt by some projecting rock; for though it was always drawn up wet, as well as the end of the line to which it was tied, this proves nothing at all, as the water which precipitates itself from the mountain, rises very high in foam. For my own part, after having

examined it on a'l fides, where it could be viewed
to the greateſt advantage, I am inclined to think
we cannot allow it leſs than a hundred and forty, or
fifty feet.

As to its figure, it is in the ſhape of a horfe-
ſhoe, and is about four hundred paces in circumference; it is divided into two, exactly in the middle, by a very narrow iſland, half a quarter of a
league long. It is true, thoſe two parts very ſoon
unite; that on my fide, and which I could only
have a fide view of, has ſeveral branches which project from the body of the caſcade, but that which
I viewed in front, appeared to me quite entire.
The baron de la Hontan mentions a torrent, which
if this author has not invented it, muſt certainly
fall through ſome channel on the melting of the
ſnows.

You may eaſily gueſs, Madam, that a great way
below this Fall, the river ſtill retains ſtrong marks
of ſo violent a ſhock; accordingly, it becomes only navigable three leagues below, and exactly at the
place which M. de Joncaire has choſen for his reſi-
dence. It ſhould by right be equally unnavigable
above it, ſince the river falls perpendicular the whole
ſpace of its breadth. But beſides the iſland, which
divides it into two, ſeveral rocks which are ſcattered
up and down above it, abate much of the rapidity
of the ſtream; it is notwithſtanding ſo very ſtrong,
that ten or twelve Outaways trying to croſs over to
the iſland to ſhun the Iroquoiſe who were in purſuit
of them, were drawn into the precipice, in ſpite of
all their efforts to preſerve themſelves.

I have

I have heard fay that the fifh that happen to be
entangled in the current, fall dead into the river,
and that the Indians of thofe parts were confiderably
advantaged by them; but I faw nothing of this
fort. I was alfo told, that the birds that attempted
to fly over were fometimes caught in the whirlwind
formed, by the violence of the torrent. But I obferved quite the contrary, for I faw fmall birds flying very low, and exactly over the Fall, which yet
cleared their paffage very well.

This fheet of water falls upon a rock, and there
are two reafons which induce me to believe, that it
has either found, or perhaps in time hollowed out
a cavern of confiderable depth. The firft is, that
the noife it makes is very hollow, refembling that
of thunder at a diftance. You can fcarce hear it
at M. de Joncaire's, and what you hear in this place,
may poffibly be only that of the whirlpools caufed
by the rocks, which fill the bed of the river as far
as this. And fo much the rather as above the cataract, you do not hear it near fo far. The fecond
is, that nothing has ever been feen again that has
once fallen over it, not even the wrecks of the
canoe of the Outaways, I mentioned juft now. Be
this as it will, Ovid gives us the defcription of fuch
another cataract fituated according to him in the
delightful valley of Tempe. I will not pretend that
the country of Niagara is as fine as that, though
I believe its cataract much the nobleft of the two *.

* Eft nemus Hæmoniæ, prærupta quod undique claudit
    Sylva, vocant Tempe, per quæ Peneus ab imo
    Effufus Pindo fpumofis volvitur undis.
    Dejectifque gravi tenues agitantia fumos
    Nubila conducit, fummifque afpergine fylvas
    Impluit, et fonitis plufquam vicina fatigat.   MET. Liv. 1.

Befides

Befides I perceived no mift above it, but from behind, at a diftance, one would take it for fmoke, and there is no perfon who would not be deceived with it, if he came in fight of the ifle, without having been told before-hand that there was fo furprifing a cataract in this place.

The foil of the three leagues I had to walk a foot to get hither, and which is called the carrying-place of Niagara, feems very indifferent; it is even very ill-wooded, and you cannot walk ten paces without treading on ant-hills, or meeting with rattle-fnakes, efpecially during the heat of the day. I think, I told you, Madam, that the Indians efteem the flefh of thofe reptiles a very great dainty. In general, ferpents are no way frightful to thefe people; there is no animal you fee oftener painted on their faces and bodies, and they feldom ever purfue them, except for food. The bones and fkins of ferpents are alfo of great fervice to their jugglers and wizards in divining; the laft of which they make ufe of for belts and fillets. It is no lefs true what we are told of their having the fecret of enchanting, or, to fpeak more properly, ftupifying thofe animals; their taking them alive, handling them, and putting them in their bofom, without receiving any hurt; a circumftance, which contributes not a little towards gaining them the great credit they have amongft thefe people.

I was going to feal this letter, when my people came to tell me, we fhould not fet out to-morrow as I expected. So I muft wait with patience, and profit what I can of my fpare time. I am therefore going to refume the article of the wars of the Indians, which will not be fo foon exhaufted. The

mo-

moment all the warriors are embarked, the canoes fail to a little diftance, keeping clofe together in one line ; then the chief rifes, holding in his hand his chichicouè, and fings aloud his own war-fong, to which his foldiers made anfwer by a treble *bé !* fetched from the bottom of their breafts. The elders and chiefs of the council who have remained on the banks, then exhort the warriors to do their duty, and above all to beware of being furprifed. This is, of all the advices which can be given an Indian, the moft neceffary, and that, by which they generally profit leaft. This admonition, however, interrupts not the chief who continues to fing all the while. Laftly, the warriours conjure their relations and friends, to remember them continually, and then raifing the moft horrid fhouts or howlings all together, they immediately fet out with fo much celerity, that they are inftantly out of fight.

The Hurons and Iroquois make no ufe of the chichicouè, but give them to their prifoners, fo that this which with other Indians is a warlike inftrument, feems with them a mark or badge of flavery. The warriors never make fhort marches, efpecially when in large bodies ; moreover, they conftrue every thing that happens into an omen, and the jugglers, whofe function it is to explain them, haften or retard their marches at pleafure. Whilft they are in a country where they have no fufpicion of an enemy, they ufe no manner of precaution, and fometimes there are fcarce half a dozen warriors together, the reft being difperfed up and down a hunting. But let them be at ever fo great a diftance from the rout, they are fure to be at the place of rendezvous at the hour appointed.

They

They pitch their camp long before fun-fet, and commonly leave in the front of it a large fpace, inclofed with a pallifade, or rather a kind of latticework, on which are placed their manitous, turned towards that fide on which their rout lies. They invoke them for the fpace of an hour, and the fame thing is done every morning before they fet out. This being done, they imagine they have nothing to fear, being perfuaded that the genii take upon themfelves the office of centinels, and the whole army fleeps fecurely under their fafeguard. No experience is able to undeceive thefe barbarians, or to draw them out of their prefumptuous confidence. This has its fource in an indolence and lazinefs which nothing is able to overcome.

Every thing in the way of the warriors is held as an enemy. In cafe, however, they fhould happen to meet with their allies, or parties of near the fame force with whom they no have quarrel, they enter in a league of mutual friendfhip. If the allies they meet are at war with the fame enemy, the chief of the ftrongeft party, or of that which has firft taken up arms, gives the other a prefent of fcalps, of which they never fail to make provifion for fuch occafions; and tells him, *You alfo have a blow here*; that is, you have fulfilled your engagements, your honour is now fecure, and you are at liberty to return; but this is to be underftood when the rencounter is accidental, and that no word or promife has paffed betwixt them, or that they have no need of a reinforcement.

When they are on the point of entering the enemy's country, they halt to perform a very extraordinary ceremony. In the evening there is a great

feaft

feaſt, after which they go to ſleep As ſoon as all
are awake, thoſe who have had any dreams go from
tent to tent, or rather from fire to fire, ſinging their
death-ſong, in which they inſert their dreams in an
enigmatical manner. Every one ſets his brains to
work to interpret them, and ſhould no one be able
to ſucceed in it, the dreamers are free to return home.
A notable opportunity for cowards truly. Afterwards new invocations are made to the genii, and
they animate themſelves anew to acquit themſelves
nobly, and to perform wonders ; they ſwear to aid
each other mutually ; laſtly, they begin their march,
and in caſe they have come thus far in canoes, they
take a great care to conceal them. If every thing
were exactly done, which is preſcribed on ſuch occaſions, it would be very difficult to ſurpriſe an Indian party in an enemy's country. There muſt no
more fires be lighted, no more ſhouting, and no
more hunting ; they are not even to ſpeak but by
ſigns ; but theſe laws are ill obſerved. The Indians
are naturally preſumptuous, and the leaſt capable of
confinement of any people in the world. They
neglect not, however, to ſend out ſcouts every evening, who employ two or three hours in excurſions
on different ſides. If theſe diſcover nothing, they
ſleep ſecurely, and once more abandon their camp
to the ſafeguard of their manitous.

As ſoon as they have diſcovered an enemy, they
ſend to reconnoitre him, and on the report of thoſe
ſent out, hold a council. The attack is generally
made at day-break. This is the time they ſuppoſe
the enemy to be in the deepeſt ſleep, and they keep
themſelves the whole night laid flat upon their faces,
without ſtirring. They make their approaches in the
ſame manner, creeping upon hands and feet, till they

Z 4   have

have got within a bow-fhot of the enemy. Then
they all ftart up, the chief gives the fignal by a
fmall cry, to which the whole body makes anfwer
by hideous howlings, and at the fame time make
their difcharge. Then without giving them time to
recover from their confufion they pour upon them
with hatchet in hand. Since the Indian have fubftituted iron hatchets to their old wooden ones,
their battles have become more bloody. The combat ended, they fcalp the dead and dying, and never think of making prifoners, till all refiftance is
over.

But when they find the enemy on his guard, or
too ftrongly intrenched they retire, provided they
have ftill time to do it. If not, they boldly re-
folve on fighting to the laft drop, and there is fometimes abundance of blood-fhed on both fides. A
camp which has been forced is the very picture of
fury itfelf, the barbarous fiercenefs of the conquerors, the defpair of the conquered, who know what
they have to expect fhould they fall alive into the
hands of the enemy, occafion prodigious efforts on
both fides, which furpafs all that can be related of
them. The figure of the combatants all befmeared
with black and red, ftill augments the horror of
the conflict, and a very good picture of hell might
be drawn from this model. When the victory is
no longer doubtful, the conquerors firft difpatch all
fuch as they defpair of being able to carry with
them, without trouble, and then try only to tire
the reft whom they are defirous of making prifoners.

The Indians are naturally intrepid, and in fpite of
their brutal fiercenefs always retain abundance of
cold

cold blood in the midſt of action; yet they never engage in an open country when they can avoid it; their reaſon for it being, ſay they, that a victory bought with blood is no victory, and that the glory of a chief conſiſts above all things in bringing back all his people ſafe and ſound, or in whole ſkins. I have heard ſay, that when two enemies who are acquaintances meet in battle, they hold dialogues together like the ſpeeches of former heroes. I do not believe this happens in the heat of the action, but it may very well happen in ſmall rencounters, or before paſſing ſome rivulet, or facing an entrenchment, in which caſe they bid one another defiance, or recall to memory what may have paſſed in ſome former action.

War is almoſt always made by ſurprize, which generally ſucceeds well enough. For if the Indians are negligent in guarding againſt ſurprizes, they are equally alert and dextrous in ſurprizing their enemies. Beſides, theſe people have a natural and a moſt admirable talent, or I might call it an inſtinct, to know whether they have paſſed any particular way. On the ſmootheſt graſs, or the hardeſt earth, even on the very ſtones, they will diſcover the traces of an enemy, and by their ſhape and figure of the footſteps, and the diſtance between their prints, they will, it is ſaid, diſtinguiſh not only different nations, but alſo tell whether they were men or women who have gone that way. I was long of opinion that what I had been told of them was much exaggerated, but the uniform voices of all who have lived and converſed much with Indians, leave me no room to queſtion the truth of them. If there are any of the priſoners wounded in ſuch manner as that they cannot be tranſported, they immediate-

ly

ly burn them, and this is done in their first tranſ-
ports of rage, and as they are often obliged to
make a haſty retreat, they generally come off
cheaper than thoſe they reſerve for a ſlower puniſh-
ment.

It is cuſtomary among ſome nations,. for the
chief of the victorious party to leave his hatchet
upon the field of battle, on which he takes care to
trace the mark of his nation, that of his family,
together with his own portrait, that is, an oval,
with all the figures he wears on his viſage repreſented within it. Others paint all theſe marks on
the trunk of a tree, or on a piece of bark, with
charcoal duſt mixed with ſome other colours. They
alſo add hieroglyphick characters by means of which
paſſengers may inform themſelves of the minuteſt
circumſtances, not only of the action but of the
whole campaign. The chief of the party may be
known by the marks above-mentioned ; the number
of his exploits by ſo many matraſſes ; the number
of his ſoldiers by ſo many lines ; that of the priſoners by ſo many ſmall figures carrying ſtaves, or
chichicoués ; that of the killed by ſo many human
figures without heads, with ſuch different marks as
ſerve to diſtinguiſh men grown from women and
children. But this is not always found very
near the place of action, for when a party is in
fear of being purſued, they place them at a dſ-
tance from their route, in order to deceive their
purſuers.

Till ſuch time as they reach a country where they
may be in ſafety, they make abundance of diſpatch,
and that the wounded may not retard their flight,
they carry them by turns on litters, or draw them

on

on fledges if it is in the winter-feafon. On entering their canoes, they make their prifoners fing,
which is alfo done as often as they meet with any
of their allies. This honour cofts thofe who receive it a feaft, and fomething ftill worfe than the
trouble of finging to the wretched captives. They
invite their allies to *carefs* them ; now to carefs a
prifoner is to do him all the mifchief they can think
of, or to maim him in fuch manner that he remains
a cripple for ever after. There are fome chiefs,
however, who take indifferent good care of thefe
unhappy people, and who do not fuffer them to be
too cruelly handled ; but nothing can come up to
their care in watching them. In the day time they
are tied by the neck and arm to the timbers of a
canoe, and when the journey is by land, there is
always one to hold them. In the night-time they
are ftretched along the ground quite naked, and
there are cords fixed to hooks planted in the ground,
which tie their legs, arms, and neck fo faft, that
they cannot ftir, and there are befides, long cords,
which are faftened to their hands and feet in fuch
manner, that the leaft motion they make wakens the
Indian who lies on thefe cords.

After the warriors have got within a certain diftance of their village, they halt, and the chief fends
to give notice of his approach. Amongft fome nations, as foon as the deputy has got near enough
to be within hearing, he makes different cries which
communicate a general idea of the principal adventures and fuccefs of the campaign. The firft fignifies the number of men killed, by fo many death-
cries. Immediately the young people come out to
inform themfelves more particularly ; and often a
whole village runs out, but only one perfon accofts
the

the envoy, learns of him the detail of the news he brings; as he relates any particular, the other turns towards the reft of the people and repeats it aloud, and they anfwer by fo many acclamations or cries of lamentation, as the news prove mournful, or the contrary.

The envoy is afterwards conducted into a cabin, where the elders put the fame queftions to him, after which a publick crier invites all the youth to go to meet the warriors, and the women to carry them refrefhments. In other parts they think of nothing at firft but bewailing thofe they have loft. The envoy makes only death-cries. No body comes out to meet him; but on his entering the village he finds all the people affembled, he relates in few words all that has paffed, and then retires to his cabin, where they bring him fomething to eat, and for fome time they are wholly occupied in mourning for the dead.

This term being expired, another cry is made, to denote the victory. Then every one wipes off his tears, and there is nothing but rejoicing; fomething like this is done, at the return from hunting; the women who have remained in the village go out to meet them, on being informed of their approach, and before they are acquainted with the fuccefs of their hunting, they fignify by their tears the number of deaths fince their departure. To return to the warriors, the moment the women join them is properly the beginning of the fufferings of the prifoners; likewife, when fome of them have at firft been appointed to be adopted, which is not lawful in every nation, their future parents, whom they take care to inform, go to a

greater

greater diftance to receive them, and conduct them
to their cabbins by round about ways. The captives are generally long in the dark with refpect to
their fate, and there are few who efcape the firft
fallies of the rage of the women. But this article
would carry me too far, and we muft fet out to-
morrow betimes.

I am, &c.

LETTER

L E T T E R XVI.

First reception of the prifoners. Triumph of the
warriors. Diftribution of the captives; in
what manner their fate is decided, with what
happens afterwards. The inhumanity with
which thofe are treated who are condemned to
death. The courage they fhew. Negotiations
of the Indians.

Entrance of Lake Erié, May 27*th,* 1721.

Madam,

I Set out this morning from the Falls of Niagara,
and had about feven leagues to make before I
got to Lake Erié, which I have done without any
trouble. We laid our account with not lying here
this night; and while my people were rowing with
all their might, I made a good progrefs in a new
letter, and now whilft they are taking a little repofe I fhall finifh, and give it to fome Canadians
going to Montreal, whom I met with in this place.
I fhall refume my account where I left it off in
my laft.

All the prifoners who are condemned to die, and thofe whofe fate is not yet determined, are, as I have already told you, Madam, abandoned to the women, who go before the warriors, and it is fur-prifing how they are able to furvive all the torments they make them fuffer. If any one has loft in the war a fon, hufband, or any other perfon who was dear to her, were it thirty years before, fhe becomes a fury, fhe fixes upon the firft who falls into her hands, and it cannot be conceived to what length her rage will tranfport her. She has no regard either to humanity or decency, and at every blow fhe gives, you would think he would fall dead at her feet, if you did not know how ingenious thefe barbarians are in protracting the moft unheard of torments. The whole night is fpent in this manner at the encampment of the warriors.

Next day is a day of triumph for the conquerors. The Iroquois and fome others affect a great modefty, and ftill a greater difintereftednefs on thefe occafions. The chiefs enter the village firft by themfelves, without any marks of victory, obferving a profound filence, and retire to their cabins, without fhewing that they have the leaft pretenfions upon any of the captives. But amongft other nations affairs are carried on in a different manner; the chief marches at the head of his company with the air of a conqueror, his lieutenant comes after him, and is preceded by a crier whofe bufinefs is to repeat the death-cry. The warriors follow two and two, the prifoners being in the middle crowned with flowers, their face and hair painted, holding a ftick in one hand and a chichicoué in the other, their body almoft naked, their arms tied above the elbow with a cord, the extremities of which are held

by

by the warriors, and finging all the while their death-fong to the beat of the chichikoué.

This fong is at the fame time extremely fierce and doleful, the captive difcovering nothing that has the leaft appearance of a perfon that has been vanquifhed, or is under affliction. The purport of this fong is as follows : " I am brave and undaunt-
" ed, and fear neither death nor the cruelleft tor-
" ments; thofe who fear them are cowards and lefs
" than women ; life is nothing to a man that has
" courage; may rage and defpair choak all my
" enemies ; why cannot I devour them and drink
" up their blood to the laft drop." The prifoners are made to halt from time to time, the Indians meanwhile flocking round them, dancing themfelves and caufing them to dance which they feem to do very chearfully, relating all the time the braveft actions of their lives, and mentioning the names of all thofe whom they have killed or burnt. They take particular notice of thofe in whom the affift-ants are moftly interefted ; and it may be faid, that their chief defign is to incenfe the arbiters of their fate more and more againft them. Thefe bravados feldom fail to provoke the fury of all who hear them, and their vanity frequently cofts them dear. But from the manner in which they bear the cruel-eft treatment, one fhould think that tormenting them is doing them a pleafure.

Sometimes they are forced to run between two rows of Indians armed with ftones and cud-gels, who ftrike them as if they intended to knock them down at every blow. This, however, never happens, for even when they feem to ftrike at random, and to be actuated only by fury, they take care never to touch any part where a blow might prove mortal. During this operation any one has the liberty to ftop the fufferer, who is likewife permitted to ftand in his defence, though it is feldom done to any purpofe. As foon as they arrive at the village, they are led from cabbin to cabbin, and are every where treated in the fame manner. Here they pluck off a nail, there they take off a finger, either with their teeth, or a bad knife which cuts like a faw ; an old man tears off their flefh to the bones, a child pierces them with an awl wherever he can, a woman beats them unmercifully till her arms fall down with fatigue ; all this time none of the warriors lay hands on them, tho' they are ftill their mafters. They are not even fuffered to be maimed without their permiffion, which is feldom granted. This excepted, every one may make them fuffer what torments he pleafes, and if they are led about in feveral villages, either of the fame nation, or of their neighbours, or allies, who happen to defire it, they every where meet with the fame reception.

These preliminaries over, they fet about dividing the captives whofe lot depends upon thofe into whofe power they are delivered up. As foon as the council, where their fate has been determined is over, a crier calls an affembly of the people in the fquare, where a diftribution is made without any noife or difpute whatfoever. Thofe women who have loft their fons or hufbands in the war, are commonly fatisfied in the firft place. Afterwards they fulfil the engagements entered into with thofe from whom they have received collars of Wampum ; if there is not a fufficient number of prifoners for this purpofe, the defect is fupplied with fcalps, which are worn by way of ornament on days of rejoicing,

but

but at other times are hung up at the gates of their cabbins. If on the other hand the number of prisoners is more than sufficient for these purposes, the overplus is sent to their allies. The place of a chief is never filled up but by a chief, or by two or three slaves, who are always burnt; even though the chief had died a natural death. The Iroquois never fail to set apart some prisoners for the use of the publick, in which case the council disposes of them as they think proper; but the matrons still have the power to abrogate their sentence, being absolute sovereigns of the life and death of those who have been condemned or absolved by the council.

The warriors, in some nations, never divest themselves entirely of the right of disposing of their prisoners, and those to whom the council has distributed them, are obliged to make restitution to them if demanded; which, however, seldom happens, but when it does, they are also obliged to restore the pledges they have received from those who had contracted for these prisoners. If upon their arrival, the warriors declare their intentions upon this point, they are seldom opposed. In general, the greatest number of the prisoners of war are condemned to die, or to a very severe slavery in which their life is never secure. Some are adopted, and from that time their condition differs in nothing from that of the children of the nation; they assume all the rights of those whose place they occupy, and frequently enter into the spirit of the nation, of which they are become members, in such a manner, that they make no difficulty of going to war against their own countrymen. By this policy, the Iroquoise have hitherto supported themselves, for having been constantly at war from time immemorial, with all the nations round them, they

A a 2

muſt have been, by this time, reduced to nothing had they not taken care to naturalize a large proportion of their priſoners of war.

It ſometimes happens that inſtead of ſending the overplus of the captives to other villages, they preſent theirs to private perſons, who did not demand any, who, in ſuch a caſe, are not ſo much their maſters as not to be obliged to conſult the chiefs of the council what they are to do with them, or elſe to adopt them. If the firſt caſe, he to whom a ſlave has been given, ſends for him by one of his family, he then ties him up to the door of his cabbin, after which he calls together the chiefs of the council, to whom he declares his intentions, and aſks their advice, which they generally give in a manner conformable to his inclinations. In the ſecond caſe, on delivering the priſoner into his hands, they tell him. " It is a long time ſince we have " been deprived of ſuch a one, your friend, or re- " lation, who was the ſupport of our village." Or, " We regret the ſpirit of ſuch a one, whom " you have loſt, and who, by his wiſdom main- " tained the tranquillity of the publick, he muſt " this day be made to appear again, he was too " dear to us, as well as too valuable a perſonage to " defer any longer bringing him back to life; we " therefore replace him upon his mattraſs in the " perſon of this captive."

There are ſome private perſons, however, probably of more credit and reputation than common, who receive the gift of a priſoner without any condition at all, and with full liberty to diſpoſe of him as they ſhall think proper; on delivering him into ſuch a perſon's hands the council addreſs him in this manner. " Behold wherewithal to repair the loſs

" of

" of such a one, and to glad the heart of his fa-
" ther, his mother, his wife and his children ; whe-
" ther you chuse to make them drink the broth
" of this flesh, or rather incline to replace the de-
" ceased upon his mattrass in the person of this cap-
" tive. You may do with him according to your
" will and pleasure."

As soon as a prisoner is adopted he is carried to
the cabbin, where he is to remain, and his bonds are
immediately loosed. He is washed with warm water, and his wounds are probed, if he has any, and
were they even full of worms he is soon cured ;
nothing is omitted to make him forget all the evils
he has suffered, victuals are set before him, and he
is properly dressed. In a word, they could not do
more for the child of the house, or even for the person whom he restores again to life, as they express
themselves. Some days after this a feast is made,
in the course of which he receives in a solemn manner the name of him whom he replaces, and from
thenceforth not only succeeds to all his rights, but
likewise becomes liable to all his obligations.

Amongst the Hurons and Iroquois those who are
condemned to be burnt, are sometimes as well treated from the first, and even till the moment of their
execution, as those who are adopted. It is probable these are victims fattened for sacrifice, and they
are indeed offered up to the god of war : the only
difference betwixt them and other captives, is that
their faces are smeared over with black. Excepting this, they treat them in the best manner possible,
setting before them the best food, never speaking to
them but with an air of friendship, calling them son,
brother, nephew, according as they themselves are
related to the person whose manes the prisoners are

to appeafe by their death : fometimes they yield the girls up to their pleafures, who ferve them as wives during the time they have yet to live. But when they are apprifed of their fate, they muft be carefully watched for fear they fhould efcape. For this reafon it is often concealed from them.

As foon as every thing is ready for the execution they are delivered up to a woman, who from the fondnefs of a mother paffes at once into the rage of a fury, and from the tendereft careffes to the moft extreme tranfports of madnefs. She begins with invoking the fhade of him whom fhe is about to a-venge. " Approach, fays fhe, thou art going to " be appeafed ; I am preparing for thee a feaft, " drink deep draughts of this broth which is now " to be poured out before thee ; receive the victim " prepared for thee in the perfon of this warrior ; " he fhall be burnt and put into the chaldron ; " burning hatchets fhall be applied to his fkin ; his " fcalp fhall be flea'd off ; they will drink out of " his fcull ; ceafe therefore thy complaining ; thou " fhalt be fully fatisfied." This formula, which is properly the fentence of death, often varies confiderably in the expreffion, but is always nearly the fame in fubftance. A crier then calls the prifoner out of his cabbin, proclaiming with a loud voice the in-tentions of the perfon to whom he belongs, and con-cludes with exhorting the youth to perform their parts well. A fecond herald then advances, and addreffing himfelf to the prifoner, tells him, " Thou " art going to be burnt, my brother, be of good " courage." He again anfwers coolly, " It is " well, I thank thee." Immediately the whole vil-lage fet up a loud fhout, and the prifoner is con-ducted to the place appointed for his execution.

The

The prifoner is commonly tied to a poft by the hands and feet, but in fuch a manner that he may turn quite round it. Sometimes when the execution is to be in a cabbin, whence there is no danger of his making his efcape, he is not tied, but fuffered to run from one end to the other. Before they begin burning him, he fings his death fong for the laft time, then he makes a recital of all the gallant actions of his life, and almoft always in a manner the moft infulting to the by-ftanders. Afterwards he exhorts them not to fpare him, but to remember that he is a man and a warrior. I am much miftaken, if the fufferer's finging with all his might, and infulting and defying his executioners, as they commonly do to their laft breath, is the circumftance that ought to furprife us moft in thofe tragical and barbarous fcenes; for there is in this a fiercenefs which elevates the mind, which tranfports it, and even withdraws it from the thoughts of what they fuffer, and at the fame time prevents their fhewing too much fenfibility. Befides, the motions they make divert their thoughts, and produce the fame effect, nay fometimes a greater, than cries and tears would do. In the laft place, they are fenfible there is no mercy to be expected, and defpair gives them ftrength, and infpires them with refolution.

This fpecies of infenfibility is not however fo univerfal as a great many have believed. It is no rare thing to hear thefe wretches crying in fuch a manner as would pierce the hardeft hearts, which however only rejoices the actors and affiftants. But as to this inhumanity in the Indians, of which human nature could hardly have been thought capable, I believe they have attained to it by degrees, and that practice has infenfibly accuftomed them to it; that the defire of making their enemy fhow a

mean-

meanness of spirit, the insults which the sufferers never fail to offer to their tormentors, the desire of revenge, a ruling passion in these people, which they never think sufficiently gratified while those who are the objects of it continue to shew the least sparks of remaining courage, and finally, superstition have all a great share in it: for what excesses will not a false zeal, inflamed by so many passions, produce!

I shall not give you a detail, Madam, of every thing that passes at these horrible executions. It would engage me too far, because there is no uniformity, nor any rules in them but what are suggested by fury and caprice. There are often as many actors as spectators, that is to say, inhabitants of the village, men, women and children, every one doing as much mischief as possible, and none but those belonging to the cabbin to which the prisoner had been delivered, refraining from tormenting him; at least this is the practice among some nations. They commonly begin with burning the feet, then the legs, thus ascending to the head, and sometimes they make the punishment last for a whole week, as happened to a gentleman of Canada among the Iroquois. Those are least spared, who having been already taken and adopted, or set at liberty, are afterwards retaken. They are looked upon as unnatural children, or ungrateful persons, who have made war upon their parents and benefactors, and no mercy whatever is shewn them. It sometimes happens that the patient is left at his liberty, even tho' he is not executed in a cabbin, and suffered to stand on his own defence, which he does less thro' hope of saving his life, than out of a desire to revenge his death before hand, and to acquire the reputation of dying like a brave man. There have been many instances to prove what a prodigious degree of strength and courage such a resolution is

capable

capable of infpiring, of which the following, atteft-
ed by perfons of credit who were eye-witneffes, is
one very remarkable.

An Iroquois captain of the canton called *Onneyouth*,
rather chofe to expofe himfelf to the worft that could
happen, than to difhonour himfelf by flying, which
he reckoned of dangerous confequence from the ill
example it would give to the youth under his command. He fought a long time like a man refolved
to die with his arms in his hands, but the Hurons
his enemies were refolved on taking him if poffible
alive. Luckily for him and thofe who were taken
prifoners with him, they were conducted to a village where there happened to be fome miffionaries,
who were allowed the full liberty of converfing with
them. Thefe fathers found them of an admirable
docility, which they looked upon as a beginning of
the grace of their converfion; accordingly they inftructed and baptized them; they were all burnt in
a few days afterwards, and teftified to their laft moments a fort of conftancy, which the Indians were
not till then acquainted with, and which, infidels as
they were, they attributed to the virtue of the fa-
crament of baptifm.

The Iroquois captain, notwithftanding, believed
he might lawfully do his enemies all the mifchief in his power, and delay his death as long as
poffible. They had made him afcend a fort of ftage
or theatre, where they began by burning his body
all over, without the leaft mercy, to which he appeared as infenfible as if he had felt no pain; but
on perceiving one of his companions whom they
were tormenting juft by him, betray fome figns of
weaknefs, he teftified a great deal of uneafinefs, and
cmitted nothing in his power to encourage him to
                                                    bear

bear his sufferings with patience, thro' the hopes of the happiness awaiting them in heaven, and he had the satisfaction to see him expire like a brave man and a christian.

Then all those who had put his companion to death fell upon him with such rage as if they would tear him to pieces. He appeared not at all moved at it, and they were now at a loss to find any part of his body that was sensible to pain; when one of the executioners, after making an incision in the skin quite round his head, tore it entirely off by mere force and violence. The pain made him fall into a swoon, when his tormentors believing him dead, left him. Upon his recovery a moment after, and seeing nothing near him but the dead body of his friend, he took up a firebrand with both hands, scorched and flead as they were, defying his executioners to come near him. This uncommon resolution terrified them, they made hideous shouts, ran to arms, some laying hold of burning coals, and and others seizing red hot irons, and all at once poured upon him; he stood the brunt of their fury with the courage of a man in despair, and even made them retire. The fire that surrounded him served him for an entrenchment, which he compleated with the ladders they had used to ascend the scaffold, and thus fortifying himself, and making a sort of citadel of his funeral pile, which was now become the theatre of his bravery, and armed with the instruments of his torture, he was for a considerable time the terror of a whole canton, and not one had the heart to approach him, tho' he was more than half burnt to death, and the blood trickled from all parts of his body.

His

His foot happening to flip, as he was endeavouring to avoid a fire-brand darted at him, delivered him once more into the hands of his murderers, who, as you may well imagine, made him pay dear for the terror he had put them into. After being tired with tormenting him, they threw him into the middle of a great coal fire, where they left him, fully perfuaded he would never be able to rife from it. But they were deceived, for when they leaft thought of it, they beheld him armed with fire-brands running towards the village, as if he was going to fet it on fire. All hearts were frozen with fear, and no one dared to face him, when juft as he had almoft reached the firft cabbin, a ftick thrown at him, and falling between his legs, brought him to the ground, and they laid hold of him before he could recover himfelf. Here they firft cut off his hands and feet, and rolled him upon burning embers, and then threw him below the burning trunk of a tree, the whole village gathering round him to enjoy the fpectacle.

He loft fuch a quantity of blood as almoft extinguifhed the fire, fo that they had now no manner of apprehenfion remaining of any future attempt. He made however another, which ftruck terror into the moft undaunted. He crept upon his knees and elbows with fo much vigour, and with fuch a threatning afpect, as made thofe who were neareft him retire to a diftance, more indeed out of aftonifhment than fear, for what could he have done mutilated and difmembered as he was? In this dreadful condition the miffionaries, who had never loft fight of him, endeavoured to put him in mind of thofe eternal truths with which he had been at firft fo much penetrated ; he liftened with attention, and feemed for fome time entirely taken up with the thoughts

of

of his falvation, when one of the Hurons taking advantage of this opportunity, ftruck off his head.

If thofe nations, Madam, make war like Barbarians, it muft however be allowed that in treaties of peace, and generally in all negociations, they difplay fuch a dexterity, addrefs and elevation of foul, as would do honour to the moft civilized nations. They never trouble themfelves about making conquefts, or extending their dominions. Some nations know no manner of dominion or fovereignty ; and thofe who have never been at a diftance from their native country, and who look upon themfelves as the lords and fovereigns of the foil, are not fo jealous of their property as to find fault with newcomers who fettle on it, provided they do not attempt to moleft them. The points which are the only fubjects of their treaties, are to make alliances againft powerful enemies ; to put an end to a war which may have become burthenfome to both parties ; or rather to treat of a fufpenfion of hoftilities, for I have already obferved, that every war is everlafting among the Indians, when it happens between different nations. Thus a treaty of peace is very little to be depended on, whilft any of the parties are capable of molefting or giving uneafinefs to the other.

During the whole time of the negociation, and even before it commences, their chief care is, that they may not feem to make the firft advances, or if they do, they ufe all their addrefs to make their enemy believe that it does not proceed from fear or neceffity ; and this laft is managed very artfully. A plenipotentiary abates nothing of his haughtinefs, even when the affairs of his country are in the worft fituation ; and he has generally the good fortune to perfuade thofe with whom he is treating, that it is their intereft to put an end to hoftilities, tho' they have been the conquerors. It is befides of the laft confequence to himfelf, to employ all his eloquence and addrefs, for fhould his propofals happen not to be relifhed, he muft keep well on his guard, a blow with a hatchet being fometimes the only anfwer given on fuch occafions. He is not out of danger even if he efcapes the firft furprife, but muft lay his account with being purfued and burnt, if taken, provided fuch an act of violence can be juftified by any pretext, fuch as that of reprifals for a like proceeding. Thus it happened to fome French amongft the Iroquois, to whom they had been fent on the part of the governor general ; and the miffionaries, who for fome years refided among thofe Barbarians, altho' they were under the fafeguard of the public faith, and in fome meafure agents for the colony, yet were every day in dread of being facrificed to fome ancient grudge, or becoming victims to the intrigues of the governors of New York.

It is furprifing, in fhort, that nations who never make war from motives of intereft, and who even carry their difintereftednefs to fuch a height, that their warriors never load themfelves with the fpoils of the vanquifhed, and if they bring home any booty, abandon it to the firft that pleafes to take it ; and laftly, who take up arms for glory only, or to revenge themfelves on their enemies ; it is, I fay, quite aftonifhing to fee them fo well verfed and practifed in the greateft refinements of policy, and even fo as to keep minifters refiding amongft their enemies at the public expence. They have one cuftom with refpect to thefe agents, which at firft fight appears fufficiently extravagant, tho' it may be reckoned

koned prudent enough at the fame time, which is that they never pay any regard to any intelligence they receive from thefe penfioners, if it is not accompanied with fome prefent. Their policy here arifes no doubt from this confideration, that in order to give an entire credit to any piece of intelligence, it is not only neceffary that he who communicates it fhould have nothing to hope from it, but even that it fhould be attended with fome expence to him, both becaufe the intereft of the public fhould be his only motive for fending it, and alfo that he may not rafhly trouble them with trifling and fuperficial matters.

I am, &c.